ARMENIAN

Armenian–English
English–Armenian

Dictionary & Phrasebook

by
Nicholas Awde
&
Peter Maghdashyan

HIPPOCRENE BOOKS INC
New York

**Historical and cultural background material
by Fred J. Hill.
Additional thanks to
Thea Khitarishvili, Tom de Waal,
Caroline Gates, and Nicholas Williams
for their help in compiling this volume.**

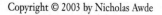

Typeset & designed by Desert♥Hearts

ISBN 0 7818 1006 X

For information, address:
HIPPOCRENE BOOKS, INC.
171 Madison Avenue
New York, NY 10016
www.hippocrenebooks.com

Printed in the United States of America

CONTENTS

- An Armenian person is a **Hay**.
- The adjective for Armenian people is **Hayeren**.
- The adjective for Armenian things is **Haykakan**.
- Armenians call themselves **Hayer**.
- The Armenian language is **Hayeren**.
- Armenia is **Hayastan**.

INTRODUCTION

Against all odds, the nation of Armenia has survived centuries of major political and social upheavals and confidently entered the 21st century with its unique cultural identity intact, which it proudly displays for all those who are willing to take the time to embrace it.

Sharing its borders with Georgia, Turkey, Azerbaijan and Iran, Armenia is a mountainous country, dominated by the mountains of the Lesser Caucasus and more than 90 percent of its surface area lies at more than 1,000 meters. The country's highest mountain, Mount Aragats, stands at 4,090 meters high.

Although the region has been populated since time immemorial—it has been called the "Cradle of Civilization"—Armenia rose gradually from the ashes of the ancient civilization of Urartu in the sixth century B.C. Yet for centuries, the local inhabitants were caught up in the bloody conflicts of a succession of rival empires and kingdoms which competed with each other to dominate the region. Among these was the Persian Achaemenid Empire, founded by Cyrus the Great in the sixth century B.C., and subsequently toppled by Alexander the Great in the fourth century B.C. Alexander's successors, the Seleucids, held sway over the land until the warring empires of Rome and Parthia transformed Transcaucasia with Armenia in the center into little more than a buffer zone.

The first Christian state

It was not until the arrival of Christianity, after King Tiridates the Great was converted by St. Gregory in 301 A.D., that Armenia really came into its own as a state. From then on the new faith became the official religion of the

Armenian kingdom, making it the earliest Christian state in the world. From then on, Christianity became a vital part of the nation's identity, which it remains to this day.

It was not long before the fledgling Christian kingdom became the target of the powerful Sasanian Empire to the East as it fought to keep the recently created Christian Byzantine Empire at bay to the West. In 428 A.D., the Sasanians annexed eastern Armenia and in the rest of the country they launched a vicious campaign to eradicate Christianity and impose their own state religion, Zoroastrianism. Although caught in the middle between these warring giants, the Armenian leadership stood their ground, simply refusing to convert.

Their bold act of defiance brought the wrath of the ruling Persian emperor, who subsequently marched his army into Armenia accompanied by eight hundred Zoroastrian priests. Desperate appeals by the Armenians for support from fellow Christians of the Byzantine Empire fell on deaf ears, a fact which was to cause lasting bitterness amongst the Armenian people.

The Golden Age of Cilicia

Down, but certainly not out, the Armenians won valuable concessions in the ensuing peace negotiations with the Sasanian leadership, and it was agreed to restore the freedom of Christian worship in Armenia, and to abolish Zoroastrian fire temples.

The seventh century brought in new overlords as the Muslim Arabs fought their way north to take over the eastern domains of Byzantium, which was slowly crumbling through political infighting. Under the fast-expanding Islamic Empire, Armenia became a key vassal kingdom and was permitted to rule itself, provided it paid the necessary taxes to the new rulers. In the ninth century, Armenia underwent a period of revival, gaining as a result a significant amount of independence from the Muslims.

The nation's fortunes changed after its incorporation

into the Turkish Seljuk Empire in the eleventh century, bringing hardship and centuries of foreign domination. Many Armenians fled to the neighboring regions to escape repressive Seljuk policies. Many of them ended up in Cilicia to the west, where Armenians were already busy carving out a new kingdom, called by some "Lesser Armenia." The kingdom, which became the only reliable ally of the Christian Crusaders, enjoyed something of a Golden Age and thrived from the eleventh century until 1375, when it finally fell to the Egyptian Mamluks who were set on consolidating their authority in their northern domains.

Caught up once again in the relentless march for power by larger neighbors, the next trial for Armenia was its absorption into the Ottoman Empire, ruled by the Sultans and their Viziers in Istanbul, and for many years its fortunes were tied to the vicissitudes of that empire's struggles with the Iranian Safavid Empire.

Occupation by the Russians

The Armenians, however, thrived during the Ottoman Empire and contributed significantly to the cultural, political and administrative life of the Empire. But their fortunes changed sharply as the Empire began to decline steadily during the nineteenth century. A new threat to its borders had emerged to the north, that of the Tsar's Russia, which greedily looked to taking Ottoman territories around the Black Sea, the Caucasus and Persia.

After a series of bloody campaigns by the Russians, a large part of Armenia was incorporated into the Russian Empire, bringing new hardships as Tsar Nicholas II confiscated Armenian Church assets and closed down Armenian schools and libraries. By the 1870s, Tsarist Russia and Ottoman Turkey had come to blows and in the fallout, during the reign of Sultan Abdul Hamid II, Armenians living in Turkey were massacred. Between 1894-1896, an estimated 300,000 were slaughtered. In 1909, a further 30,000 Armenians were massacred in Cilicia, while Armenian villages and city quarters were looted and burned. Yet, despite such a horrific fate, the Armenians continued to cling to their cherished dreams of an independent Armenia. But tragedy struck once again, between 1915–1923, when an estimated 1,500,000 Armenians were again massacred wholesale in a genocidal act by the Turkish government of the Young Turks—and 500,000 survivors were forced into exile.

The end of the First World War brought a short-lived period of independence between 1918 and 1922, but this was cut short by the victory of the Bolsheviks in the Russian Civil War, who deposed the Tsar and brought all the old Russian-occupied territories back under what was to become Soviet control. However, while under Communist rule the Armenians were fortunate enough to be spared much of the repression and hardship experienced by their Soviet neighbors.

After the collapse of the Soviet Union, Armenians finally achieved their dream of independence in 1991. Yet the happiness was tempered as an old grievance which had been simmering during the Soviet days now came to the surface. This centered on the frustration of the Armenians over the division of the Caucasus by Stalin, more particularly, the case of Nagorno-Karabagh.

Split by Nagorno-Karabagh

The Autonomous Region of Mountainous Karabagh (Nagorno-Karabagh, or "Artsakh"), which lies in western Azerbaijan close to the Armenian border, was officially made into an Autonomous Region and joined to Azerbaijan by Stalin in 1921. Some three quarters of the population were Armenian, the rest mainly Azerbaijani.

In the 1980s, the Soviet political climate thawed, but this also threatened the stability of the Caucasus as old tensions were brought to the surface by the Russians who were already jockeying for supremacy over their former colonies in the post-Soviet era they could see coming. In this unpredictable climate of transition, therefore, the regional council of Nagorno-Karabagh suddenly declared the region independent in 1988. A subsequent referendum in 1991 resulted in participating voters voting for independence from the control of the newly emerging republic of Azerbaijan. Pro-independence leaders promptly declared a new independent state, the Republic of Mountainous Karabakh and looked for support to Armenia, itself also emerging as a new, sovereign republic.

Soon Armenia and Azerbaijan were engaged in all-out war to contest the region. The terrible hostilities ended in the ceasefire of May 1994. Since then, the region and the lack of a satisfactory solution has not only remained a source of tension between the two countries but has also affected international relations.

Focus for the Diaspora

The Diaspora was born from the country's turbulent history and has given rise to the creation of innumerable Armenian communities around the world—which are a cause for celebration as they continue to flourish and keep alive their culture and traditions. There are at present an estimated six million Armenians around the world including one million in the USA, mostly in California. Thanks to the Diaspora, you will find a truly global mix of languages from all around the world in the Republic itself.

Despite the uncertainty caused by the stalemate over the Nagorno-Karabagh conflict, Armenians can look forward to a future that looks set to put their tenacious nation firmly back on the world map. ∎

For further background information, see the Introduction to "Western Armenian Dictionary & Phrasebook," by Nicholas Awde and Vazken-Khatchig Davidian, "Armenian First Names," by Nicholas Awde and Emanuela Losi, and "The Armenians—People, Culture and History," edited by Nicholas Awde.

A Very Basic Grammar

Eastern Armenian belongs to the Iranian branch of the Indo-European family of languages. Its closest relative is Western Armenian – speakers of the two languages can understand each other with varying ease and also share a long history of common literature. Other members of this family include Greek, Albanian, and, more distantly, English, German, French, Italian and Spanish. Armenian is written in its own unique script (see page 22) — this book uses an easy-to-understand transliteration throughout.

– Structure

Like English, the linguistic structure of Armenian is basically a simple one. In word order, the verb is usually put at the end of the sentence, e.g.

> **Duk' rradio unenk'?**
> "Do you have a radio?"
> (literally: "You radio have?")

– Nouns

"THE" — Armenian has no words for "a" or "an" in the same way as English does — instead the meaning is generally understood from the context, e.g. **rradio** can mean "a radio" or just simply "radio". The main way of conveying the meaning of "the" is by adding **-ë** (if the word ends in a consonant) or **-n** (if the word ends in a vowel) to the end of a word, e.g. **vart'ë** "<u>the</u> rose", **rradion** "<u>the</u> radio".

PLURALS — Nouns form their plural by adding **-er** or **-ner**, e.g. **vart'** → **vart'er** "roses," **rradio** → **rradioner** "radios".

There are some irregular plurals — analogous to occurrences in English like "man/men" or "child/children", e.g. **kin** "woman" → **kanaykʻ** "women", **mard** "person" → **mardikʻ** "people", **durr** "door" → **dërrner** "doors."

CASE — Nouns (and sometimes adjectives) change their endings depending on how they are used in a sentence. Like German or Russian, these endings change according to the position of a word in a sentence, what is being done with or to a word, or whether a postposition (see below) is present. This is generally predictable – triggered by rules of grammar – and the various "declensions" are best left for more advanced study, but a few essential examples are given in the following sections. The most commonly seen basic forms with their grammatical descriptions are as follows:

Nominative/Accusative	*no special ending*
Genitive/Dative	**-i***
Instrumental	**-ov** *or* **-amb**
Ablative	**-itsʻ**
Locative	**-um**

e.g.
stadion	stadium
stadioni	of the stadium, to a stadium
stadionov	with the stadium
stadionitsʻ	from the stadium
stadionum	at/in the stadium

Some nouns may change slightly according to the form they take, e.g. **akhchʻik** "girl"/**akhchʻëka** "girl's", **kin** "woman"/**kënochʻ** "woman's", **yekhpayr** "brother"/ **yekhpor** "brother's", **tun** "house"/**tan** "house's".

* Since this is an extremely commonly used case (see the section overleaf for "of"), it will be useful to help you recognize a few other commonly occurring variants of this ending: **-in**, **-u**, **-an**, and **-tsʻ**.

Plurals simply add the case endings to the plural marker **-(n)er**, e.g. **rradioner** "radios"/**rradioneri** "of radios"/**rradionerov** "with radios".

The genitive, instrumental, ablative and locative cases more or less parallel where English uses the prepositions "of", "with", "from", and "at/in" respectively, e.g. **Yes Amerikayits' yem.** "I am from America." Note that the instrumental also has a particular sense of "by", e.g. **otayin post'ov** "by airmail". The remaining cases have broader uses, and we'll outline a few of them here.

"Nominative" refers to the subject of a verb while "accusative" is the object of that verb, e.g. in the sentence **Yerevan k'aghak' e** ("Yerevan is a city"), "Yerevan" is the subject/nominative of "is", and "city" is the object/accusative of "is".

The "dative" is used in many cases where English would use "to", "for", or "at" – note especially the use of **zhamë yerekin** "at three o'clock". Similar to Spanish, where "a" is used before human objects of verbs (i.e. "veo nubes" is "I see clouds" but "veo a Aram" is "I see Aram"), the dative case is also used to mark human objects in the same slot as the accusative above.

As in languages like German, postpositions trigger a variety of case changes – for more see the special section below.

"OF" — There is no separate word for "of" but the genitive **-i** gives you "of" in the same way that English " -'s" does, e.g. **Arami rradio** = "Aram's radio" (or "the radio of Aram"), **firmayi hasts'en** "the (= **-n**) firm's address" or "the address of the firm", **atami khozanak** "toothbrush" (literally: "tooth's brush"), **Yerevani k'artez** "map of Yerevan", **kaghak'i kentron** "city center".

– Adjectives

Adjectives are like nouns in that they can take the same endings. They always come before the noun, e.g.

"new" **nor** — **nor mek'ena** "new car"
"old" **hin** — **hin mek'ena** "old car"

Some other basic adjectives are:

open **bats'**	quick **arag**
shut **p'ak**	slow **dandagh**
cheap **ezhan**	expensive **t'ankarzhek'**
hot **t'ak**	old *person* **tser**
cold **sarrë**	old *thing* **hin**
near **mot**	young **yeritasard**
far **herru**	good **lav**
big **mets**	bad **vat**
small **p'ok'ër**	rich **harust**
long **yerkar**	short **karch'**

– Adverbs

Adverbs have a single form which does not change. Some examples:

here **aystegh**	up **verev**
there **ayntegh**	down **nerk'ev**
well **lav**	now **hima**
badly **vat**	tomorrow **vaghë**
again **kërkin**	truly **iskut'yamb**
probably **havanabar**	immediately **anmijapes**

– Postpositions

Armenian has postpositions – where words like "in", "at" and "behind" come after the noun and not before it as in English (though remember that you can say "who *with*?" as well as "*with* who?" – and there is no change in meaning). They generally take genitive/dative endings and most are joined to the word itself:

for **hamar**	opposite **dimats'**
in/at/on **mech'**	near **mot**
on **vĕra**	with **het**

e.g. **kayarani mot** "near the station", **ays p'oghots'i vĕra** "on this street", **rrestorani mech'** "at the restaurant", **Yes gnats'i nĕra het.** "I went with him/her." (literally "I went him/her with.")

The sense of English prepositions is also rendered by the noun endings (see above in the section on Case).

– Pronouns

Basic forms are as follows:

SINGULAR	PLURAL
I **yes**	we **menk'**
you *singular* **du**	you *plural* **duk'**
he/she/it **na**	they **nĕrank'**

Like French "vous", also use **duk'** for anyone you don't know well or who is older or more senior. As subject pronouns, like Spanish or Italian, you tend to use them for emphasis only, since the verb already tells you who is speaking (see page 16).

Possessive pronouns are generally used with **ĕ/-n** ("the") attached (in some cases Italian also does this, e.g. "la mia casa" as a substitute for "mia casa"):

SINGULAR	PLURAL
my **im**	our **mer**
your **k'o**	your **dzer**
his/her/its **nĕra***	their **nĕrants'****

e.g.   **dzer yekhpayrĕ** "your brother"
      im girk'ĕ "my book"
      mer mek'enan "our car"
      mer mek'enanerĕ "our cars"

* You may also hear **ir**.
** You may also hear **irents'**.

There is also a system of "streamlined" forms that join onto the noun and function for both singular and plural:

my/our	**-(ë)s**
your *sing/plural*	**-(ë)t**
his/her/its/their	**-ë** *or* **-n**

e.g.   **rrestoranë** "his/her/their radio"
         tert'ës "my newspaper"

Simple demonstratives in Armenian are:

this **ays**	these **sërank'**
that **ayt'**	those **dërank'**
that over there **ayn**	those over there **nërank'**

In the spoken language, people tend to use the simpler system of **ays** for both "this" and "these", and **ayn** for "that" and "those", e.g. **ays rradio** "this radio", **ays rradioner** "these radios", **ayn mek'ena** "that car", **ayn mek'enaner** "those cars".

— Verbs

Verbs are easy to form, adding a number of prefixes and suffixes to the basic verb form. In fact the underlying structure of Armenian verbs shares similiar concepts to those of the majority of European languages and so its system of regularities and irregularities may appear familiar.

Every Armenian verb has a basic form that carries a basic meaning. To this are added smaller words or single vowels/consonants that add further information to tell you who's doing what and how and when, e.g.

gërel* "to write"
gërem "I should write"
gërum em "I am writing"
kë gërei "I would write"
kë gërel em "I will write"**

* The ending **-el** gives the most common infinitive form for verbs. Other verbs also end in **-al**, e.g. **unenal** "to have".
** **Piti** is another word meaning "will/shall".

Some verbs, as in Western European languages, have sound changes for different tenses, completely different forms, or combinations of these, e.g. **tal** "to give"/**tvets'i** "I gave", **gal** "to come"/**galis em** "I'm coming"/**eka** "I came".

We saw the personal pronouns above, but these are only used for emphasis. Like French or Spanish, the verb already gives this information:

SINGULAR	PLURAL
I **-em/-am**	we **-enk'/-ank'**
you *singular* **-es/-as**	you *plural* **-ek'/-ak'**
he/she/it **-i/-a**	they **-en/-an**

e.g.

gërem I write	**gërenk'** we write
gëres you write	**gërek'** you write
gëri he/she/it writes	**gëren** they write

These are the most commonly used endings, but note they can take different forms according to the tense used.

"Not" is **ch'-**. This is joined to the following word, e.g. **da herru ch'e** "it's not far", **yes zhamanak ch'unem** "I don't have time". You may also see the forms **ch'i** and **ch'e**.

Mi is used with commands, e.g. **mi kangnek'!** "don't stop!", **mi këpek'!** "don't touch that!"

—Essential verbs
—"To be" **linel**
The present is:

SINGULAR	PLURAL
I am **em**	we are **enk'**
you are **es**	you are **ek'**
he/she/it is **e**	they are **en**

The negative form is:

SINGULAR	PLURAL
I'm not **ch'em**	we aren't **ch'enk'**
you aren't **ch'es**	you aren't **ch'ek'**
he/she/it isn't **ch'e**	they aren't **ch'en**

The simple past is:

SINGULAR	PLURAL
I was **eyi**	we were **eyink'**
you were **eyir**	you were **eyik'**
he/she/it was **er**	they were **eyin**

e.g. **Yes bëzhishk em.**
"I am a doctor."
Duk' bëzhishk ch'eyik'.
"You were not a doctor."
Vortegh e hyuranots'ë?
"Where is the hotel?"

—"To have" **unenal**

SINGULAR	PLURAL
I have **unem**	we have **unenk'**
you have **unes**	you have **unek'**
he/she/it has **uni**	they have **unen**

e.g. **Duk' unek' azat hamar?**
"Do you have any rooms free?"
Yes unem bëjëshkakan apahovagrut'yun.
"I have medical insurance."

—"To go" **gënal**

SINGULAR	PLURAL
I'm going **gënum em**	we're going **gënum enk'**
you're going **gënum es**	you're going **gënum ek'**
he/she/it's going **gënum e**	they're going **gënum en**

—"To come" **gal**

SINGULAR	PLURAL
I'm coming **galis em**	we're coming **galis enk'**
you're coming **galis es**	you're coming **galis ek'**
he/she/it's coming **galis e**	they're coming **galis en**

PRONUNCIATION GUIDE

Armenian letter	Armenian example	Approximate English equivalent
a	**azat** "free"	*fa*ther, as in South British English
b	**barev!** "hello!"	*b*ox
ch'	**ch'anapar** "road"	*ch*urch, aspirated
ch	**chisht** "right"	*ch*urch, unaspirated or glottalized
d	**durr** "door"	*d*og
dz	**dzëmerr** "winter"	a*dz*e
e	**ek'spres** "express"	p*e*t
ë	**ënker** "friend"	*a*bove
f	**futbol** "soccer"	*f*at
g	**gini** "wine"	*g*ot
gh	**ghek** "steering wheel"	*see note on page 21*
h	**haryur** "hundred"	*h*at
i	**institut** "institute"	h*ea*t
j	**jur** "water"	*j*et
k'	**k'aghak'** "city, town"	*k*ick, aspirated
k	**kin** "woman"	*k*ick, unaspirated or glottalized
kh	**khanut'** "shop"	a*ch*, as in German
l	**lezu** "language"	*l*et
m	**metro** "metro"	*m*at
n	**naft'** "oil"	*n*et
o	**or** "day"	c*o*t, in South British English
p'	**p'oghots'** "street"	*p*et, aspirated
p	**panir** "cheese"	*p*et, unaspirated or glottalized
r	**sirel** "to love"	*r*at, but "rolled" as in Spanish "pe*r*o"
rr	**rradio** "radio"	*r*at, but "rolled" as in Spanish "pe*rr*o"

s	**sar** "mountain"	*s*it
sh	**shabat'** "week"	*sh*ut
t'	**tert'** "newspaper"	*t*en, aspirated
t	**tak'si** "taxi"	*t*en, unaspirated or glottalized
ts'	**ts'urt** "cold, coldness"	hi*ts*, aspirated
ts	**tsarr** "tree"	hi*ts*, unaspirated or glottalized
u	**utelik'** "food"	sh*oo*t
v	**vart'** "rose"	*v*an
y	**yerkir** "country"	*y*es
z	**zbosaygi** "park"	*z*ebra
zh	**zhamanak** "time"	a*z*ure

Nothing beats listening to a native speaker, but the following notes should help give you some idea of how to pronounce the following letters. Like English, the spoken language has a range of variations in pronunciation that are not reflected in the written language – these are not only from the various regions in Armenia but also from the various forms of Armenian spoken outside the republic's borders, including, of course, Western Armenian. The standard language in this book, however, will enable you to be understood clearly wherever you may be.

– Vowels

1) There is a degree of variation in Armenian vowels which is not reflected in the transliteration used in this book. However, this does not affect meaning.
2) The combination **ay** is pronounced as the "y" in English "why", e.g. **hay** "Armenian".

– Consonants

dz, ts — Note that, as in other Caucasian languages and Russian, the combinations of letters in each case represent a single consonant.

ch', k', p', t', ts' — These are all pronounced as in English but are always clearly "aspirated" – i.e. with just a little more "breath". You may also hear the term "breathed" used to describe them. Practise by fusing the "h" plus preceding consonants in "rich horse", "backhand", "hiphop", "hothouse", "hits hall".

ch, k, p, t, ts — The pronunciation of these consonants can be interpreted as being "unaspirated" or "glottalized" – depending on where the speaker comes from, or on the linguist's point of view. Both are right, as long as you ensure that you make enough of a distinction between these consonants and their aspirated counterparts described above. As already mentioned, "aspiration" means when consonants are pronounced with a discernable, heavy puff of air, and these contrast with their "unaspirated" counterparts, which are pronounced far "lighter" than in English. A good comparison is the different way these consonants are pronounced in English (aspirated) and Spanish (unaspirated). English can have approximates to both, sometimes in the same word, e.g. for many speakers the first "p" in "peep" will tend to be aspirated and the final "p" unaspirated, likewise "kick", "church", and so on. You may also hear these Armenian sounds pronounced in a different way, referred to as "glottalized" or "ejective". These terms simply mean that each consonant's basic sound is modified in a similar way to produce a less breathy, "harder" version. As an example, begin making the sound "k" as you normally would in English, but momentarily stop the breath going into your mouth by closing the fleshy bits (your glottis) at the very back. Hold your tongue and lips in the position they should be in to pronounce the "k". Rather than letting out a slow stream of breath with the English sound there should be instead an "explosion" simultaneously accompanying it. At first you may find it easier to do this for consonants at the ends of words.

kh — is the rasping "ch" in Scottish "loch" and German "ach". It is also pronounced like the Spanish/Castillian "jota" in "jamás". [= Georgian ხ; Persian خ]

gh — is pronounced like a sort of growl in the back of your throat — like when you're gargling. Frequently transcribed into English as "gh" for other languages that have this sound, the German or Parisian "r" is the easy European equivalent. [= Georgian ღ; Arabic غ]

r — tends to be a light tap, like the Spanish "pero" ("but") a lightly breathed tap of the tongue that sometimes sounds similar to **zh**. This is the same **r** found in Persian and Turkish.

rr — is a more strongly "rolled" **r**, as in the Castillian Spanish "perro" ("dog"), which contrasts with "pero" above. This is the same **r** found in Scottish English.

A note on spelling

The transliteration used in this book generally reflects the pronunciation of spoken Eastern Armenian and not the actual spelling, which is not always predictable and can also be subject to different interpretations by different speakers. Aside from the presence of West Armenian speakers with their own differences in pronunciation and grammar, as in English there are personal and regional variations in Eastern Armenian of consonants and vowels. These usually have no effect on meaning, and are easily picked up once you have found your "Armenian ear." It is a feature of Western Armenian, but there is also a marked tendency in conversational Eastern Armenian to overlap certain sounds. The most common you'll here are **b** and **pʻ**, **d** and **tʻ**, **dz** and **tsʻ**, **j** and **chʻ**, **g** and **kʻ**, **rr** and **r**. Examples are **martʻ** "person", written as **mard** մարդ; **mechʻ** "in", written as **mej** մեջ; **yerkʻ** "song", written as **yerg** երգ; **yerpʻ** "when?", written as **yerb** երբ. In many cases you'll hear **v** alternating with the sound **w**, also without any change in meaning, e.g. the name of the letter Ո is **vo** or **wo**. **E** and **o** can be realised in different ways, and occasionally **u**. ■

The Armenian alphabet

Armenian letter	Roman equivalent		Armenian letter	Roman Equivalent	
Ա ա	a	*ayb*	Մ մ	m	*men*
Բ բ	b	*ben*	Յ յ	y, h	*yi*
Գ գ	g	*gim*	Ն ն	n	*now*
Դ դ	d	*da*	Շ շ	sh	*sha*
Ե ե	e, ye	*ech'*	Ո ո	o, vo, wo	*vo*
Զ զ	z	*za*	Չ չ	ch	*che*
Է է	e	*e*	Պ պ	p	*pa*
Ը ը	ë	*et*	Ջ ջ	j	*je*
Թ թ	t'	*t'o*	Ռ ռ	rr	*rra*
Ժ ժ	zh	*zhe*	Ս ս	s	*se*
Ի ի	i	*ini*	Վ վ	v	*vew*
Լ լ	l	*liwn*	Տ տ	t	*tiwn*
Խ խ	kh	*khe*	Ր ր	r	*re*
Ծ ծ	ts	*tsa*	Ց g	ts'	*ts'o*
Կ կ	k	*ken*	Ւ ւ	v, w	*yiwn*
Հ h	h	*ho*	Փ փ	p'	*p'iwr*
Ձ ձ	dz	*dza*	Ք f	k'	*ke*
Ղ ղ	gh	*ghad*	Օ o	o, vo, wo	*o*
Ճ ճ	ch'	*ch'a*	Ֆ ֆ	f	*fe*

NOTES:

1) Frequently added to the alphabet list are two letters which are composites of a pair of letters each: Ու ու **ou, u, v**; and Եւ **ev, yev** (generally not given a capital form).

2) Some letters take slightly different shapes depending on the style of font used. The Armenian font used in this book has more modern shapes; the most common shapes of traditional fonts you'll encounter are:

ՙ for h **h**, ՙ for ն **n**, ՙ for ն **ch'**, and ՙ for f **k'**.

ARMENIAN
Dictionary

NOTE: For ease of reference, the different sounds **r** and **rr**, and **e** and **ë** are treated as the same letters for alphabetical order in the dictionary sections.

ARMENIAN-ENGLISH
HAYEREN – ANGLEREN

A

ach right; right-wing; **ach dzerrk'** right hand
ach'el to rise; to grow (up)
achk' eye; **achk'er** eyes
adapter *electric* adapter
Adërbejan Azerbaijan
adërbejanakan *thing* Azerbaijani
adërbejaneren *language* Azerbaijani/Azeri
adërbejants'i *person* Azerbaijani
administrator administrator
administrats'ia administration
agarak farm
agh salt
aghal to grind
aghander dessert
aghats' mill
aghavni dove; pigeon
aghb trash
aghbyur source
aghchik girl
aghchikner girls
aghet disaster
aghi salty
aghik' gut; intestine; **aghik'ner** guts
aghk'at poor
aghk'atut'yun poverty
aghmuk noise
aghot'el to pray
aghot'k' prayer
aghp' rubbish
aghp'yur spring *of water*
aghtot dirty
aghts'an salad
aghves fox

aghyus brick
agrrav crow
agronom agronomist
ahabekchut'yun hijacking
ahabekich hijacker
ahavor terrible
akademia academy
ak'aghagh rooster; cock
akan *explosive* mine; **hakahetevakayin akan** anti-personnel mine; **hakatankayin akan** anti-tank mine
akan t'akard booby trap
akanadasht minefield
akanates witness
akanj ear; **akanjner** ears
akanjogher earrings
akënhayt evident
akënkalel to expect
akënt'art time; an instance
akër acre
akhorzhak appetite
akhtanish *medical* symptom
akhtoroshum *medical* diagnosis
ak'is weasel
aknots' glasses; spectacles
akos furrow
akrat snack
akumb club
alani saltless
alarkot lazy
alarkutut'yun laziness
alergik allergic
alik' channel; T.V. channel
alkohol alcohol
alraghats' flour mill
alyur flour
amachets'nel to shame

Amanorya p'arraton New Year festival

amarr summer

ambartak dam

ambarts'ich crane *machine*

amboghchakan complete

amboghj entire; whole

amen each; every; **amen mekë** everybody; **amen mekë** everyone; **amen inch** everything

amenap'ok'ër erekha youngest child

AMëNë U.S.A.

amenorya daily

Amerika America

amerikats'i *person* American

Amerikayi Miats'yal Nahangner United States of America

amerikyan *thing* American

amis month

amot' shame

amot'ahar ashamed

amp cloud

amprop' rain shower; thunderstorm

amragrel to reserve; **Yes karogh em tegh amragrel?** Can I reserve a place/seat?

amrats'nel to fasten

amrots' fort

amsagir magazine; glossy magazine

amsakan bokhk radish

amsat'iv: **zhamanman amsat'iv** date of arrival; **meknelu amsat'iv** date of departure; **tsënëndyan amsat'iv** date of birth

amsekan monthly

amusin husband

amusnalutsut'yun divorce

amusnanal to marry

amusnats'ats married; **Yes amusnats'ats em.** I am married.

amusnut'yun marriage

an- -less

analiz *medical* test; **aryan analiz** blood test

anapat *noun* desert

anavart incomplete

anbaryats'akam unfriendly

anbërrënkeli inflammable

andamahatel amputate

andërpayt'el detonate

andërpayt'um detonation

andorragir receipt

andravartik' trousers

andz person

andzër femur

andzerrots'ik napkin

andzerots'ikner tissues

andznagir passport; **andznagri hamar** passport number

andznakazm staff

andznatur linel to surrender

andzrev rain; **Andzrev e galis.** It is raining.

anel to do; to make

anëndunakut'yun disability

anep' uncooked

aner father-in-law

anerdzak brother-in-law *wife's brother*

angëgh vulture

angëraget illiterate

angleren *language* English

Anglia England

angliakan *thing* English

angliats'i Englishman; Englishwoman

anhajogh unsuccessful

anhajoghut'yun failure

anham tasteless

anhangëstats'ats worried; **anhangëstats'ats linel** to be worried

anhangëstut'yun trouble; inconvenience

anharmar uncomfortable

anhavat unbeliever

anhayt unknown

anhënarin impossible

anhetadzëgeli urgent

anhrazhesht necessary; da anhrazhesht e it's necessary

anhrazheshtut'yun necessity

anisoni serm aniseed

anitsel to swear; to curse

aniv wheel

anjatel to cut off; to switch off; Elektrakanut'yunë anjatvel e. The electricity has been cut off.

anjatich *electric* switch

ank'aghak'avari impolite

ankakh independent; ankakh petut'yun independent state

ankakhut'yun independence

ankanon disorderly

ankaskats *adverb* sure

ankent'an lifeless

ankoghin bed

ankyun corner

anmarsoghut'yun indigestion

anmegh innocent

anmijapes immediately

anmit thoughtless; unwise

annëshan insignificant

anot' pot

anot'evan homeless

anshusht certainly

ant'am member

antarr wood; forest

anteghyak uninformed

antibiotik antibiotic

antifriz anti-freeze

antsanot' stranger

ants'ats *adjective* past

ants'ats dar the past century

ants'at'ught' pass; I.D.

ants'nel to pass

ants'ord passer-by

ants'yalë *noun* past

anun name; Inchpes e dzer anunë? What is your name?; Im anunë Fred e. My name is Fred.

anvadogh tyre/tire

anvëch'ar free of charge

anvëtang safe

anvëtangut'yun safety; security

ap' palm *of hand*; shore

apaga future

apahovagrut'yun insurance; Yes unem bëjëshkakan apahovagrut'yun. I have medical insurance.

apahovagrvats insured; Im unets'vatsk'ë apahovagërvats e. My possessions are insured.

apaki glass *substance*

apakoghmnoroshel to mislead

apaku shërjanak window pane

aparanjan bracelet

apastan shelter

apats'uts'el to prove

apats'uyts' proof

ap'ion opium

aporini illegal

aprel to live; to be alive

aprelakerp way of life

april April

ap'se dish; plate

apstamb *noun* rebel

apstambut'yun riot

Arab *person* Arab

arabakan *thing* Arab

araberen *language* Arabic

arag fast; quick

aragats'rek'! hurry up!!

aragoren quickly

aragut'yun speed; rate

arahet path

araj forward(s); araj go!

arraj ago; mi shabat arraj a week ago; yerku or arraj two days ago

arrajark proposal

arrajënt'ats' progress

arrajin first; arrajin ognut'yun first aid

arrajnakarg first class
arakan *adjective* male
arrak'elut'yun mission
arrandzin *adjective* separate
arrandznahatuk distinct
arrants' without; **arrants'
ashkhatank'i** without work;
arrants' shak'ar no sugar
arrarka matter; subject
arraspel legend
arrastagh ceiling
arravelut'yun advantage
arravot morning; **ays arravot**
this morning
arbanyak satellite
arbanyakayin herrakhos
satellite phone
arch bear
arch'ich' lead *metal*
arden already
ardyunaberut'yun industry
arev sun
arevamut sunset
arrevangel to hijack; to kidnap
arrevangich kidnapper
arrevangum kidnapping
arevapashtpan aknots'
sunglasses
arevapashtpan k'ësuk'
sunblock
arevatsak' sunrise
arevayruk sunburn
arevelk' *noun* east
arevelyan *adjective* east(ern)
arevmëtyan *adjective* west(ern)
arevmutk' *noun* west
arevot sunny; **Arevot e.** It is
sunny.
arrevtrakan trader
argand womb
argelak brake(s)
argelakel to brake
arhest handicraft
arhestakan artificial; **arhestakan
vot** artificial leg; **arhestakan
dzerr** artificial arm; **arhestakan achk'** artificial eye

arhestavarzh professional
person
arhestavor craftsman
ark *military* shell
ark'ayazn prince
arkëgh chest; box
ark'elel to forbid
ark'elk' veto; **ark'elk' dënel** to
veto
ark'elvats forbidden
armat root
armiut'yun trade union
armunk elbow
arrnet rat
arrokhch healthy
arrokhchapahut'yun healthcare
arrokhchut'yun health
arsenal arsenal
arshav campaign
artadrank' product
artahanel to export
artahanum exports
artahaytut'yun expression
artakark' iravich'ak
emergency
art'arut'yun justice
artarzhuyt' currency
artasahmants'i foreigner
artasahmanyan foreign
artasanel to pronounce
artasanut'yun pronunciation
artazhayt'k'um exhaust/
muffler *of car*
arteria artery
art'nanal to wake up
arts'akel to release
arts'akurt holidays; vacation
arts'an monument; statue
artsat' silver
artsiv eagle
arts'unk' tear(s)
art'uk iron *for clothes*
art'un awake
art'yok' whether
art'yunk' result
arvarts'an suburb

arvest art

aryun blood; **aryan khumb** blood group; **aryan ch'ënshum** blood pressure; **aryan stugum/aryan analiz** blood test; **aryan p'okhnerarkum** blood transfusion; **aryan bardëzr ch'ënshum** high blood pressure; **aryan ts'atsër chënshum** low blood pressure

aryunahosel to bleed

arryuts lion

arzhel to be worth

arzhenal to cost

asats'vatsk' proverb

asegh needle; **Duk' unek' t'el yev asegh?** Do you have a needle and thread?

asel to say; to tell

ashakert *school* pupil

ashkharh world

ashkhatank' occupation; job; work

ashkhatel to work; **Yes ashkhatum em bankum.** I work in a bank.; **Herrakhosë chi ashkhatum.** The phone doesn't work.

ashkhatogh worker

ashora rye

ashtarak tower

ashun autumn; fall

Asia Asia

aspirin aspirin

astarr lining *of clothes*

astëgh star; **astgher** stars

astghaditak telescope

astich'an *academic* degree

astich'anner stairs

ast'ma asthma

Astvats God

astvatsashunch Bible

ataghdzagorts carpenter

atam tooth; **atamner** teeth; **atami khozanak** toothbrush;

atami matsuk toothpaste

atamnabuyzh dentist

atamnak'ëchp'orik toothpick

atamnats'av toothache

at'eist atheist

atel to hate

atelut'yun hate

atërch'anak pistol

at'letika athletics

atomayin atomic

at'orr chair

at'orrak stool; seat

atsakan adjective

atsukh coal

avak' elder; senior; **avak' ekhbayr** elder brother

avanak donkey

avandakan traditional

avanduyt' custom; tradition

avart *noun* final

avartel to finish

avaz sand

avazak bandit

avel more; **aveli shat** more; **aveli k'ich** little, less; **aveli lav** better; **Yes indz aveli lav em zgum.** I feel better.

avelats'nel to add

avelats'um addition

avelts'uk excess

aviats'ia aviation

aviaughi airline

avlel to sweep

avlets'uts'ich sweeper

Avstralia Australia

avstraliakan *thing* Australian

avstraliats'i *person* Australian

avtobus bus

avtobusov by bus

avtokayan bus station

avtomat machine gun

avtomatavor gunman

avtomek'enayi dimats'i apaki windshield/windscreen

avtomek'enayi gërants'um car registration

avtomek'enayi p'asta-t'ëght'er car papers

aygegorts gardener

aygi garden; yard

ayn that; those

ayntegh there

ayo yes

ayrel to burn

ayri widow

ayri tghamard widower

ayrvatsk' *medical* burn

ays this; these

aysk'an this much

aysor today

aystegh here

ayt cheek

aytk'an shat so much/many

aytpes so

aytpisi such

aytsamis goat *meat*

ayts'elel to visit

ayts'elu visitor

aytuts' edema

azat free; liberated; azat zhamanak free time; Ayn nëstaranë azat e? Is this seat free?

azatagrel to liberate

azatel to free; to sack; to dismiss

azatut'yun freedom; liberty

azdër hip; thigh

azg state; nation

azgakts'ut'yun *blood* relationship

azganun surname; family name

azgayin national

azgut'yun nationality

ß

bach'kon jacket

bad *noun* duck

bagazhategh trunk; boot *of car*

bah spade; shovel

baits' but

bajanagh brother-in-law *wife's sister's husband*

bak yard; courtyard

bakht luck

bakteria bacteria

bal cherry; plum

bambak cotton wool

bamper bumper/fender

banak army

banakanut'yun *noun* mind

banakts'ogh negotiator

banali key

banan banana

banasteghts poet

banavech' argument; row

banjareghen *fresh* vegetables

banjaregheni khanut' vegetable shop

bank bank

bankir banker

bant prison

bantarkyal prisoner

bar bar; pub

barr word

barakut'yun thinness

barraran dictionary

bardz pillow

bardzër high; loud; loudly

bardzraguyn dëprots high school

bardzranal to climb; to mount

bardzrats'nel to lift

bardzrut'yun height

baregortsakan kazmakerp-ut'yun charity *organization*

baregortsut'yun charity *action*

barekam relative; barekamner relatives

barel *storage* barrel

barev! hello!

bari *adjective* kind; good; bari galust welcome!; bari gisher! good night!

barik' ev charik' good and evil

barts' cushion

barts'rahasak tall

barts'rakhos speaker

barur diaper; Yerekhayis barurë petk' e p'okhrm. I need to change my baby's diaper.

basketbol basketball

bats' *adjective* open; light *in color*

bats'akajut'jun absence

bats'atrel to explain

bats'atrut'yun explanation

bats'atrut'yunner explanations

bats'el to open

bats'i *preposition* besides; except (for)...

bats'ich bottle-opener; can opener

bats'ik postcard

bavakan enough; bavakan linel to be enough

bavarar sufficient; satisfactory

bavararvats satisfied

bay verb

baze falcon

bazhak *drinking* glass; cup; mi bazhak jur glass of water

bazhanel to divide; to share

bazhanmunk' department

bazhanum division

bazhin portion

bazmapatkel to multiply

bazmapatkum multiplication

bëghavel to shout

bëjëjajyin herrakhos cell phone

bëjëjayin herrakhos mobile phone

bëjij insect; bëjijner insects

bekakal *medical* splint

bekh mustache

bëlur hill

bem *theater* stage

bëmbulayin vermak duvet

bënakan natural; bënakan aghet natural disaster;

bënakan pasharner natural resources

bënakaran apartment

bënakchut'yun population

bënakich tenant

bënakvel to live; to dwell

bënut'yun nature; the natural world

benzin petrol; gasoline

berr cargo; load; luggage

beran mouth

berel bring

bërrënkvel to flash

berk' harvest

bërrnak handle

berrnakir dzi packhorse

berrnarkëgh *freight* container

berrnatar mek'ena lorry; truck

bërrnel to catch

bërrnut'yun violence

bërt'ya woolen

bërrunts'k' fist

bët'amat thumb

bëzhëshkakan *adjective* medical; bëzhëshkakan apahovagrut'yun medical insurance

bëzhishk doctor

bib pupil *of eye*

birt coarse

blank *official* form

bobik barefoot

boghok'arkel to protest

boghok'arkum protest

bok's boxing

bolor all; bolor miasin all together

boloragëlkhark hat

borbos must; to have to

bots' fire

brindz rice; mak'tars brindz hulled rice; yep'ats brindz cooked rice

britanakan *thing* British

britanats'i Briton

Britania Britain
broshyurr brochure
bu owl
buk'sirayin ch'opan tow rope
buk'sirel to tow
bun stem; trunk *of tree*
burr handful
burd wool
burmunk' fragrance
busaker mard vegetarian; Yes busaker mard em. I am a vegetarian.
buys herb; plant
buzhel to cure; to heal
buzhum medication
byuje budget
byurokratia bureaucracy

CH/CH'

ch'agar rabbit
chagh *adjective* fat
ch'ahich' marsh; swamp
ch'akat forehead; front
ch'akatagir destiny; faith
ch'akatamart battle
ch'akndegh beetroot
chalma turban
ch'ambar camp; Menk' karoghenk' aystegh ch'ambar dënel? Can we camp here?
chamich raisins
ch'amp'ord traveler; ch'amp'ordner travelers; ch'amp'ord cheker traveler's checks
ch'ampruk trunk; box; suitcase
chamusnats'ats single *not married*
ch'anachel to recognize
ch'anachvats known; well-known
ch'anapar road; route; way
ch'anaparayin nëshan road sign
ch'anaparayin vostikanut'yun traffic police
ch'anaparordakan gortsakalut'yun travel agency
ch'anaparordel to travel
ch'anaparordut'yun travel; ch'anaparort'ut'yan nëpatak reason for travel
ch'anj *noun* fly
chap'el to measure
ch'aponakan *thing* Japanese
ch'aponats'i *person* Japanese
ch'aponeren *language* Japanese
Ch'aponiya Japan
chap's size
ch'artarakhos eloquent
ch'artarapet architect
ch'ash dinner
ch'ashak taste
ch'asharan dining room
chëghchik bat
cheghyal hamarel to cancel; T'rrichk'ë cheghyal e hamarvel. The flight is canceled.
chëhashvats apart from
chek bill; check
ch'ekhk'el to split
ch'ëk'nazham crisis
ch'ëkuyt little finger
ch'enapaki chinaware
chënayats although
ch'ënch'ghuk sparrow
ch'ënshel to press
chënshum pressure
chëpayt'ats rumb unexploded bomb
ch'ëshgërit correct; true; certain
ch'ëshmartut'yun truth
chëvats'uts'ak travel timetable
chil kak'av partridge
chinakan *thing* Chinese
Chinastan China

chinats'i *person* Chinese
chineren *language* Chinese
chisht right; correct
chor dry; arid; stale; **chor khot** hay
chorek'shap't'i Wednesday
chorrord fourth
chors four
chorut'yun dryness
ch'purr dragonfly
ch'yugh branch

D/DZ

dadarets'nel quit
daghdz mint
dahuknerov sahel to ski
danak knife
dandagh slow; **dandagh!** slowly!
daniakan Danish *thing*
daniats'i Dane
danieren Danish *language*
dar century
darak drawer; shelf
daran ambush
darrë bitter
darrnal become
darpas gate
darp'in blacksmith
das class; period; lesson
dasagirk' manual *book*
dasak platoon
dasakargum arrangement
dasakhosut'yun lecture
dasaran *academic* class
dashnamur piano
dasht field
dashtanashërjan *menstrual* period
dashuyn dagger
dastak wrist
datapartel condemn
dataran *law* court

datark empty
datarkel to empty
datavarut'yun *legal* trial
datavor judge *noun*
dayak nurse
dazhan severe; cruel; **dazhan shok'** severe heat
deghamijots' cure
deghatun pharmacy
deghdz peach(es)
deghin yellow
deghorayk' *medical* drug; medicine
dëghyak palace; castle
dekada decade
deklarats'ia declaration
dektember December
demkh face
dëndasegh pin; safety pin
dënel to put; **ts'ats dënel** to put down
depi: depi ach to the right; **depi dzakh** to the left
dëprots' school; **dëprots'i ashakert** school pupil; **dëprots'i usuts'ich** school teacher
derr yet
derrahas infant
dërakht paradise
dërrnapan janitor
derts'ak dressmaker; tailor
despan ambassador
despanatun embassy
dët'um pumpkin
dëzhbakht unfortunate
dëzhbakhtabar unfortunately
dëzhokhk' hell
dëzhvar hard; difficult
diabetik diabetic
dialekt dialect
diarea diarrhea
dieta diet
dimadrel to resist
dimakayel to face
dimanëkar portrait
dimats'ë in front of

dinamo dynamo
dIrk' position
ditel to watch
ditord observer
divaharut'yun rabies
divaharvel to catch rabies
divanaget diplomat
divanagitakan kaper diplomatic ties
dizel diesel; to save *money*
dizenteria dysentery
dogh fever
dogherots'k' malaria
dollar dollar
dondoghak jelly
dram money
dramapanak wallet
dramarkëgh booth; cashier's booth; ticket office
droshmakënik' *official* stamp
du you *singular*; **du ink'ëd** yourself
duk' you *plural*; **duk' ink'nerëd** yourselves
dunch chin; jaw
durr door; **durrë tsatskel** to close a door
dur gal to like
durs *preposition* beyond; **durs gal** to exit; to go out; **durs hanel** to pull out; **durs netel** to throw out
dursë outside
dustër daughter; **dëstrer** daughters
duyl bucket
dyurinut'yun ease
dyuzhin dozen
dzakh left; left-wing
dzakhlik left-handed
dzayn voice; sound; **dzayn tal** to cast a vote
dzaynagrel to reconcile
dzeghnahark loft
dzëk'el to pull
dzëknorsut'yun fishing;

dzëknorsakan ts'ants' fishing net
dzëmerr winter
dzëmeruk watermelon
dzer your *singular*
dzerr hand
dzerbakalum arrest
dzerë your *plural*
dzerrk' arm
dzerrk'i jamats'uyts' wristwatch
dzerrk'i lapter flashlight
dzerrnap'ayt walking stick
dzerrnark instructions *on use*
dzerrnarkutyun business; enterprise
dzerrnots'ner gloves
dzerp'akalel to take prisoner
dzev shape; form; manner; mode
dzi horse; **dzier** horses; **dzi nëstel** to ride a horse
dziagënats'ut'yun horseback riding
DZIAH AIDS
dziapan stable-groom
dziarshav horse racing
dziastats' hornet
dzit'agortsaran dairy
dzoghik plank
dzu egg; **khashats dzu** boiled egg
dzuk fish
dzyan p'at'ilner snowflakes
dzyun snow; **Dzyun e galis.** It is snowing.

Ɛ

ej page
ek'spres express; fast
elektrakan shok electric shock
elektrakanut'yun electricity
elektralamp lightbulb
elektronayin p'ost e-mail

elektronayin p'osti hasts'e e-mail address
ëmbshamart wrestling
emigrant immigrant
ëmpelik' drink; liquor
ënddimut'yun opposition
ëndmijel to break
ëndmijum recess; break
ëndunaran reception *desk/area*
ëndzarryuts leopard
ënker *male* friend; boyfriend
ënkerk' placenta
ënkeruhi *female* friend; girlfriend
ënkerut'yun friendship
ënknavorut'yun epilepsy
ënknel to fall
ënt'anali passable; Ays ch'anaparë ënt'anali e? Is the road passable?
ëntani domestic *animal*
ëntanik' family
ënt'anrapes generally
ënt'anur *adjective* general
ënt'erts'um reading
ëntrel to choose; to elect
ënt'rik' supper
ëntrogh voter
ëntrut'yun election
erekhaner children
ev and
evakuats'nel to evacuate
ezhan cheap; **aveli ezhan** cheaper

F

fak's fax; **fak'si mek'ena** fax machine; **fak's ugharkel** to fax
fakultet faculty *of university*
farsi Farsi
fayl *computer* file
federatsia federation
fen hairdryer
fermer farmer
festival festival
fik'sel fix
finansakan gortser financial affairs; finance
finansner finance; money
firma firm; company
fizika physics
fizikakan physical
fiziot'erapia physiotherapy
flomaster felt-tip pen
folklor folklore
fransiakan *thing* French
fransiats'i Frenchman; Frenchwoman
fri french fries
funt pound *weight/sterling*
fut' foot *measurement*
futbol football; soccer; **futboli mërts'akhagh** soccer match

G/GH

gagat' peak; top; **gagat'nazhoghov** summit
gaghap'ar idea
gah throne
gakhtni *adjective* secret; **gakhtni vostikanut'yun** secret police
gakhtnik' *noun* secret; **gaghtnik'ner** secrets
gal to come
gala gala
galon gallon
gamp'ërr sheepdog
gandzapah cashier
gandzapetaran treasury *ministry*
gang skull
gangat complaint
gangatvel to complain
gangrena gangrene
garr lamb
garazh garage
garejur beer
garejur patrastel to brew

gari barley
garri mis lamb *meat*
garun spring *season*
gavarr province
gavat‘ bowl; mug
gayl wolf
gaz gas
gazananots‘ zoo
gazar carrot
geghets‘ik beautiful
geghets‘kut‘yun beauty
gëlkhak‘anak livestock
gëlkhapëtuyt dizzy
gëlkhats‘av headache
gëlkhavor main
gëlkhavor klerk head clerk
gëlukh head; chapter; **Gëlukhës pëtëtvum e.** I feel dizzy.
gënahatel to estimate; to value
gënal to go; **gënal ayntegh** to go *over there*; **gënal k‘ënelu** to go to bed
gënats‘k‘ train
gënats‘k‘asharzh locomotive
gëndak ball; bullet; **gëndak khëp‘el** *sports* to score; **Ov khëpets‘ gëndak‘ë?** Who scored?
gëndaki netum *football* pitch
gënel to buy
general *noun* general
gënord buyer
genots‘id genocide
gënum buying
gënumner shopping
ger thick; wide
gëradaran library
geradasel prefer
gërakanut‘yun literature
gëramek‘ena typewriter
geran beam; girder
gerandi scythe
gërants‘um check-in; **gërants‘man byuro** check-in counter
gërasenyak office;

gërasenyaki ashkhatogh office worker
gërasenyakayin pituk‘ner stationery
gërasenyakayin pituk‘neri khanut‘ stationer's shop
gëratakhtak blackboard
gërav mortgage
gëravel yerkir to occupy a country
gëravogh uzher occupying forces
gerazants‘ excellent
gërchahat penknife
gërel to write
gerezman *noun* grave
gerezmanatun cemetery
gërich pen
gërk‘eri khanut bookshop
germanakan *thing* German
Germanatsi *person* German
germaneren *language* German
Germania Germany
gërogh writer
gërpan pocket
get river; **geti ap‘** riverbank
getak‘ar rubble
gët‘al spoon
getin floor; ground
gëtnel to find
ghek steering wheel
ghekavar boss; head
ghekavarel to direct
gid guide
gin price; worth
gindz coriander
ginekolog gynecologist
gini wine
gipsakap *medical* plaster cast
gir writing
girk‘ book
gisher night; **ants‘ats gisher** last night; **ays gisher** tonight
gisherayin akumb nightclub
gitakan scientific
gitakts‘el to realize

gitenal to know; **Du nëran gites?** Do you know him/her?; **Yes chëgitem.** I don't know.; **Yes gitem.** I know.

gitelik' knowledge

gitnakan scientist

gits line

gitut'un science

gogh thief; **gogher** thieves

goghanal to steal

goghut'yun theft

gol *football* goal

gomaghb manure

gorg rug

gort frog

gorts work; business

gortsadir executive

gortsadul strike *from work*; **gortsadul anel** to strike *from work*

gortsaran factory

gortsarar businessman; businesswoman

gortsats gorg carpet *woven*

gortsatsut'yun use

gortsazërkut'yun unemployment

gortsazurk unemployed

gortsel knit

gortsënker colleague; companion

gortsik'ner tools

gortsvatsk' cloth; material

goti belt

gotkategh loins

govazdel to advertise

govergank' praise

goyakan noun

gram gram

greypfrut grapefruit

grip flu

gudronapatats khëch'ughi tarmac road

gulpaner socks

gumar amount; sum

gumarel *maths* to add

gumarum *maths* addition

gunavor matit crayon

gut'an plow

guyn color

gyugh village; countryside

gyughapet head *of village*

gyughatëntesut'yun agriculture; farming

gyughats'i villager

gyughum in the country

H

hab pill; tablet

hach'akh often

hach'akhakioren frequently

hach'eli nice

hach'uyk' pleasure

haghordagrut'yun *news* report

haghordakts'ut'yun communications

haghordap'ok fan belt

haghordel to report; to transmit

haghordich transmitter

haghordum program; **radio haghordum** radio program

haghort'agrut'yun message

haghort'avar speaker *on radio/TV*

haght'aharel to conquer; to overcome

haght'anak victory

haght'el to win; to beat; **Ov e haght'el?** Who won?

hajoghut'yun success

hajord next; **hajord shap'at'** next week

hakadir opposite

hakahërt'irrajin t'ndanot' anti-aircraft cannon

hakanekhich antiseptic

hakarrakord opponent

hak'nel to wear

hak'nëvel to get dressed

hak'ust clothes; **hak'usti khanut'** clothes shop

hamach'arak epidemic

hamadzaynut'yun agreement

hamagortsakts'ut'yun co-operation

hamakark' system

hamakark'chayin computer virus; **hamakark'chayin tsëragir** computer program

hamakark'ich computer

hamalërum reinforcements

hamalsaran university

hamapataskhan according to; appropriate

hamar for

hamarë havak'el to dial; **Karogh em ughigh hamar havak'el?** Can I dial direct?

hamarya almost; nearly

hamarzhek' equivalent

hamaynk' community

hamazgest uniform *clothing*

hamazhoghov conference

hamburel kiss

hamegh tasty

hamematel to compare

hamemunk' spice

hamenayndepës however

hamerg concert

hamergayin srah concert hall

hamest modest

hamozvats *adjective* sure

hamp'eratar *adjective* patient

hamp'erek'! be patient!

hamtesel to taste

handart *adjective* quiet

handartoren quietly

handartvats conciliated

handerts'ank' munitions

handipel meet

handipum meeting

handzënvel to give oneself up

handznel to hand over; to extradite; to submit

hanel to take out; to subtract

hangëstanal to relax; to rest

hangëstats'uts'ich deghamijots' tranquilizer

hangist rest; relaxation

hank' mineral

hank'ap'or miner

hank'aran *mineral* mine

hankartsaki suddenly

hank'ayin jur mineral water

hanrach'anach famous

hanragir petition

hanrakats'aran hostel

hanrapetut'yun republic

hants'agorts criminal

hants'agortsut'yun crime

hanum subtraction

hanun for the sake of

hanvel to get undressed; to undress

hap'shtakel to loot

haraberut'yun relationship

haraf *noun* south

harafayin *adjective* south(ern)

hardzakum attack; assault

hardzakvel to attack

harevan neighbor

hargank' respect

hark floor; story; tax

harkel to tax

harkerits' azatvats tax-free

harmar suitable

harmarank' accommodation

harmaravet comfortable; **Ays nstateghë harmaravet e.** This car seat is comfortable.

hars bride; daughter-in-law; sister-in-law *brother's wife/ husband's brother's wife*

harsanik' wedding

harst'um inquiry

hart' level; smooth

hart'avayr *noun* plain

harts' question

harts'azruyts interview

harts'munk' inquiry

harts'nel to ask

hart'ut'yun plane

harust rich

harvatsel to hit; to strike

haryur hundred

hasarak simple

hasarakakan social

hasarakut'yun society

hashish hashish

hashiv *sports* score; **Inchk'an e hashivë?** What's the score? *in football*

hashmandam disabled; **hashmandami bazkat'orr** wheelchair

hashtets'um reconciliation; **azgayin hashtut'yun** national reconciliation

hashvarkich calculator

hashvarkum calculation

hashvel count

hashvich meter *dial*

haskanal to understand; **Duk' haskanum ek'?** Do you understand?; **Yes haskanum em.** I understand.; **Yes ch'em haskanum.** I don't understand.

hasnel to overtake *by car*

hast shorer thick cloth

hastap'or paunchy

hasts'e address

hasun ripe

hatapëtugh berry

hatel to cross

hatkapes especially

hator book; volume

hats' bread; loaf; **hats' t'ëkhel** to make bread

hats'abuyser ach'ets'nel to grow crops

hats'ahatik corn; grain

hats'i p'urr bakery

hav chicken; hen; **havi mis** chicken *meat*

havanabar probably

havanakan probable; **Da havanakan e.** It is probable.

havanakanut'yun probability

havasar equal

havat belief

havatal to believe

havatats'yal believer

havelyal extra

haverzh eternal

hay *person* Armenian

Hayastan Armenia

Hayastani Azgayin Zhoghov Armenian National Assembly

hayeli mirror

hayeren *language* Armenian; **Duk' gitek' hayeren?** Do you know Armenian?

haykakan *thing* Armenian

hayr father; **hayrer** fathers

hayrenik' homeland

haytnaberel discover

haz cough

hazal to cough

hazar thousand

hazaramyak millennium

heghap'okhut'yun revolution

heghasërjum coup d'etat

heghegh avalanche

hëghi pregnant; **Yes hëghi em.** I'm pregnant.

heghinak author

heghuk liquid

hëmtut'yun skill

hëmut skilled

hënaravor e perhaps; possibly

hënaravorut'yun possibility

hënavurts' ancient

hëndik *person* Hindu; Indian

hëndkahav turkey

hëndkakan *thing* Indian

Hëndkastan India

hëndzum reaping

hents' ays this (very)

hents' hima just now; right now

henvel to lean
hëpart proud
hëpartut'yun pride
herraditak binoculars
herradzaynel to telephone
herragir telegram
herrahaghordagrut'yun telecommunications
hërahang directions
herrakhos telephone
herrakhosavar telephone operator
hëraman order; command
hëramayel to order; to command
hëraparak town square
hërashk' miracle
hëratarakel to publish
hëratarakich publisher
hërats'an gun; rifle
hëraver invitation
hëravirel to invite
herravor distant
hërel to push
herkel to plow
hërmështuk' jam
heros hero
hert' queue; line
hërt'irr rocket; missile; **hërt'irrayin ardzakich** rocket-launcher; missile launcher
herru far
herrustats'uyts' television
hëstak exact
het with; **Yes gënats'i nëra het.** I went with him.
hetagayum afterwards
hetak'ënnel investigate
hetak'ënnum investigation
hetak'ërk'ërel to interest
hetak'ërk'ir interesting
hetak'ërk'rut'yun interest
hetapëndel to chase
hetazotum research

hetevapes therefore
hetlotën pedestrian
hetk' track; trail
heto after; then
hetsan girder
hetsaniv bicycle
higiyena hygiene
hima now
himar fool; foolish
himk' base; bottom; basis; foundation *of building*
himnadram foundation *organization*
himnel to establish
hin k'aghak' old city
hindi Hindi
hinduizm Hinduism
hing five
hingshabti Thursday
hishel to remember
hishoghut'yun memory
hisun fifty
hivand ill; sick; **hivand linel** to be ill; **Yes hivand em.** I am ill.
hivandanots' hospital
hivandut'yun illness; disease
hod joint
hodvats article; paper; item
hog care
hogehangëstyan funeral prayer
hogh soil
hognats tired
hognel to get tired
hoktember October
holandakan Dutch *thing*
holandats'i Dutchman; Dutchwoman
holanderen Dutch *language*
horak'uyr aunt *father's sister*
horeghbor: horeghbor aghjik cousin *father's brother's daughter*; horeghbor vordi cousin *father's brother's son*; horeghbor kin

aunt *father's brother's wife*
horekhbayr uncle *father's brother*
hort' *animal* calf
hort'i mis veal
hosal to flow
hosk' stream
hot smell; herd
hotazertsich deodorant
hov cool; cold
hovanots' umbrella
hovatak stallion
hovit valley
hoviv cowherd; shepherd
hrea Jew
hreakan *thing* Jewish
hreakanut'yun Judaism
hretani artillery
hrushak cake
hugharkavorut'yun funeral
hulis July
hum raw
humanitar humanitarian; **humanitar ok'nut'yun** humanitarian aid
humor humor
hunakan *thing* Greek
Hunastan Greece
huneren *language* Greek
hunis June
hunvar January
huyn *person* Greek
huys hope; braid
hyupatosaran consulate
hyur guest
hyuranots' hotel; guesthouse
hyurënkal hospitable
hyusats carpet *knotted*
hyusel to weave
hyusis *noun* north
hyusisayin *adjective* north(ern)
Hyusisayin Irlandia Northern Ireland
hyut' juice; **mërk'ayin hyut'** fruit juice

I

ichats anvadogh flat tire; **Anvadoghës ijel e.** I have a flat tire.
ichnel to descend
igakan *adjective* female
im my; mine
imanal to know
imastun wise
imastut'yan atam wisdom tooth
imastut'yun wisdom
inch? what?; **inch e da?** what's that?; **inch vor** whatever; **Sa inch arje?** How much is it?; How much does this cost?
inchk'an? how many?; how much?
inchpes? how?
inchpisi? what kind?
inchu? why?
inchvor ban something
inchvor kerp somehow
inchvor mekë somebody; someone
inchvor tegh somewhere
indz me
inë nine
inësun ninety
infekts'ia infection
ink'nahos gërich ballpoint
ink'natirr to board *a plane*
insektits'id insecticide
institut institute
internet internet
interval interval
inzhener engineer
ir thing
Irak' Iraq
irak'akan *thing* Iraqi
irakan real
irakanut'yun reality
irak'ts'i *person* Iraqi
Iran Iran
iran waist

iranakal waistband
iranakan *thing* Iranian
iranats'i *person* Iranian
iravaban lawyer
iravakan legal; iravakan masnagitut'yun legal profession
iravats'i : Duk' iravats'i ek'. You are right.
iravich'ak situation
iravunk'ner rights
irlandakan *thing* Irish
irlandats'i Irishman; Irishwoman
irlanderen *language* Irish
Irlandia Ireland
irok' indeed
iskakan original
Islam Islam
ispanakan *thing* Spanish
ispanats'i Spaniard
ispaneren *language* Spanish
israelakan *thing* Israeli
israelats'i *person* Israeli
Isrrayel Israel
italats'i *person* Italian
italekan *things* Italian
italeren *language* Italian
Italia Italy
izh viper

J

jakhjakhel to destroy
jardvel to break down; Mer mek'enan jardvel e. Our car has broken down.
jaz jazz
jentëlmen gentleman
jëraghats' watermill
jëraghats'ak'ar millstone
jëraghats'pan miller
jërapomp water pump
jërheghegh *noun* flood
jërhor well *of water*

jërhosk' drain
jërl shish water bottle
jermachap' thermometer
jermut'yun temperature; Amrranë jermut'yunë bardzr e. The temperature in summer is high.; Dzëmrranë jermut'yunë ts'atsr e. The temperature in winter is low.
jërov shish bottle of water
jërp'os pool
jërvezh waterfall
jori mule
jur water; Khëmelu jur ka? Is there drinking water?; jurë pompov k'ashel to pump water

K/K'/KH

ka ... there is/are ...
kabinet *political* cabinet
k'aghak' city; town; k'aghak'i kentron city/town center; k'aghak'i k'artez city/town map; k'aghak'i hëraparak city/town square
k'aghak'akan political; k'aghak'akan gortsich politician
k'aghak'akanut'yun politics
k'aghak'apetaran city hall; town hall
k'aghak'ats'i citizen
k'aghak'ats'iakan *noun/ adjective* civilian; civil; k'aghak'ats'iakan iravunk'ner civil rights; k'aghak'ats'iakan paterazm civil war
k'aghak'ats'iut'yun citizenship
k'aghak'avari polite
kaghamb cabbage
k'aghts'ats hungry
k'aghts'kegh cancer
k'ahana priest; pope

kahuyk' furniture
kakharan clothes hanger
kakhel to hang
k'akhëts'r *adjective* sweet
k'akhts'reghen *noun* noun
kam or
kam ... kam either ... or
kamats'-kamats' little by little
kamera camera
k'ami wind
k'amot windy
kampus campus
kamurj bridge
k'an than; **Ays girk'ë aveli lavn e k'an ayn.** This book is better than that one.
kanach green
Kanada Canada
kanadakan *thing* Canadian
kanadats'i *person* Canadian
kanats' iravunk'ner women's rights
kanayk' women; *and see* kin
kanchel to call; **Vostikanutyun kanchek'!** Call the police!
kanch'rak *noun* rape
kangarr bus stop
kangnel to stop; to stand; **kangnek'!** stop!; **mi kangnek'!** don't stop!
kankhel prevent
kanon rule; regulation
kanonakark'um regulation
kap connection
kapel to tie
kapik monkey
kapital *financial* capital
kaptuk *noun* bruise
kapuyt blue
k'ar stone
karak' butter
k'arrakusi square
k'arandzav cave
k'arrasun forty
karravarakan governmental

karravarich manager
karravarum *act of* direction
karravarut'yun government
karch' short
karel to sew
karer *surgical* stitches
karevor important
karevorut'yun importance
kari mek'ena sewing machine
karich' scorpion
karik' unenal to need
kark' arrangement; order
karkut hail
karmir red
Karmir Khach Red Cross
Karmir Mahik Red Crescent
karogh: Karogh em utel? Can I eat?; **Yes karogh em...** I can...
k'arrord quarter; **k'arrord jam** quarter of an hour
karpet t'aghik'e carpet *felt*
k'arsh tal drag
kart' hook
kart'al to read
k'artez map; **Yerevani k'artez** map of Yerevan
kartofil potatoes
kartses likely
k'artughar secretary
karruts'el to build
karruts'vatsk' structure
kaset; kaseta cassette
k'ash weight
kashi leather
kashve koshikner rubber boots
kaskats suspicion
kaskatsel doubt
kat' milk; human milk; **kovi kat'** cow's milk; **aytsi kat'** goat's milk; **kat'i p'oshi** powdered milk
katak *noun* joke
katarel to perform
katarum performance
kataryal perfect

kat'eter catheter
kat'nashorr cottage cheese
kat'nasun mammal
k'ats'akh vinegar
katu cat
kat'vatsahar paralyzed
kat'vatsel to paralyze
kavagortsut'yun pottery
kavich' chalk
kayanategh car park
kayaran station
kayazor garrison
k'ayk'ayel corrupt
k'ayk'ayel to walk; to hike;
  k'aylelu p'ayt walking stick
k'aylvatsk' pace
kaytsak lightning
kaytsakach'armand zipper;
  fastener
kazdurum recreation
kazino casino
kechup ketchup
keghts false; Ays dramë keghts
  e. This money is counterfeit.
keghtsanun penname
keghtsik' counterfeit
këlor round
k'ëlung pickax
kënaber degh sleeping pill(s)
kënch'it'avor ch'pur cicada
k'ënel to sleep; gënal k'ënelu
  to fall sleep
kënerek'! sorry!
k'eni sister-in-law *wife's sister*
kënkokh sleepy
k'ënnarkel to discuss
k'ënnarkum discussion
k'ënnel *academic* to test;
  medically to examine
k'ënnut'yun exam;
  k'ënnut'yunë handznel to
  pass an exam
kent'ani animal; kent'aniner
  animals
kentron center
kentronakan hëraparak
  main square

k'erakanut'yun grammar
kërakayrich lighter
kërakë varrel to light a fire
kërakel to shoot; Mi kërakek'!
  Don't shoot!
k'errakin *mother's brother's wife*
kerakrakat'sa cooking pot
kerakrel to feed
keramika ceramics
kërch'at briefly
k'erri uncle *mother's brother*
kërriv fight; fighting
kërkin again
kërknapatkel to double
kërknel to repeat
kërrtats khoz boar
k'ërtink' sweat
kërtser junior
kërtskal bra/brassiere
kërtsk'avandak chest; thorax
kërt'ut'yun education
k'erru: k'erru aghjik cousin
  mother's brother's daughter;
  k'erru vordi cousin *mother's
  brother's son*
kërunk heel
kërrvarar cockerel
kërrvel to fight
kes half
kesgisher midnight
kesor afternoon; noon; midday;
  ays kesorin this afternoon
kesorits' heto p.m.
kesrar father-in-law
kestari half year
k'ësuk' cream; ointment
keszham half-hour
ket point
këtërtel to chop
këtor piece
këtrel to cut
këtsel to bite
këts'ort'ich clutch *of car*
këtsu spicy; hot
këzak'is ferret
khachmeruk crossroads;
  intersection

khumb

khagh game
khaghagh banakts'ut'yunner peace talks
khaghaghapah zork'er peace-keeping troops
khaghaghut'yun peace; **khaghaghut'yun berel** to bring peace
khaghal to play
khaghogh grapes
khaki khaki
khal mole
khanut' shop; store; **khanut'i ter** shopkeeper
khap'el to deceive
kharrnel to mix
kharrnel to stir
kharrnurd mixture
khayt'el to sting
khëch'ëch'vats twisted
khëch'ughi highway; motorway
khëch'ughineri k'artez road map
kheghdvel to choke; **Na kheghdvum e!** He/She is choking!
khëkhunj snail; *snail/sea* shell
khelagar crazy
khelagarrvats insane
khelamit intelligent
khëlarar silencer/muffler *of car*
khëlats'uts'ich silencer/muffler *of car*
khëlel to take away; to take off *something*
khëmats drunk; intoxicated; **khëmats linel** to be drunk/intoxicated
khëmbagir editor
khëmel to drink
khëmelu jur drinking water
khëmor dough
khënamel to tend *to the sick*
khëndir problems; trouble; **Inchumn e khëndirë?** What's the trouble?

khëndzor apple
khënt'ir problem
khënt'ir ch'ëka! no problem!
khënt'rum em! please!
khëp'el to beat
khëramat trench
khërel to stick
khërrëmp'ots' snore
khëtrakanut'yun distinction
khëts'an bath plug; cork
khëts'anahan corkscrew
khit antarr thick forest
khizakh brave
khizakhut'yun courage
khoghovak pipe; tube
khohanots' kitchen
khohanots'ayin paharan cabinet; cupboard
khoharar *noun* cook
kholera cholera
khonav damp; humid
khor deep
khorërdaran parliament
khorërt'akts'el to consult
khorërt'atu consultant
khorhel to consider
khorhurd council
khort': khort' hayr stepfather; khort' k'uyr half-sister; khort' mayr stepmother; khort' yeghbayr half-brother; khort' yekhpayr stepbrother
khorut'yun depth
khosal to speak; **Duk' khosum ek' angleren?** Do you speak English?; **Yes khosum em angleren.** I speak English.
khoshor anasun cattle
khot grass
khots' ulcer
khoy ram
khoz pig; khozi mis pork
khozuk porcupine
khul deaf
khumb group

khuzel to shear

k'ich less; **k'ich t'e shat** more or less

kilogram kilogram

kilometr kilometer

k'imia chemistry

k'imiakan chemical

kin woman; wife; female; *and see* kanayk'

kinofestival film festival

kinonëkar movie

kinonëkarich filmmaker

kinot'atron cinema

kiosk kiosk; newsstand

kiraki Sunday

kirch' mountain pass; ravine

k'it' nose

kit'ron lemon

klan clan

klerk clerk

klient client

klima climate

klinika clinic

k'nats asleep

kobra cobra

koch' ankle

koch'ak button

koch'kamer buttonhole

k'ochvor nomad

kod code; **mijazgayin herrakhosakod** international dialing code

koghm side

koghmnats'uyts' compass

koghoptel to rob

koghoptich robber

koghoput robbery

koghoskër rib(s)

koghp'ek lock; padlock

kokord throat

k'olej college

komite committee

kompakt disk C.D.; **kompakt-disk pleyer** C.D. player

kompania company; firm

k'onë yours *singular*

konferents' dahlich' conference room

konfet candy

konk' *noun* sink; pelvis

kontakt contact

kontaktayin linzaner contact lenses

kontuzia *medical* concussion

kopich' pebble

kopit rude

K'oran Quran

korek millet

kortsanel to crash

korts'nel to lose; to mislay; **Yes banalis korts'rel em.** I have lost my key.

korrupts'ia corruption

k'os itch

koshik shoe; boot; **koshikner** shoes; boots

koshiki khanut' shoeshop

koshkakar cobbler

kosht hard; rough; coarse

kosmetika make-up; cosmetics

kostyum suit *of clothes*

kotërvatsk' fracture

kotërvel to fracture

kov cow

Kovkas Caucasus

kovkasyan *thing* Caucasian

kreditayin k'art credit card

kret wasp

kriket cricket *game*

k'ristoneakan *thing* Christian

k'ristoneut'yun Christianity

k'ristonya *person* Christian

kron religion

kronakan religious; **kronakan aghand** religious sect

k'san twenty

k'suk' ointment

kul tal to swallow

kurtsk' breast

kusakts'ut'yun *political* party

kusht: kusht linel to be full up; **Yes kusht em!** I am full up!

kutakel to collect; to gather
kuyr *adjective* blind
k'uyr sister; **k'uyrer** sisters
kuyrats'nel to blind
kuyrer blind people
kuzh jug
k've vote
k'vearkel to vote
k'yabab kebab
kyank' life

l

laboratoria laboratory
lakot puppy
lamp lamp
lanch lunch
lanj hillside
lapter torch; flashlight
lar wire
larvatsut'yan tak lar live wire
lastanav ferry
lats' linel to cry; to weep
lav *adjective/adverb* good; well
lavaguyn best
lavats'nel to improve
lavik pretty
layn wide
lëch'ak pond
leghapark gall bladder
lëpëstel to lick
lep't'op' laptop computer
lëragrogh journalist
lërats'nel to fill; **dzevë lërats'nel** to fill in a form
lërrelyayn silent
lëriv lusin full moon
lerrnakhbyur mountain stream
lerrnants'k' mountain pass
lerrnayin vëtak mountain stream
lërtes spy
lërrut'yun silence
lësap'oghak stethoscope
lësel to hear; to listen

lëtsak lever
lëts'anav tanker
lëts'nel to pour
lëts'vats linel to be full
lëvanal to wash
lëvatsaran washbowl; basin
lëvats'ats washed
lëvats'k'arar laundry person
lëvats'k'atun laundry
lëvats'k'i p'oshi washing powder
lëvats'oghakan mijots'ner detergent
lezu language; tongue
lezvaban linguist
lezvabanut'yun linguistics
li full
Libanan Lebanon
libananakan *thing* Lebanese
libanats'i *person* Lebanese
lich' lake
lider leader
lind gum
linel to be
linza lens
litër liter
lobi green beans
logaran bathroom
logh swimming
loghal to swim
loghanal to bathe
loghavazan swimming pool
loghazgest swimsuit
lolik tomato
lu flea
lurj serious; **Iravich'akë lurj e.** The situation is serious.
lusabats' dawn
lusakir traffic lights
lusanëkar photo
lusanëkarich photographer
lusanëkarum photography
lusatsërogh gëndak tracer bullet
lusavor bright; light
lusavorel to light
lusavorvats alight

lusayin indikator

lusayin indikator indicator light; blinker
lusin moon
lutsel to solve
luts'ki matches *for fire*
luys *noun* light
lyard liver
lyart'i borbok'um hepatitis

⅏

machet'e machete
magnisayin magnetic
magnitofon tape recorder
mah death
mahats'ats dead
mahch'akalik cot
mahmedakan *thing* Muslim; Islamic
makagrut'yun inscription
makanun nickname
makardak *noun* level
mak'rel to clean; to clear
mak'saneng smuggler
mak'satun duty *customs*
mak'saturk' *border* customs
mak'ur clean; fresh; cool
malukh cable
mamul (the) press; **azat mamul** the free press
manër p'ogh coins
mangagh sickle
mankabardzuhi midwife
mankabuyzh pediatrician
mankabuzhut'yun pediatrics
mankavarzh *primary school* teacher
manrakhich' gravel
manyak necklace
marrakhogh mist; fog
mardaspan killer; assassin
mardaspanut'yun killing; assassination
mardu iravunk'ner human rights
margarit pearl

mark'agetin meadow
mark'are prophet
marmin body
mart' human; human being
mart March
martarshav raid
mart'aspan murderer
mart'aspanut'yun murder
martik fighter
mart'ik people
mart'kayin *adjective* human; **mart'kayin iravunk'ner** human rights
martkots' *electric* battery
marzum exercise; activity
mas part
mashk skin
mashkakht eczema
masnaget specialist
masnagitut'yun profession
masnakts'el to participate
mat finger; toe; **mater** fingers; toes
matakararel to supply
matakararumner supplies
mat'ematika mathematics
matit pencil
matnots' thimble
matras mattress
matsun yogurt
matuts'ogh waiter
matuts'oghuhi waitress
mayis May
mayr mother; **mayrer** mothers
mayrak'aghak' capital *city*
mayt' footpath
mazer hair
mazeri khozanak hairbrush
mechtegh middle
mechteghi mid-
mëgdakats' vermak quilt
meghadrel to accuse; to denounce
mëghdzavanj nightmare
meghër honey
mëghon mile
meghu bee

mejë inside
mejk' *noun* back
mek one
mek hok'u senyak single room
mëkan muscle; **mëkanner** muscles
mek'ena car; machine
mekh *metal* nail
mekhak pink
mekhanikakan mechanic
meknabanut'yun commentary
meknel to leave
meknum departure; **meknumner** departures
mëkrat scissors
mekusats'vats blocked; **Zuk'aranë zbaghvats e.** The toilet is blocked.
mënal to stay; to remain
mënats'ogh remaining
mënatsordë rest; remainder
menk' we; us
menk' ink'neres ourselves
menyu menu
mer our
mërchyun ant
merk naked
mërk'ahyut' syrup
mërk'ayin hyut' fruit juice
mërrsats kokord sore throat
mërrsel: Yes mërrsel em. I have a cold.
mërrsum: Yes mërrsum em. I am cold.
mërts'akhagh *football* match
mërts'aktsut'yun competition
mërts'anak prize
mërts'avar referee
mërts'um contest
mërts'uyt' tender
mësavach'arr butcher
mëshakats banjareghen vegetables *ready to eat*
mëshakel to cultivate
mëshakuyt' culture
mështakan constant

mëshushot foggy
mëtadrut'yun intention
mëtadrvel to intend
metagh *noun* metal
metaghadram coin
metaghya *adjective* metal
metak's silk
metak'se silken
mëtek'i' come in!
metër metre/meter *distance*
mëtnel to enter
metro metro; subway; underground
mets big; great; **mets masë** most
mets sërunk'oskër tibia
metsabekorner lumps *of earth*
metsamasnut'yun majority
mëts'ënel to put in
mët'ut'yun dark; darkness
mez us; urine
mëzkit' mosque
mi ... do not...!
miakoghmani p'oghots' one-way: one-way street
miapet monarch
miapetut'yun monarchy
miasin together
miats'nel to connect; to switch on
Miavorvats Azger United Nations
miayn *adverb* only
miaynak only; alone; single
mich'ants'k' corridor
michat bug; insect
michev among
mijazgayin international; **mijazgayin karravarich** international operator; **mijazgayin kod** international code; **mijazgayin tërrichk'** international flight
mijev between; through
mijin *adjective* average

mijots' media
mijots'ov through; by means of
milion million
minchderr still; yet; while
minchev before; until; minchev vor ch-... unless
mirk' fruit
mis meat
misht always
Miss Miss
mistik mystic *person*
mitk' thought
miut'yun union
modem modem
moghes lizard
mokhraguyn grey
molorvets'i: Yes molorvets'i. I am lost.
mom candle; momer candles
momakal candlestick
morak'ëroj aghjik cousin *aunt's daughter*
morak'ëroj vordi cousin *aunt's son*
morak'uyr aunt *mother's sister*
morranal to forget
morrats'vats forgotten
morekh locust
mort' sheepskin coat
mort'e boloragëlkhark fur hat
moruk' beard
mot near
motavorapes approximately
motik *adjective* close (to)
mototsʻiklet motorbike; motorcycle
motsak mosquito
motsakneri ts'ants' mosquito net
mtatsel think
muk mouse
murats'kan beggar
murch' hammer
musulman *person* Muslim
mut' *adjective* dark
mutk' entrance; mutk' chëka no entry

Ո

na he; she; it; na ink'ë himself; herself; itself
naft' *engine* oil
naft'ahank' oilfield
naft'ahor oil well
naft'amëshakogh gortsaran oil refinery
naft'amugh oil pipeline
nahanj tari leap year
nahanjel to retreat
nakhabazuk forearm
nakhach'ash breakfast
nakhadasut'yun sentence *of words*
nakhagah president *of country/ organisation*; speaker *of parliament*
nakhagahakan t'iknazor presidential guard
nakhants'yal orë the day before yesterday
nakhapap great-grandfather
nakharar minister
nakhararutyun ministry
nakhatat great-grandmother
nakhorok' previously
namak *written* letter
namakanish *postal* stamp
napastak hare
narënjaguyn orange *color*
nargile hookah
narinj orange *fruit*
narkayats'uts'chut'yun representation
nav ship
navahangist port
navap'okhadraberr freight *noun*
nayel to look
negh narrow
nëkar drawing; painting; picture
nëkaragrel to describe
nëkarel to draw *an image*
nëkarich artist; painter

nekhats rotten
nëkugh cellar
nëman like; similar
nëmush model; example
nengali treacherous
nënjapark sleeping bag
nënjasenyak bedroom
nëparavach'arr greengrocer
nëpatak goal; aim; objective
nëra his; her; hers; its; **nëra girk'ë** his book
nëran him; her; it
nërank' they
nërank' inknerë themselves
nërants' their; theirs; them
nerarkots' syringe
nerarryal included
nërbagegh *adjective/adverb* fine
nerel to forgive
nerets'ek'! excuse me!
nergaght' immigration
nerk paint
nerka present; current
nerkak'ogharkum camouflage
nerkayats'nel to introduce; to represent
nerkayats'uts'ich representative
nerkel to paint
nerkërel to import
nerk'ev below; down
nerk'evi under; bottom
nerkhuzhel to invade
nerkhuzhum invasion
nerk'in *adjective* interior; internal; **nerk'in gortseri nakhararutyun** ministry of the interior
nerk'nazgest underwear
nërrnak grenade
nërp'ants'k' sidestreet
nershënchel to infuse
nerum excuse
nëshan sign
nëshanakel to mean; Inch e

sa nëshanakum? What does this mean?
nëshanakut'yun sense; meaning; **Da nëshanakut'yun chuni!** It doesn't matter!
nëshanneri lezu sign language
nëshel mark
nëstakëtron boarding pass
nëstaran bench
nëstashërjan session
nëstats seated
nëstel to sit; to get in *to a vehicle*
nëstelategh seat
nëstots' seat *in vehicle*
netel to throw
nëvagel to play *a musical instrument*
nëvazanal to decrease
nëver present; gift
nëviratvut'yun gift
nihar thin
nist sitting
nokhaz goat
nor new; **nor tari** new year
Nor Zelandia New Zealand
noradzevut'yun fashion
noralusin new moon
noratsin yerekha newborn child
normal normal
norut'yun news; news story
Norvegia Norway
not'atetër notebook
noyember November
nurr pomegranate(s)
nush almond
nuyn same
nuynakanats'um identification; I.D.
nuynisk even; even if
nuynpes too; also
nyart' nerve
nyut' material

O

och'arr soap
odap'okhich *electric* fan
odzik' collar
ogh *noun* ring
ognut'yun aid
ogtavetut'yun utility
ok'nakan *noun* second
ok'nel to help; **ok'nets'ek'!** help!; **Duk' karogh ek' indz ok'nel?** Can you help me?
ok'nut'yun help
ok'tagortsats secondhand
ok'tagortsel to use
ok'takar useful
ok'takarut'yun usefulness
operator operator
or day; **Inch or e aysor?** What day is it?
orran cradle
orat'ert' daily newspaper; *and see* t'ert'
orats'uyts calendar
orenk' law
organ organ *of body*
orhnel bless
orinak example; edition; copy; **orinaki hamar** for example
orinakan iravunk' legal right
Oriord Ms.
ot' air
ot'achu pilot
ot'akayan airbase
ot'anav airplane
ot'anavakayan airport; airfield
ot'anavashenk' aircraft hangar
ot'arakich air conditioner
ot'arakum air conditioning
ot'ayin harts'akum air-raid
ot'ayin p'ost air mail
ot'ayin uzh air force
ots' snake
otsanelik' perfume

ots'i khayt'um snakebite
ov? who?
ovkianos ocean
ozhit dowry

P/P'

pah moment
pahanj need
paharan cupboard
pahel to hold; to keep
pahest store; storehouse
pahestatup' magazine *of gun*
pahestayin aniv spare tire
pahesti yelk' emergency exit
pahpanak condom
pahpanel to maintain
pait'el to blow up; to explode
paitsarr intelligent
p'ak closed
pakasut'yun lack; shortage
p'akel to lock
p'ak'et' packet; package
p'akhchel to escape; to flee
p'akhëstakan refugee; **p'akhëstakanner** refugees; **p'akhëstakanneri ch'ambar** refugee camp
pakhpaghak ice cream
p'akhust escape; flight
p'amp'ështakal cartridge belt *of gun*
p'amp'usht cartridge *of gun*
panir cheese
pap grandfather
p'ap'uk soft
par dancing
paran rope
parartanyut' fertilizer
parashyut parachute
parek patrol
parel to dance
parenayin aprank'ner provisions
park sack; bladder
parrkel to lie down

p'armani teenager *girl*

parmanuhi young girl

parpel to pump

parsavagir pamphlet

parsik *person* Persian

parskeren *language* Persian; Farsi

partakanut'yun obligation

partez garden

partizan guerrilla

partk' debt; **partk' verts'ënel** borrow; **partk'ov tal** to lend

partut'yan matnel to defeat

partut'yun defeat

partvats defeated

parunakel contain

parz clear

pas fasting; fast; **pas pahel** to fast; **Yes pas em pahum.** I am fasting.

pasharum siege

pashton *political* seat

pashtonakan *adjective* official

pashtonya *noun* official; **pashtonyaner** officials

pashtpanel to protect; to defend; to guard

pashtpanut'yun protection

p'asian pheasant

p'ast fact

pasta pasta

p'astat'ught' document

p'astat'ught'ë droshmel to stamp a document

p'astel to state

pat wall

patahar accident

patahel to happen

patand hostage; **patand verts'nel** to take hostage

patani teenager *boy*

patarak'agh fork

pataskhan answer

pataskhanel to answer

p'at'at'el to roll up; to wrap; **pat'at'el t'elë** to wind thread

patch'arr cause; reason

patch'arrel to cause

patch'arrov because of

patch'en copy; photocopy

patch'enahanel to copy; to photocopy

patch'enahanman mek'ena photocopier

paterazm war; **paterazm varel** to wage war

paterazmi hërdzig warmonger

patëshgamb balcony

patgarak *hospital* stretcher

pativ honor

patker image

patmaban historian

patmëvatsk' story; tale; novel

patmut'yun history

patrast ready; **Yes patrast em.** I am ready.

patrastut'yunner preparations

patrastvats cooked

patrastvel to prepare

patrrel to tear

patshach' proper; tactic

pats'ient *medical* patient

patsparvel to take shelter

patuhan window

patvastel vaccinate

patviratoms reservation *ticket/place/room*

patvirel to order; **utelik patvirel** to order a meal

patzhel to punish

payk'ar struggle

p'aylatakum flash *of camera*

p'aylel to shine

payman condition; term

paymanagir contract; treaty

paymanavorvatsut'yun arrangements

p'ayt wood; stick

p'aytatsukh charcoal(s)

paytel to shoe *a horse*

payt'el to explode

paytsarr *adjective* light; bright

payt'uts'ik nyut'er explosives

payt'yun explosion

payusak bag; handbag

p'ëchats'nel to spoil

p'ëchel to blow

pëghindz copper

p'ëlatakner ruins

penits'ilin penicillin

p'ëntrel to look for; to search; andz p'ëntrel to search a person; tun p'ëntrel to search a house

p'ërrështal to sneeze

p'ërrështum sneeze

p'ërkel to save; to rescue

p'esa bridegroom; brother-in-law *sister's husband*; son-in-law

p'ëshalar barbed wire

p'ëskhel to vomit; Yes p'ëskhum ei. I have been vomiting.

p'etërvar February

pëtëtum spin

pëtghaber fertile

pëtghatu aygi orchard

petk': indz petk' e... I need...

pëtutak screw

pëtutakabanali spanner; wrench

pëtutakich screwdriver

petut'yan ghekavar head of state

petut'yun *federal* state

pëtuyt turn

pies play *of theater*

p'igh elephant

pind tough; tight; Ays misë pind e. This meat is tough.

plastik plastic

platforma *railway* platform; platformai hamar platform number

plita cooker

p'och'ok beans

poem poem

poezia poetry

p'ogh gun barrel

p'oghots' street

p'ok'ër little; small

p'okhadrel to transport

p'okhanakum exchange; Duk' artarzhuyt' p'okhanakum ek'? Do you change money?

p'okhants'um gear *car*

p'okharen instead

p'okharinel to replace

p'okharkich transformer

p'okhel to change; Yes uzum em mi k'ich dollar p'okhel. I want to change some dollars.

p'okhhatuts'um compensation

p'okhnakhagah vice-president *of country*

p'ok'ramasnut'yun minority

p'ok'rik mas a bit

polo polo

pomp pump

poni pony

popok nut

p'op'okhut'yun change

p'ordzarkum test; trial

p'ordzel to try

p'orel to dig; to drill; jërhor p'orel to drill a well

p'orkap constipation

p'orp'akvats constipated; Dzez mot p'orkaput'yun e? Are you constipated?

port navel

portalar umbilical cord

porrt'kum gust

p'oshi powder

p'ost mail; post office

p'ostarkëgh mailbox

p'ostov by post

p'ot'orik storm; blizzard; gale

Pr Mr.

profesor professor

prot'ez prosthesis

proyektor projector

p'ush thorn

R/RR

rradiator radiator
rradio radio
rradio haghordum radio program
rradiokayan radio station
rradiolokator radar
rradio yet'er radio broadcast
RRamadan Ramadan
rrazmageri prisoner-of-war
rrazmakan *adjective* military; rrazmakan tsarrajut'yun military service
rrazmakayan military base
rregbi rugby
rrejim regime
rrëmbakotsum bombardment
rrëmbanetum bomb disposal
rrentgenyan ch'arragayt'ner X-rays
rrestoran restaurant
rretin rubber; eraser
rrisk risk
rriski dimel to risk
rope *noun* minute
rrumb bomb
rrus *person* Russian
rrusakan *thing* Russian
RRusastan Russia
rruseren *language* Russian

S/SH

sag goose
saghm germs
sahman border; frontier; limit; **sahmani ants'um** border crossing; **sahmanner** limits
sahmanadrut'yun constitution
sahmanapah border guard
sakavaryunut'yun anemia
salat' lettuce
sandalner sandals
sandukhk' ladder
sandzel tame
sanrel comb
sap'ërvel to shave
sap'ërvelu k'suk' shaving cream
sap'rich razor
sar mountain
sard spider
sarrë *adjective* cold; **sarrë jur** cold water
sarrel to freeze
sarrets'um freezing
sark'avorum equipment
sarrnamanik' frost
sarrnaran fridge
sarrts'adasht glacier
sarrts'akalats icy
sarruyts' ice
satana devil
savan sheet
sayl cart
sayt'ak'el to fall over
sayt'ak'un slippery
seghan table
seghmel to grasp; to squeeze
sëghots' *noun* saw
sekh melon
sëkhal mistake; wrong; **sëkhal tuyl tal** to make a mistake
sëkhtor garlic
sëmbuk aubergine; eggplant
seminaria seminary
sendvich sandwich
senyak room
sep'akan *adjective* own
sep'akanater owner *of building*
sep'akanut'yun ownership *of property*
sëpërt'nats pale
sëp'ot'el to confuse
sëp'rrel scatter
sëp'rrots' tablecloth
september September
septik septic

ser love
serr sex; gender
serrakan akt (act of) sex
serrakan organner genitals
sërats'nel to sharpen
sërënk'amis calf *of leg*
sërënt'ats' rapid
serial series *radio/TV*
sermer seeds
sërp'azan holy
sërp'ich towel
sev black; **sev shuka** black market
sevanerk mascara
shabat' week; **ays shabat'** this week
shafran saffron
shaganakaguyn brown
shaghgam turnip
shahen hawk
shahuyt' gain
shak'ar sugar
shak'arakht diabetes
shak'araman sugar bowl
shakhmat chess
shal shawl
shampun shampoo
shap'at'akan weekly
shap'at'or Saturday
shapik shirt
sharahyusut'yun syntax
sharan range
sharravigh sprout
sharf scarf
sharjvel to move
shark' row; line
sharunakel to continue; **sharunakek'!** continue!
sharzhich engine
shat very; too; too much/many; **shat k'ich** too little; **voch shat** not much
shëchak car horn
sheghp' razor blade
shëkht'a chain
shënagayl jackal

shënchap'ogh trachea; windpipe
shënchel to breathe
shenk' building
shëp'ot'vats confused
sheram silk worms
sherep' ladle
shërjakayk' nearby
shërjan circle; district; period *of time*
shërjapatel to surround
shërjel to turn; to reverse; **shërjek' dzakh!** turn left!; **shërjek' aj!** turn right!
shërt'nak'suk' lipstick
shërt'unk' lip
shinarar builder
shish bottle
shnorakalut'yun thanks; **shnorakalut'yun!** thank you!; **shnorakalut'yun haytnel** to thank
shog: Shog e. It is hot.; **Yes shogum em.** I am hot.
shok *medical* shock
shokolad chocolate
shor dress
shoshapel advert
shotlandakan *thing* Scottish
shotlandats'i Scot
Shotlandia Scotland
shrapnel shrapnel
shtab headquarters; **shtap ok'nut'yun** ambulance
shtapel to be in a hurry; **Yes shtapum em.** I'm in a hurry.
shtapoghakanut'yun hurry
shuka market
shun dog
shutov soon
sigaret cigarette(s)
simbol symbol
sinagoga synagogue
siramarg peacock
sirel to love; **Yes sirum em...** I like...

t'ak'avorakan

sireli dear; loved
Siria Syria
siriakan *thing* Syrian
siriats'i *person* Syrian
sirt heart; **sërti harvats** heart attack; **sërti vich'ak** heart condition
skësats since
skësel to start
skëzbunk'ayin principal
skisur mother-in-law
skizb beginning
skutegh tray
skyurrik squirrel
soghvatsk' landslide
sokh onion(s)
sokhak nightingale
sosindz glue
sous sauce
sov hunger; famine
sovats hungry; **Yes sovats em.** I'm hungry.
sovorabar normally
sovorakan normal
sovorel to study; to learn; **angir sovorel** to learn by heart
spa *military* officer
spanakh spinach
spand slaughter
spanel to kill; to murder
sparrvel to run out (of)
spasel to wait (for); **spasets'ek'!** wait a moment!
spasum waiting
speghani *medical* plaster; cast
spirt *medical* alcohol
spitak white
spitakavun whitish
sport sports
sportsmen sportsman
spung sponge
sp'yurrk' diaspora
stadion stadium
stamok's stomach; **stamok'si khots'** stomach ulcer; **stamok'si ts'av** stomachache

stanal to get; to receive; to gain
steghtsel to create
steik' steak
sterling sterling
stipvats linel to have to
storagrel to sign *a document*
storagrut'yun signature
struk slave
stugel to check; **Yughë stugek'.** Check the oil.
stugel to test
stugoghakan ashkhatank' *academic* test
stvarat'ught' carton
stver shade
sulots' whistle
sult'an sultan
sup soup
supermarket supermarket
sur sharp
surch' coffee; **kat'ov surch'** coffee with milk
surp' saint
sut *noun* lie
suzvel to sink
svin bayonet
sviter sweater

T/T'/TS/TS'

tach'ar temple
t'agavor king
t'agavorum reign
t'aghamas quarter *area*
t'aghel to bury
taghvats stuck
t'aghvel to be stuck; **Mer mek'enan t'aghvel e.** Our car is stuck.
t'aguhi queen
tak' warm; hot; **tak' jur** hot water
tak *preposition* under
takarr butt
tak'ats'nel to heat
t'ak'avorakan royal

tak'degh pepper
t'akel knock
t'aknëvats hidden
t'aknëvel to hide
tak'si taxi
taktika tactics
tal sister-in-law *husband's sister;* to give; *and see* **tur indz**
t'alanel: Indz t'alanel en! I've been robbed!
t'an buttermilk
t'anak' ink
tandz pear
t'andzër sup thick soup
t'andzramokank' gravy
tanel carry
t'angaran museum
tanik' roof
tanjank' torture
tanjel to torture
tank tank *military*
t'ankarzhek' expensive
tanker oil tanker
tap' heat
t'ap'aharel to shake
tap'akashish flask
tapakel to fry; to roast
tapar ax
t'ap'el to spill
t'ap'vel to leak
tarr letter *of alphabet;* **tarrer** letters *of alphabet*
tarakan cockroach
taranjatel to separate
tarants'ik t'ërrichk' flight transfer
tarrapyal martyr
taratsashërjan region
taratsel spread
taratsk' area; space; territory
tarber different
tarberut'yun difference
taredarts' anniversary
tarekan annual; **K'ani tarekan ek' duk'?** How old are you?; Yes ... tarekan em. I am ... years old.

t'argmanel to interpret; to translate
t'argmanich interpreter; translator
t'argmanut'yun interpretation; translation
tari year; **ays tari** this year; **nahanj tari** leap year
tarik' age
t'arm recent; fresh *e.g. food*
tarorinak strange
t'art'ichner eyelashes
tarvel to lose; to be defeated
tas ten
taserort' tenth
t'ashkinak handkerchief
tasnëchors fourteen
tasnëhing fifteen
tasnëinë nineteen
tasnëmek eleven
tasnerek' thirteen
tasnerku twelve
tasnëvets' sixteen
tasnëyot' seventeen
tasnut' eighteen
tat grandmother
t'at' foot; sole
t'atron theater
t'ats' wet
tavar beef
tegh place
tëgha boy
teghadrel to place
teghakan local
teghakayvats situated
tëghamard; tëghamart' man; male
tëghamart'ik men
teghamasayin khanut' a local shop for local people
teghap'okhvats andz displaced person
teghatarap' torrent
teghayin local anesthetic
teghekatu directory
teghekatvut'yun information;

tirapetel

teghekatvakan grasenyak information office
t'ëght'adram banknote
t'ëght'akits' reporter
t'ëght'apanak *paper* file
t'ëk'el to spit
tek'ër brother-in-law *husband's brother*
t'ëkhavun blackish
tekhnika technique
tekhnikakan technical
t'ëkht'e ot'aparuk kite
tëkhur sad
tek'st text
t'ek'vatsk' slope
t'el string; thread
telek's telex
t'ëmbuk drum
t'ëmp'kat'aghant' eardrum
t'ëmramol drug addict
t'ëmranyut' drug; narcotic
tënater landlord
tënayin ashkhatank' homework
tënayin t'ërrchun poultry
t'ëndanot' cannon
tenis tennis
tënkel to plant
tënki seedling
tënkum planting
tënoren director; headmaster; principal
tënoreni grasenyak director's office
tënorinum directorship
tent tent
tëntesaget economist
tëntesagitut'yun economics
tëntesakan payusak carrier bag
tëntesel to spare
tëntesut'yun economy *of country*
tëpel to print; to type
tëpich *computer* printer
ter host; owner

t'ërrchel to fly
terev leaf
t'ërrichk' flight *plane*
termit termite
tërohum separation
tërorel to rub; to knead
t'ert' newspaper; sheet *of paper*; t'ert' **anglerenov** newspaper in English; *and see* orat'ert'
t'ërt'ur caterpillar
tesak kind; sort
tesakan theoretical
tesamagnitofon video player
tesaran view
tesazhapaven video cassette
tëshnami enemy
t'ëshnamut'yun feud
tesnel to see
tesoghut'yun sight; eyesight
test test
tesut'yun theory
tetër exercise book
t'et'ev easy; light *not heavy*
t'et'evats'nel to earn
t'ët'u sour
t'ët'vatsin oxygen
t'ev bumper/fender *of car*
t'ëvakan date *time*
t'ëval to seem
t'evk' sleeve
t'ey tea; sev t'ey black tea; kanach t'ey green tea; kat'ov t'ey tea with milk
t'eyaman saucer
t'eyaran tea house
t'eyi gët'al teaspoon
t'eynik kettle; teapot
t'iak shoulder blade
Tikin Mrs.
t'iknapah guard
t'iknapayusak backpack
tiknik doll
t'iknots' cloak
t'im team
tirakal ruler *person*
tirapetel to possess

tirapetut'yun *government* rule
tirel to own
t'it'egh *noun* can
t'it'err butterfly
t'iv number
t'ok' lung
tokosadruyk' *financial* interest
toms ticket
toms mek ughghut'yamb one-way ticket
ton holiday; feast
tonavach'arr show; fair; trade show
tonel to celebrate
tonna ton; tonne
t'orr granddaughter; grandson
tost toast *bread*
traktor tractor
transport transport
t'romboz thrombosis
tsaghik flower
tsaghkabuyts florist
tsaghkakaghamb cauliflower
tsaghkakarel embroider
tsak hole
tsakhsel to spend *money*
tsak'um origin
ts'amak' land
tsamel to chew
tsamon chewing gum
ts'anel to sow
ts'ankanal to wish
ts'ankanal to want; **Inch ek' ts'ankanum?** What do you want?; **Yes uzum em...** I want ...; **Yes chem uzum...** I don't want ...
ts'ankapat fence
tsanot'ut'yun acquaintance
tsanr heavy
tsanrots' parcel
ts'ants' net; **dzëknorsayin ts'ants'** fishing net
tsarr tree; **tsarrer** trees
tsarra servant
tsarav thirst; thirsty; **Yes tsarav em.** I'm thirsty.

tsarrayut'yun service
ts'atkotan jumper; sweater
ts'atsër low
tsatskel to close
tsatskots' bonnet/hood *of car*
ts'atsradasht *noun* sink
ts'atsrats'nel to lower
ts'av hurt; pain
ts'aval to hurt; **Aystegh ts'avum e.** It hurts here.; **Mejk'ës ts'avum e.** My back hurts.
tsaval volume; size
ts'avazërkogh painkiller
ts'avazertsum ëndhanur general anesthetic
ts'avi bërrnkum *medical* stitch *in one's side*
ts'aytkum leap
tseghik straw
tsëghrid cricket; grasshopper
ts'ekh mud
tsëkhakhot tobacco
tsëkhamorch' pipe *for tobacco*
tsëkharan chimney
tsëkhel to smoke
tsëkhelë smoking
tsëkheln ark'elvum e no smoking
tsëkhogh smoker
tsënel to give birth to
tsëneliutyan hëskum birth control
tsënëndaberel to give birth (to)
tsënëndavayr place of birth
tsënëndyan vëkayakan birth certificate
tsënoghner parents
ts'ënts'ugh shower *bath*
tsënund birth; birthday
tsënvel to be born; **Vortegh ek' tsënvel?** Where were you born?; **Yes tsënvel em Nyu York'um.** I was born in New York.
tser old; **tser kin** old woman; **tser mard** old man

tsërar envelope
tsërrel to bend
tsërtaharel frostbite
ts'ërtarrut'yun *medical* cold
ts'ëtesutyun good-bye!
tsetsats beaten
tsëtsel to suck
tsiatsan rainbow
tsiran apricot
tsirani purple
tsistaghal laugh; laughter
ts'isterrn tank *petrol*
tsit bird
tsitsagheli funny
tsitserrnak swallow *bird*
ts'ogh dew
tsorr great-grandchild
tsorak tap; faucet
ts'oren wheat
ts'oreni hatik wheat bin
tsotsrak nape *of neck*
tsov sea
tsovakhets'getin crab
tsovap' coast
tsughak trap
tsukh smoke
ts'ul bull; ox
tsunk knee; **tsunk chok'el** to kneel
ts'urt *noun* cold; **Ts'urt e.** It is cold.
ts'uts'adrel to show
ts'uts'ahandes exhibition
ts'uts'ak list; timetable
ts'uts'amat index finger
ts'uts'ararner *political* demonstrators
ts'uyts' *political* demonstration
tuberkulyoz tuberculosis
tugank' fine *of money*
t'ught' paper *substance*
t'uk' saliva
tun house
tunel tunnel
tur indz ... give me...; *and see* tal
t'urk' Turk
t'urk'akan *thing* Turkish

t'urk'eren *language* Turkish
T'urk'ia Turkey
t'ut' mulberry
t'ut'ak parrot
t'uyl weak
t'uylatrel to let; to allow
t'uyn poison

U

ugharkel to send
ugheberr baggage
ughegh brain
ughekal roadblock
ughekts'el to guide
ughets'uyts' girk' guidebook
ughevor passenger
ughghat'irr helicopter
ughghel to correct
ughghut'yun destination; direction
ughigh straight; direct; upright; **ughigh yet'er** live broadcast
ughighut'yun straightness
ught camel
uik-end weekend
ukhtagënats' pilgrim
ukhtagënats'ut'yan gënal to go on a pilgrimage
ukhtagënats'ut'yun pilgrimage
ul kid *goat*
unak able; **unak linel** to be able
unakut'yun ability
unenal to have
unikal unique
unk' eyebrow; **unk'er** eyebrows
unkëndrogh listener
unts'ia ounce
urrchel to swell
urish other; another
urp'at Friday
urts' cumin

urvagits essay

us shoulder

usanogh *university* student

ush late; Yes ushats'a. I am late.

ushats'um *noun* delay

usumnasirel to research; to survey

usumnasirogh surveyor

usumnasirum study

usumnasirut'yun survey

usuts'anel teach

usuts'ich teacher

usutsum study; instruction

ut' eight

ut'anasun eighty

utel to eat

uteli edible

utelik' food; meal; **utelik' patvirel** to order a meal

uzh strength; power

uzhasparrum exhaustion

uzhegh strong

U

vach'arrel to sell

vach'arrogh salesman

vach'arroghuhi saleswoman

vagh early; Na shut e yekel. He is early.

vaghë tomorrow; vaghë che myus orë the day after tomorrow

vagon carriage

vagonavar carriage driver

vakh fear

vakhats'nel to frighten

vakhch'anvel to die

vakhenal to fear

vakts'inayov patvastum vaccination; Indz vakts'inayov patvastel en. I have been vaccinated.

vank' monastery

varaguyr curtain

varakvats infected; Sa varakvats e. It is infected.

varraran stove; oven; jerruts'ogh varraran heating stove

varchapet prime minister

varchararakan administrative

varel to drive; to lead

varrelap'ayt firewood

varrelik' fuel

vark credit

vark' behavior

varord driver; chauffeur

varordakan iravunk' driver's license

varsavir barber; hairdresser

vart' rose

vart'ak electric plug

varts'el to hire; to rent *for oneself*

varts'ov tal to rent *to someone*

varts'kan mercenary

varung cucumber

varveladzev way; manner

varvelakarg etiquette

varzhut'yun *school* exercise

vastakel to earn

vat bad; badly; **aveli vat** worse; Yes aveli vat em zgum. I feel worse.

vatsun sixty

vaverats'nel to confirm; Yes uzum em im t'ërrichk'ë hastatel. I want to confirm my flight.

vayr location; vayr gëlorvel to overturn

vayrechk' katarel to land *aircraft*

vayri wild *animal*; vayri sag wild goose

vazel to run

vech' argument; dispute

vëch'ar pay; payment; commission; fare; Inchk'an e

vëch'arë? What is the fare?
vëch'arel to pay
vëch'arovi herrakhos pay-phone
vëkayel to testify
vëkayut'yun evidence
vënasatu harmful
vënasel to injure
vënasvats injured
vënasvatsk' injury; trauma
venerakan hivandut'yun venereal disease
ver above; up
vëra *preposition* onto
veradarts'nel to return
verahëskel to control
veranda veranda
veranorok'el to repair
veranorok'um repair
verarku coat; overcoat
Vërastan Georgia
vercherës recently
verchin; verchnakan *adjective* final; last
verelak lift; elevator
verev up
verevum upon; above
verin over
verj end
verjats': Im benzinë verjats'el e. I have run out of petrol.
verjats'nel to end
verjavorut'yunner limbs *of body*
verk' sore; injury
verkenal to get up
vermak blanket
vërts'in brush
verts'nel to take
vëtang danger
vëtangavor dangerous
vëtarel to expel
vëtit *adjective* lean
vets' six
vets'erord sixth
vëzkap tie; necktie

vich'ak state; condition
vich'akakhagh lottery
vich'el quarrel
virabuyzh surgeon
virabuzhakan dahlich' operating theater/room
virabuzhut'yun surgery *subject*
virahatut'yun surgery *operation*
virakap bandage; dressing
viravorel to wound
virus virus
visht grief; sorrow
vit' gazelle
vitaminner vitamins
viz neck
viza visa
voch no; not; **derr voch** not yet; **voch mi** none; **voch... voch** neither ... nor
vochënchats'nel to demolish
vochil louse; lice
vochinch nothing
vochkhar ewe; sheep; **vochkhari mis** mutton
vochmek nobody
vochmekë none
vochmitegh nowhere
voghj alive
voghnashar spine; spinal column
voghnoskër vertebra
vok'i soul
volork' twist
volorvel to wind
vor that; which; **vor mekë?** which (one)?
vorder worms
voreve mekë anyone
vorevits'e tegh anywhere
vork'an herru? how far?; **Vork'an herru e hajord gjughë?** How far is the next village?
voroshel to decide
voroshum decision

vorot thunder

vorovayn uterus

vorovhetev because

vorp' orphan

vorp'anots' orphanage

vors hunt

vorsagoghut'yamb zbaghvel to poach *animals/game*

vorskan shun hound

vorsordut'yun hunting

vort' vine

vortegh? where; **vortegh e?** where is?; **vortegh en?** where are?

vorteghits'? where from?

vort'i son

vort'iner sons

voskerchut'yun jewelry

voskerich jeweler

voski gold

voskor bone

voskratsuts marrow *of bone*

vosp lentils

vostikan policeman

vostikanatun police station

vostikanut'yun police

vot leg

votk'ov on foot

votnalat' nappy; diaper; **Yes petk' e p'okhem yerekhayis taki shorë.** I need to change my baby's nappy.

vozni hedgehog

vra on

vrats'akan *thing* Georgian

vrats'eren *language* Georgian

vrats'i *person* Georgian

vripel to miss *to not hit*

Y

yard yard *distance*

yeghanak weather; season

yeghbayr brother; **yeghbayr-ner** brothers

yeghjeru deer; stag

yeghjyur horn

yeghung nail *of finger/toe*

yegiptats'oren maize

yekeghets'i church

yekek' gënank'! let's go!

yelak strawberry

yelk' exit

yent'aka *noun* interior

yent'astamok'sayin geghdz pancreas

yep'el to cook

yepiskopos bishop

yerak vein

yerakhtapart grateful; **Yes yerakhtapart em.** I am grateful.

yerral to boil

yeram flock

yerramsya quarterly

yerasht heat wave

yerazank' dream

yerazel to dream

yerazhështakan p'arrat'on music festival

yerazhështut'yun music

yerb? when?

yerbemën occasionally

yerek yesterday

yerek' three

yerekam kidney; **yerekamner** kidneys

yerekha baby; child; **amena p'ok'ër yerekha** youngest child

yerek'nuk clover

yereko evening; **ays yereko** this evening

yerek'shabt'i Tuesday

yerekuyt' party; celebration

yerekva yesterday's

yerresun thirty

yerevakayut'yun imagination

yereval to appear

yeritasard young; **yeritasard mard** young person

yerjanik happy

yerk' song; **siro yerk'** love song

yerkamya biannual
yerkar long
yerkarats'nel to lengthen
yerkarut'yun length
yerkat' steel
yerkat'eghen ireri khanut' hardware store
yerkat'ughayin kayaran railway station
yerkat'ughi railway
yerk'el to sing
yerkink' sky; heaven
yerkir country
yerkraban geologist
yerkrabanut'yun geography
yerkragund earth
yerkrasharzh earthquake
yerkrord *adjective* second
yerku two; **yerku angam** twice; **yerku shabat'** fortnight
yerkushap't'i Monday
yerkushap'tiorvanits' since Monday
yerkusn el both
yerkvoryakner twins
yerrord third
yerp'ek' never
yerp'emn sometimes
yershik sausage
yert'evekut'yun traffic
yert'um tal to swear an oath
yerrum *medical* boil
yes I; **yes ink'ës** myself
yetadardz backwards
yet'e if; **yet'e voch** if not; **yet'e miayn** if only; **yet'e hënaravor e** if possible
yetevel follow
yetevum behind
yevro euro *currency*
Yevropa Europe
yevropakan European
Yevropakan Miut'yun European Union
yevs mek shish another bottle

yezër hem
yot' seven
yot'anasun seventy
yugh fat; cooking oil
yughamas oilcan

Z/ZH

zambik mare
zambyugh basket
zang bell
zangaharel to ring; to phone; **Yes uzum em Emmayin zangaharel.** I want to ring Emma.; **Khënt'rum em zangaharek' indz.** Please phone me.
zangvatsayin lëratvut'yan mijots'ner mass media
zargatsum development
zarmanali surprising; **zarmanali linel** to be surprising
zarmats'ats surprised
zarmik nephew
zarmikuhi niece
zartughi roundabout *in road*
zart'uts'ich alarm clock
zaveshtakan humorous
zavt'el to seize
zayrats'ats angry
zbaghvats busy
zbosakhënjuyk' picnic
zbosashërjik tourist; **zbosashërjikner** tourists
zbosashërjikayin grasenyak tourist office
zbosashërjikut'yun tourism
zbosaygi park
zenjefil ginger
zenk' weapon
zërahapatvats mek'ena armored car
zëro zero
zëruts'el to talk
zëruyts' conversation

zëspanak spring *metal*
zeteghel to lay (down)
zëtich *noun* filter
zëzvank' aversion
zgal to feel
zgestavorel to dress
zgushut'yun caution
zguysh careful; gently
zham hour; o'clock; Zhamë vets'ën e. It is six o'clock.
zhamanak time; during; nuyn zhamanakin at the same time; yerkar zhamanakov for a long time; zhamanakin on time; Yes zhamanak chunem. I don't have time.; Zhamë k'anisn e? What time is it?; Avtobusë zhamanakin yekav? Has the bus arrived on time?
zhamanak ants'kats'nel to pass time
zhamanakakits' modern
zhamanel to arrive
zhamats'uyts' clock; watch
zhang rust

zhantahotel to stink
zhapaven tape
zhayrr rock
zhilet waistcoat; vest
zhoghov *government* assembly
zhoghovërdayin yerazhështut'yun folk music
zhoghovërt'avarut'yun democracy
zhoghovërt'ayin par folk dancing
zhoghovurd *noun* folk
zinadat'ar ceasefire; truce
zinvor soldier
zinvorakan handerts'ank' ammunition
zoh victim; zoher victims; yerkrasharzhi zoher earthquake victims
zoramas unit *military*
zork'er troops
zugagulpaner; zuk'agulpaner tights; pantyhose
zuk'aran toilet(s)
zuk'arani t'ught' toilet paper

ENGLISH-ARMENIAN
ANGLEREN – HAYEREN

A

ability unakut'yun
able unak; **to be able** unak linel
about mot; **about 50 miles** motavorapes 50 mëghon; **about town** k'aghak'in mot
above *up* ver; *upon* verevum
absence bats'akajut'jun
academy akademia
accident patahar
accommodation harmarank'
according to hamapataskhan
accuse meghadrel
acquaintance tsanot'ut'yun
acre akër
adapter *electric* adapter
add avelats'nel; *maths* gumarel
addition avelats'um; *maths* gumarum
address hasts'e
adjective atsakan
administration *organization* administrats'ia
administrative varchararakan
administrator administrator
advantage arravelut'yun
advert shoshapel
advertise govazdel
after heto
afternoon kesor; **this afternoon** ays kesorin
afterwards hetagayum
again kërkin
age tarik'
ago arraj; **a week ago** mi shabat arraj; **two days ago** yerku or arraj
agreement hamadzaynut'yun
agriculture gyughatëntesut'yun

agronomist agronom
aid ognut'yun; **aid agency** baregortsakan gortsakalut'yun; **relief aid** humanitar ok'nut'yun
AIDS DZIAH
aim nëpatak
air ot'
airbase ot'akayan
air conditioner ot'arakich
air conditioning ot'arakum
airfield ot'anavakayan
air force ot'ayin uzh
airline aviaughi
air mail ot'ayin p'ost
airplane ot'anav
airport ot'anavakayan
air-raid ot'ayin hardzakum
alarm clock zart'uts'ich
alcohol alkohol; *medical* spirt
alight lusavorvats
alive voghj
all bolor; **all together** bolor miasin
allergic alergik
allow t'uylatrel
almond nush
almost hamarya
alone miaynak
already arden
also nuynpes
although chënayats
always misht
ambassador despan
ambulance shtap ok'nut'yun
ambush daran
America Amerika
American *person* amerikats'i; *thing* amerikyan
ammunition zinvorakan handerts'ank'

among michev

amount gumar

amputate andamahatel

ancient hënavurts'

and ev

anemia sakavaryunut'yun

anesthetic *general* ts'avazertsum ëndhanur; *local* teghayin

angry zayrats'ats

animal kent'ani; **animals** kent'aniner

aniseed anisoni serm

ankle koch'

anniversary taredarts'

annual tarekan

another urish; **another bottle** yevs mek shish

answer *noun* pataskhan; *verb* pataskhanel

ant mërchyun

anti-aircraft cannon hakahërt'irrajin t'ndanot'

antibiotic antibiotik

anti-freeze antifriz

antiseptic hakanekhich

anyone voreve mekë

anywhere vorevits'e tegh

apart from chëhashvats

apartment bënakaran

appear yereval

appetite akhorzhak

apple khëndzor

appropriate hamapataskhan

approximately motavorapes

apricot tsiran

April april

Arab *person* Arab; *thing* arabakan

Arabic *language* araberen

architect ch'artarapet

area taratsk'

argument *row* banavech'

arid chor

arm dzerrk'

Armenia Hayastan

Armenian *person* hay; *thing* haykakan; *language* hayeren;

Do you know Armenian? Duk' gitek' hayeren?

armored car zërahapatvats mek'ena

arms zenk'

army banak

arrangement dasakargum; **arrangements** paymanavorvatsut'yun

arrest dzerbakalum

arrive zhamanel

arsenal arsenal

art arvest

artery arteria

artificial arhestakan; **artificial limb** prot'ez; **artificial leg** arhestakan vot; **artificial arm** arhestakan dzerr; **artificial eye** arhestakan achk'

artillery hretani

artist nëkarich

ashamed amot'ahar

Asia Asia

ask harts'nel

asleep k'nats

aspirin aspirin

assassin mardaspan

assassination mardaspanut'yun

assault hardzakum

assembly *government* zhoghov

asthma ast'ma

astonished zarmats'ats

atheist at'eist

athletics at'letika

atomic atomayin

attack *noun* hardzakum; *verb* hardzakvel

aubergine sëmbuk

aunt *father's sister* horak'uyr; *father's brother's wife* horeghbor kin; *mother's sister* morak'uyr; *mother's brother's wife* k'errakin

Australia Avstralia

Australian *person* avstraliats'i; *thing* avstraliakan

author heghinak
autumn ashun
avalanche heghegh
average *adjective* mijin
aversion zëzvank'
aviation aviats'ia
awake art'un
ax tapar
Azerbaijan Adërbejan
Azerbaijani *person* adërbejants'i;
  thing adërbejanakan; *language*
  adërbejaneren

B

baby yerekha
back *noun* mejk'
backache: I have a backache.
  Mejk'ës ts'avum e.
backpack t'iknapayusak
backwards: to go backwards
  yetadardz
bacteria bakteria
bad vat
badly vat
bag payusak
baggage ugheberr
bakery hats'i p'urr
balcony patëshgamb
ball gëndak
ballpoint ink'nahos gërich
banana banan
bandage *medical* virakap
Band-Aid *plaster* speghani
bandit avazak
bank *financial* bank
banker bankir
bar *pub* bar
barbed wire p'ëshalar
barber varsavir
barefoot bobik
barley gari
barrel *of gun* p'ogh; *storage* barel
base *bottom* himk'; *military*
  base rrazmakayan
basin lëvats'aran
basis himk'

basket zambyugh
basketball basketbol
bat chëghchik
bathe loghanal
bathroom logaran
battery *electric* martkots'
battle ch'akatamart
bayonet svin
be linel
beam *girder* geran
beans p'och'ok; **green beans**
  lobi
bear arch
beard moruk'
beat khëp'el; *to overcome*
  haght'el
beautiful geghets'ik
beauty geghets'kut'yun
because vorovhetev; **because
  of** patch'arrov
become darrnal
bed ankoghin; **to go to bed**
  gënal k'nelu
bedroom nënjasenyak
bee meghu
beef tavar
beer garejur
beetroot ch'akndegh
before minchev
beggar murats'kan
begin skësel
beginning skizb
behavior vark'
behind yetevum
belief havat
believe havatal
believer havatats'yal
bell zang
below nerk'ev
belt goti; **cartridge belt**
  p'amp'shtakal
bench nëstaran
bend *verb* tsërrel
berry hatapëtugh
besides *adverb* nuynpes;
  preposition bats'i

best lavaguyn

better aveli lav; **I feel better.** *health* Yes indz aveli lav em zgum.

between mijev

beyond *preposition* durs; **beyond the river** geti myus ap'in

biannual yerkamya

Bible *Gospel* astvatsashunch

bicycle hetsaniv

big *large* mets; *long* yerkar

bill *check* chek

binoculars herraditak

bird tsit

biro *see* pen

birth tsënund; **to give birth to** tsënel; **birth certificate** tsënëndyan vëkayakan; **birth control** tsëneliutyan hëskum

birthday tsënund

bishop yepiskopos

bit; a bit p'ok'rik mas

bite *verb* këtsel

bitter darrë

black sev

blackboard gëratakhtak

blackish t'ëkhavun

black market sev shuka

blacksmith darp'in

bladder park

blanket vermak

blasphemer astvatsanargogh

bleed aryunahosel

bless orhnel

blind *adjective* kuyr; **blind people** kuyrer; *verb* kuyrats'nel

blizzard p'ot'orik

blocked mekusats'vats; **The toilet is blocked.** Zuk'aranë zbaghvats e.

blood aryun; **blood group** aryan khumb; **blood pressure** aryan ch'ënshum; **blood test** aryan stugum; **blood transfusion** aryan p'okhnerarkum

blow *verb: wind* p'ëchel; k'ami

blow up *to explode* pait'el

blue kaputy

boar kërrtats khoz

board *a plane* ink'natirr

boarding pass nëstakëtron

body marmin

boil *noun* yerrum; *verb* yerral

bomb rrumb; **bomb disposal** rrëmbanetum

bombardment rrëmbakotsum

bone voskor

bonnet *of car* tsatskots'

booby trap akan t'akard

book girk'

bookshop gërk'eri khanut

boot *of car* bagazhategh

booth: cashier's booth dramarkëgh

boots koshikner; **rubber boots** kashve koshikner

border sahman; **border crossing** sahmani ants'um; **border guard** sahmanapah

born: to be born tsënvel; **Where were you born?** Vortegh ek' tsënvel?; **I was born in New York.** Yes tsënvel em Nyu York'um.

borrow partk' verts'ënel

boss ghekavar

both yerkusn el

bottle shish; **bottle of water** jërov shish

bottle-opener bats'ich

bottom *level* nerk'evi

bowl gavat'; **sugar bowl** shak'araman

box arkëgh

boxing bok's

boy tëgha

boyfriend ënker

bra kërtskal

bracelet aparanjan

braid huys

brain ughegh

brake *noun* argelak; *verb*

argelakel
branch ch'yugh
brassiere kërtskal
brave khizakh
bread hats'; to bake bread
  hats' t'ëkhel
break *for refreshments*
  ëndmijum; *verb* ëndmijel
break down: Our car has
  broken down. Mer mek'enan
  jardvel e.
breakfast nakhach'ash
breast kurtsk'
breathe shënchel
brew garejur patrastel
brick aghyus
bride hars
bridegroom p'esa
bridge kamurj
briefly kërch'at
bright *light* lusavor; *intelligent*
  paitsarr
bring berel
Britain Britania
British *person* Britanatsi; *thing*
  britanakan
Briton britanats'i
brochure broshyurr
brother yeghbayr; brothers
  yeghbayrner
brother-in-law *sister's husband*
  p'esa; *husband's brother* tek'ër;
  wife's brother anerdzak; *wife's
  sister's husband* bajanagh
brown shaganakaguyn
bruise *noun* kaptuk
brush vërts'in
bucket duyl
budget byuje
bug *insect* michat
build karruts'el
builder shinarar
building shenk'
bull ts'ul
bullet gëndak
bumper *fender* bamper
bureaucracy byurokratia

burn *medical* ayrvatsk'; *verb* ayrel
burst payt'yun
bury t'aghel
bus avtobus
bus station avtokayan
bus stop kangarr
business *enterprise* dzerrnarkutyun; *work* gorts
businessman gortsarar
businesswoman gortsarar
busy zbaghvats; *telephone call*
  zbaghvats e
but baits'
butcher mësavach'arr
butt *of rifle* takarr
butter karak'
butterfly t'it'err
buttermilk t'an
button koch'ak
buttonhole koch'kamer
buy gënel
buyer gënord
buying gënum
by *see pages 11-14;* by bus
  avtobusov; by post p'ostov

C

cabbage kaghamb
cabinet *cupboard* khohanots'ayin
  paharan; *political* kabinet
cable malukh
cake hrushak
calculation hashvarkum
calculator hashvarkich
calendar orats'uyts
calf hort'; *leg* sërënk'amis
call kanchel; Call the police!
  Vostikanutyun   kanchek'!;
  What are you called? Inch e
  dzer anunë?
camel ught
camera kamera
camouflage nerkak'ogharkum
camp ch'ambar; Can we camp
  here? Menk' karoghenk'
  aystegh ch'ambar dënel?

campaign arshav

campus kampus

can *noun* t'it'egh; **I can...** Yes karogh em...; **Can I eat?** Karogh em utel?

can opener bats'ich

Canada Kanada

Canadian *person* kanadats'i; *thing* kanadakan

canal khoghovak

cancel cheghyal hamarel

canceled: The flight is canceled. T'rrichk'ë cheghyal e hamarvel.

cancer k'aghts'kegh

candle mom; **candles** momer

candlestick momakal

candy konfet

cannon t'ëndanot'

capital *city* mayrak'aghak'; *financial* kapital

car mek'ena; **car papers** avtomek'enayi p'astat'ëght'er; **car park** kayanategh; **car registration** avtomek'enayi gërants'um

care hog

careful zguysh

carefully! zguysh!

cargo berr

carpenter ataghdzagorts

carpet *felt* karpet t'aghik'e; *knotted* hyusats; *woven* gortsats gorg

carriage vagon

carriage driver vagonavar

carrier bag tëntesakan payusak

carrot gazar

carry tanel

cart sayl

carton stvarat'ught'

cartridge *of gun* p'amp'usht

cartridge belt p'amp'ështakal

cashier gandzapah

casino kazino

cassette kaseta

cast: plaster cast *medical* gipsakap

castle dëghyak

cat katu

catch bërrnel

caterpillar t'ërt'ur; **caterpillar track** t'ërt'ur

catheter kat'eter

cattle khoshor anasun

Caucasian kovkasyan

Caucasus Kovkas

cauliflower tsaghkakaghamb

cause *noun* patch'arr; *verb* patch'arrel

caution zgushut'yun

cave k'arandzav

C.D. kompakt disk; **C.D. player** kompakt-disk pleyer

ceasefire zinadat'ar

ceiling arrastagh

celebrate tonel

cell phone bëjëjayin herrakhos

cellar nëkugh

cemetery gerezmanatun

center kentron

century dar

ceramics keramika

certain ch'ëshgërit

certainly anshusht

chain shëkht'a

chair at'orr

chalk kavich'

change *noun* p'op'okhut'yun; *money* manër; *verb* p'okhel; **I want to change some dollars.** Yes uzum em mi k'ich dollar p'okhel.

channel: T.V. channel alik'

chapter gëlukh

charcoal(s) p'aytatsukh

charge: What is the charge? gin: Inch arzh e?

charity *action* baregortsut'yun; *organization* baregortsakan kazmakerput'yun

chase *verb* hetapëndel

chauffeur varord

cheap ezhan

cheaper aveli ezhan

check *bank* chek; *verb* stugel;
Check the oil. Yughë stugek'.

check-in gërants'um; **check-in
counter** gërants'man byuro

cheek ayt

cheese panir; **cottage cheese**
kat'nashorr

chemical k'imiakan

chemistry k'imia

cherry bal

chess shakhmat

chest *box* arkëgh; *of body*
kërtsk'avandak

chew tsamel

chewing gum tsamon

chicken hav; *meat* havi mis

chief *of village* gyughapet

child yerekha; **youngest child**
amena p'ok'ër yerekha

children erekhaner

chimney tsëkharan

chin dunch

China Chinastan

chinaware ch'enapaki

Chinese *person* chinats'i; *thing*
chinakan; *language* chineren

chocolate shokolad

choke kheghdvel; **He/She is
choking!** Na kheghdvum e!

cholera kholera

choose ëntrel

chop këtërtel

Christian *person* k'ristonya;
thing k'ristoneakan

Christianity k'ristoneut'yun

church yekeghets'i

cicada kënch'it'avor ch'pur

cigarette(s) sigaret

cinema kinot'atron

circle shërjan

citizen k'aghak'ats'i

citizenship k'aghak'ats'iut'yun

city k'aghak'; **city center**
k'aghak'i kentron; **city hall**
k'aghak'apetaran; **city map**
k'aghak'i k'artez

civil rights k'aghak'ats'iakan
iravunk'ner

civil war k'aghak'ats'iakan
paterazm

civilian *noun/adjective* k'aghak'-
ats'iakan

clan klan

class *academic* dasaran

clean *adjective* mak'ur; **clean
sheets** mak'ur; *verb* mak'rel

clear *adjective* parz; *verb* mak'rel

clerk klerk; **head clerk**
gëlkhavor klerk

client klient

climate klima

climb *verb* bardzranal

clinic klinika

cloak *woman's/man's* t'iknots'

clock zhamats'uyts'

close (to) *adjective* motik

close *verb* tsatskel; **to close a
door** durrë tsatskel

closed p'ak; *door* p'ak durr

cloth gortsvatsk'

clothes hak'ust; **clothes shop**
hak'usti khanut'

cloud amp

clover yerek'nuk

club akumb

clutch *of car* këts'ort'ich

coal atsukh

coarse birt

coast tsovap'

coat verarku; *sheepskin* mort'

cobbler koshkakar

cobra kobra

cock ak'aghagh

cockerel kërrvarar

cockroach tarakan

code kod; **international
dialing code** mijazgayin
herrakhosakod

coffee surch'; **coffee with milk**
kat'ov surch'

coin metaghadram; **coins**
manër p'ogh

cold

cold *adjective* sarrë; *noun* ts'urt; *medical* ts'ërtarrut'yun; **cold water** sarrë jur; **It is cold.** Ts'urt e.; **I am cold.** Yes mërrsum em.; **I have a cold.** Yes mërrsel em.

collar odzik'

colleague gortsënker

collect kutakel

college k'olej

color guyn

comb sanrel

come gal; **come in!** mëtek'!

comfortable harmaravet; **This car seat is comfortable.** Ays nstateghë harmaravet e.

commentary meknabanut'yun

commission vëch'ar; **What is the commission?** Inchk'an e vëcharë?

committee komite

communications haghordakts'ut'yun

community hamaynk'

companion gortsënker

company *firm* kompania

compare hamematel

compass koghmnats'uyts'

compensation p'okhhatuts'um

competition mërts'aktsut'yun

complain gangatvel

complaint gangat

complete amboghchakan

computer hamakark'ich; **computer program** hamakark'chayin tsëragir; **computer virus** hamakark'chayin

concert hamerg; **concert hall** hamergayin srah

conciliated handartvats

concussion *medical* kontuzia

condemn datapartel

condition *state* vich'ak; *term* payman

condom pahpanak

conference hamazhoghov

conference room konferents' dahlich'

confirm: I want to confirm my flight. vaverats'nel: Yes uzum em im t'ërrichk'ë hastatel.

confuse sëp'ot'el

confused shëp'ot'vats

connect miats'nel

connection kap

conquer haght'aharel

consider khorhel

constant mështakan

constipated p'orp'akvats

constipated: Are you constipated? Dzez mot p'orkaput'yun e?

constipation p'orkap

constitution sahmanadrut'yun

consulate hyupatosaran

consult khorërt'akts'el

consultant khorërt'atu

contact kontakt

contact: I want to contact my embassy. Yes uzum em kapnëvel despanatan het.

contact lenses kontaktayin linzaner

contain parunakel

container *freight* berrnarkëgh

contemporary zhamanakakits'

contest mërts'um

continue sharunakel; **continue!** sharunakek'!

contract paymanagir

control *verb* verahëskel

conversation zëruyts'

converse hakarrak

cook *noun* khorarar; *verb* yep'el

cooked patrastvats

cooker plita

cooking pot kerakrakat'sa

cool *adjective* hov

cooperation hamagortsakts'ut'yun

copper pëghindz

copy *noun* patch'en; *edition*

orinak; *verb* patch'enahanel
coriander gindz
cork khëts'an
corkscrew khëts'anahan
corn hats'ahatik
corner ankyun
correct *adjective* ch'ëshgërit; *verb* ughghel
corridor mich'ants'k'
corrupt k'ayk'ayel
corruption korrupts'ia
cost *verb* arzhenal
cot mahch'akalik
cottage cheese kat'nashorr
cotton wool bambak
cough *noun* haz; *verb* hazal
council khorhurd
count *verb* hashvel
counterfeit keghtsik'; **This money is counterfeit.** Ays dramë keghts e.
country yerkir
countryside gyugh
coup d'etat heghasërjum
courage khizakhut'yun
court *law* dataran
cousin *aunt's daughter* morak'ëroj aghjik; *aunt's son* morak'ëroj vordi; *father's brother's daughter* horeghbor aghjik; *father's brother's son* horeghbor vordi; *mother's brother's daughter* k'erru aghjik; *mother's brother's son* k'erru vordi
cow kov
cowherd hoviv
crab tsovakhets'getin
cradle orran
craftsman arhestavor
crane *machine* ambarts'ich
crash *verb* kortsanel
crayon gunavor matit
crazy khelagar
cream *ointment* k'ësuk'
create steghtsel
credit vark; **credit card**

kreditayin k'art
cricket *game* kriket; *insect* tsëghrid
crime hants'agortsut'yun
criminal hants'agorts
crisis ch'ëk'nazham
cross *verb* hatel
crossroads khachmeruk
crow agrrav
cruel dazhan
cry *to weep* lats' linel
cucumber varung
cultivate mëshakel
culture mëshakuyt'
cumin urts'
cup bazhak
cupboard paharan
cure *noun* deghamijots'; *verb* buzhel
currency artarzhuyt'
curtain varaguyr
cushion barts'
custom avanduyt'; *border* mak'saturk'
cut *verb* këtrel
cut off: The electricity has been cut off. Elektrakanut'yunë anjatvel e.

D

dagger dashuyn
daily amenorya
dairy dzit'agortsaran
dam ambartak
damp khonav
dance parel
dancing par
Dane daniats'i
danger vëtang
dangerous vëtangavor
Danish *thing* daniakan; *language* danieren
dark *adjective* mut'
darkness *noun* mët'ut'yun
date *fruit* khurma; *time* t'ëvakan;

date of arrival zhamanman amsat'iv; **date of departure** meknelu amsat'iv; **date of birth** tsënëndyan amsat'iv; **What's the date?** Aysor amsi k'anisn e?

daughter dustër; **daughters** dëstrer

daughter-in-law hars

dawn *noun* lusabats'

day or; **What day is it?** Inch or e aysor?

dead mahats'ats

deaf khul

dear *loved* sireli

death mah

debt partk'

decade dekada

deceive khap'el

December dektember

decide voroshel

decision voroshum

declaration deklarats'ia

decrease *verb* nëvazanal

deep khor

deer yeghjeru

defeat *noun* partut'yun; *verb* partut'yan matnel

defeated partvats

defend pashtpanel

degree *grade* astich'an; *academic* astich'an

dehydration jërazërkum

delay *noun* ushats'um

delayed: The plane is delayed. Tërrichk'ë hetadzëk'vum e.

democracy zhoghovërt'avarut'yun

demolish vochënchats'nel

demonstration *political* ts'uyts

demonstrators *political* ts'uts'ararner

denounce meghadrel

dentist atamnabuyzh

deodorant hotazertsich

department bazhanmunk'

departure meknum;

departures meknumner

depth khorut'yun

descend ichnel

describe nëkaragrel

desert *noun* anapat

desk seghan

dessert aghander

destination ughghut'yun

destiny ch'akatagir

destroy jakhjakhel

detergent lëvats'oghakan mijots'ner

detonate andërpayt'el

detonation andërpayt'um

development zargatsum

devil satana

dew ts'ogh

diabetes shak'arakht

diabetic diabetik

diagnosis *medical* akhtoroshum

dial *verb* hamarë havak'el; **Can I dial direct?** Karogh em ughigh hamar havak'el?

dialect dialekt

diaper barur; **I need to change my baby's diaper.** Yerekhayis barurë petk' e p'okhrm.

diarrhea diarea

diaspora sp'yurrk'

dictionary barraran

die vakhch'anvel

diesel dizel

diet dieta

difference tarberut'yun

different tarber

difficult dëzhvar

dig p'orel

dining room ch'asharan

dinner ch'ash

diplomat divanaget

diplomatic ties divanagitakan kaper

direct *adjective* ughigh; *verb* ghekavarel

direction *to a place* ughghut'yun; *act of* karravarum

directions hërahang

director tënoren; **director's office** tënoreni grasenyak

directorship tënorinum

directory teghekatu

dirty aghtot

disability anëndunakut'yun

disabled hashmandam

disaster aghet

discover haytnaberel

discuss k'ënnarkel

discussion k'ënnarkum

disease hivandut'yun

dish ap'se

disorderly ankanon

displaced person tegha-p'okhvats andz

dispute *noun* vech'

distant herravor

distinct arrandznahatuk

distinction khëtrakanut'yun

district shërjan

divide *verb* bazhanel

division bazhanum

divorce *noun* amusnalutsut'yun

dizzy gëlkhapëtuyt; **I feel dizzy.** Gëlukhës pëtëtvum e.

do anel; **do not ...!** mi ...!

doctor bëzhishk

document p'astat'ught'

dog shun

doll tiknik

dollar dollar

domestic *animal* ëntani

donkey avanak

door durr; **door lock** koghp'ek

double *verb* kërknapatkel

doubt *noun* kaskatsel

dough: to make dough khëmor

dove aghavni

down nerk'ev

dowry ozhit

dozen dyuzhin

drag *verb* k'arsh tal

dragonfly ch'purr

drain *noun* jërhosk'

draw *an image* nëkarel

drawer darak

drawing *picture* nëkar

dream *noun* yerazank'; *verb* yerazel

dress *noun* shor; *verb* zgestavorel

dressed: to get dressed hak'nëvcl

dressing *medical* virakap

dressmaker derts'ak

drill *verb* p'orel; **to drill a well** jërhor p'orel

drink *noun* ëmpelik'; *verb* khëmel

drinking water khëmelu jur

drive *verb* varel

driver varord

driver's license varordakan iravunk'

drug *medical* deghorayk'; *narcotic* t'ëmranyut'; **drug addict** t'ëmramol

drum *noun* t'ëmbuk

drunk: to be drunk khëmats: khëmats linel

dry *adjective* chor

dryness chorut'yun

duck *bird* bad

during zhamanak

Dutch *thing* holandakan; *language* holanderen

Dutchman; Dutchwoman holandats'i

duty *customs* mak'satun; *obligation* partakanut'yun

duvet bëmbulayin vermak

dynamo dinamo

dysentery dizenteria

Ɛ

each amen

eagle artsiv

ear akanj; **eardrum** t'ëmp'kat'aghant'

early vagh; **She is early.** Na shut e yekel.

earn vastakel
earrings akanjogher
ears akanjner
earth yerkragund
earthquake yerkrasharzh
ease *noun* dyurinut'yun; *verb* t'et'evats'nel
east *noun* arevelk'
Easter zatik
east(ern) *adjective* arevelyan
easy t'et'ev
eat utel
economics tëntesagitut'yun
economist tëntesaget
economy *of country* tëntesut'yun
eczema mashkakht
edema aytuts'
edible uteli
editor khëmbagir
education kërt'ut'yun
egg dzu; **boiled egg** khashats dzu
eggplant sëmbuk
eight ut'
eighteen tasnut'
eighty ut'anasun
either ... or kam ... kam
elbow armunk
elder brother avak' ekhbayr
elder avak'
elect ëntrel
election ëntrut'yun
electric shock elektrakan shok
electricity elektrakanut'yun
elephant p'igh
elevator verelak
eleven tasnëmek
eloquent ch'artarakhos
e-mail elektronayin p'ost; **e-mail address** elektronayin p'osti hasts'e
embassy despanatun
embroider tsaghkakarel
emergency artakark' iravich'ak
emergency exit pahesti yelk'
empty *adjective* datark; *verb* datarkel

end *noun* verj; *verb* verjats'nel
enemy tëshnami
engine sharzhich
engineer inzhener
England Anglia
English *thing* angliakan; *language* angleren
Englishman; Englishwoman angliats'i
enough bavakan; **to be enough** bavakan linel
enquiry harts'munk'
enter mëtnel
enterprise dzerrnarkut'yun
entire amboghj
entrance mutk'
envelope tsërar
epidemic hamach'arak
epilepsy ënknavorut'yun
equal havasar
equipment sark'avorum
equivalent hamarzhek'
eraser rretin
escape p'akhchel
especially hatkapes
essay urvagits
establish himnel
estimate *verb* gënahatel
eternal haverzh
etiquette varvelakarg
euro *currency* yevro
Europe Yevropa
European yevropakan
European Union Yevropakan Miut'yun
evacuate evakuats'nel
even: even if nuynisk
evening yereko; **this evening** ais yereko
every amen
everybody amen mekë
everyone amen mekë
everything amen inch
evidence vëkayut'yun
evident akënhayt
ewe vochkhar
exact hëstak

exam k'ënnut'yun

examine *medically* k'ënnel

example orinak; **for example** orinaki hamar

excellent gerazants'

except (for) ... bats'i...

excess avelts'uk

exchange p'okhanakum; **Do you exchange money?** Duk' artarzhuyt' p'okhanakum ek'?

excuse *noun* nerum; **excuse me!** Nerets'ek'!

execute *verb* katarel

executive gortsadir

exercise *noun: activity* marzum; *school* varzhut'yun; **exercise book** tetër

exhaust *of car* artazhayt'k'um

exhaustion uzhasparrum

exhibition ts'uts'ahandes

exit *noun* yelk'; *verb* durs gal

expect akënkalel

expel vëtarel

expensive t'ankarzhek'

explain batsa'trel

explanation bats'atrut'yun; **explanations** bats'atrut'yunner

explode payt'el

explosion payt'yun

explosives payt'uts'ik nyut'er

export *verb* artahanel

exports artahanum

express *fast* ek'spres

expression artahaytut'yun

extra havelyal

extradite handznel

eye achk'; **eyes** achk'er

eyebrow unk'; **eyebrows** unk'er

eyeglasses aknots'

eyelashes t'art'ichner

eyesight tesoghut'yun

f

fabric gortsvatsk'

face *noun* demkh; *verb* dimakayel

fact p'ast

factory gortsaran

faculty *of university* fakultet

failure anhajoghut'yun

faith ch'akatagir

falcon baze

fall *autumn* ashun; *verb* ënknel; **to fall over** sayt'ak'el

false keghts

family ëntanik'

famine sov

famous hanrach'anach

fan *electric* odap'okhich; **fan belt** haghordap'ok

far herru

fare vëch'ar; **What is the fare?** Inchk'an e vëch'arë?

farm agarak

farmer fermer

farming gyughatëntesut'yun

Farsi *language* farsi

fashion noradzevut'yun

fast *quick* arag; *verb* pas pahel; **I am fasting. Yes pas em pahum.**

fasten amrats'nel

fastener *for clothes* kaytsakach'armand

fasting *noun* pas

fat *adjective* chagh; *noun* yugh

father hayr; **fathers** hayrer

father-in-law aner; kesrar

faucet tsorak

fax faks ugharkel; **fax machine** fak'si mek'ena

fear *noun* vakh; *verb* vakhenal

feast ton

February p'etërvar

federation federatsia

feed *verb* kerakrel

feel zgal

felt-tip pen flomaster

female *adjective* igakan; *noun* kin

femur andzër

fence ts'ankapat

fender *of car* t'ev

ferret këzak'is

ferry lastanav

fertile pëtghaber
fertilizer parartanyut'
festival festival
feud t'ëshnamut'yun
fever dogh
field dasht
fifteen tasnëhing
fifty hisun
fight *verb* kërrvel; *noun* kërriv
fighter martik
fighting kërriv; *argument* vech'
file *computer* fayl; *paper* t'ëght'apanak
fill lërats'nel; **to fill in a form** dzevë lërats'nel
film *movie/camera* kinonëkar/zhapaven
film festival kinofestival
filmmaker kinonëkarich
filter *noun* zëtich
final *adjective* verchnakan; *noun* avart
finance *money* finansner; *financial affairs* finansakan gortser
find gëtnel
fine *adjective/adverb* nërbagegh; *of money* tugank'
finger mat; **fingers** mater
fingernail yeghung
finish *verb* avartel
fire bots'
firewood varrelap'ayt
firm *noun* firma
first arrajin; **first aid** arrajin ognut'yun; **first class** arrajnakarg
fish dzuk
fishing dzëknorsut'yun
fishing net dzëknorsakan ts'ants'
fist bërrunts'k'
five hing
fix fik'sel
flash *camera* p'aylatakum; *verb* bërrënkvel

flashlight dzerrk'i lapter
flask tap'akashish
flat tire ichats anvadogh; **I have a flat tire.** Anvadoghës ijel e.
flea lu
flee p'akhchel
flight *plane* t'ërrichk'; *escape* p'akhust
flock yeram
flood *noun* jërheghegh
floor *ground* getin; *story* hark
florist tsaghkabuyts
flour alyur; **flour mill** alraghats'
flow hosal
flower tsaghik
flu grip
fly *noun* ch'anj; *verb* t'ërrchel
fog marrakhugh
foggy mëshushot
folk *noun* zhoghovurd
folk dancing zhoghovërt'ayin par
folklore folklor
folk music zhoghovërdayin yerazhështut'yun
follow yetevel
food utelik'
fool *noun* himar
foot t'at'; *measurement* fut'
football futbol
footpath mayt'
for hamar; **for the sake of** hanun
forbid ark'elel
forbidden ark'elvats
force uzh
forearm nakhabazuk
forehead ch'akat
foreign artasahmanyan
foreigner artasahmants'i
forest antarr
forget morranal
forgive nerel
forgotten morrats'vats
fork patarak'agh
form *official* blank; *shape* dzev

fort amrots'
fortnight yerku shabat'
forty k'arrasun
forward(s) araj
foundation *building* himk'; *organization* himnadram
four chors
fourteen tasnëchors
fourth chorrord
fox aghves
fracture *noun* kotërvatsk'; *verb* kotërvel
fragrance burmunk'
free *liberated* azat; **free of charge** anvëch'ar; **free time** azat zhamanak; **Is this seat free?** Ayn nëstaranë azat e?; *verb* azatel
freedom azatut'yun
freeze sarrel
freezing sarrets'um
freight *noun* navap'okhadraberr
French *thing* fransiakan
french fries fri
Frenchman fransiats'i
Frenchwoman fransiats'i
frequently hach'akhakioren
fresh *food* t'arm'; *cool* mak'ur
Friday urp'at
fridge sarrnaran
friend ënker; *male* ënker; *female* ënkeruhi
friendship ënkerut'yun
frighten vakhats'nel
frog gort
from *see pages 11-14.*
front *noun* ch'akat
frontier sahman
frost sarrnamanik'
frostbite tsërtaharel
fruit mirk'; **fruit juice** mërk'ayin hyut'
fry *something* tapakel
fuel varrelik'
full li; **full moon** lëriv lusin; **to be full** lëts'vats linel
full up *satisfied* kusht linel; **I am full up!** Yes kusht em!
funeral hugharkavorut'yun
funny tsitsagheli
furniture kahuyk'
furrow akos
future apaga

G

gain *noun* shahuyt'; *verb* stanal
gala gala
gale p'ot'orik
gall bladder leghapark
gallon galon
game khagh
gandana leek
gangrene gangrena
garage garazh
garden partez
gardener aygegorts
garlic sëkhtor
garrison kayazor
gas gaz; *petrol* benzin
gasoline benzin
gate darpas
gather kutakel
gazelle vit'
gear *car* p'okhants'um
general *adjective* ënt'anur; *noun* general
generally ënt'anrapes
genitals serrakan organner
genocide genots'id
gentleman jentëlmen
gently! zguysh!
geography yerkrabanut'yun
geologist yerkraban
Georgia Vërastan
Georgian *person* vrats'i; *thing* vrats'akan; *language* vrats'eren
German *person* Germanatsi; *thing* germanakan; *language* germaneren
Germany Germania
germs saghm

get stanal; **to get in** *to a vehicle* nëstel; **to get up** verkenal

gift nëviratvut'yun

ginger zenjefil

girder hetsan

girl aghchik; **girls** aghchikner

girlfriend ënkeruhi

give tal; **give me...** tur indz...; **to give oneself up** handzënvel; **to give birth (to)** tsënëndaberel

glacier sarrts'adasht

glass *substance* apaki; *drinking* bazhak; **glass of water** mi bazhak jur; **glasses** *spectacles* aknots'

gloves dzerrnots'ner

glue sosindz

go gënal; **to go over there** gënal ayntegh; **to go out** durs gal; **to go to bed** gënal k'ënelu; **go!** arraj!

goal *aim* nëpatak; *football* gol

goat nokhaz; *kid* ul; *meat* aytsamis

God Astvats

gold voski

good lav; **good and evil** barik' ev charik'

good night! Bari gisher

good-bye! Ts'ëtesutyun!

goose sag

government karravarut'yun

governmental karravarakan

grain hats'ahatik

gram gram

grammar k'erakanut'yun

granddaughter t'orr

grandfather pap

grandmother tat

grandson t'or

grapefruit greypfrut

grapes khaghogh

grasp seghmel

grass khot

grasshopper tsëgrid

grateful yerakhtapart; **I am grateful. Yes yerakhtapart em.**

grave *noun* gerezman

gravel manrakhich'

gravy t'andzramokank'

gray mokhraguyn

great mets

great-granddaughter tsorr

great-grandfather nakhapap

great-grandmother nakhatat

great-grandson tsorr

Greece Hunastan

Greek *person* huyn; *thing* hunakan; *language* huneren

green kanach

greengrocer nëparavach'arr

grenade nërrnak

grey mokhraguyn

grief visht

grind *verb* aghal

groom *horses* dziapan

ground getin

group khumb

grow ach'el; **to grow crops** hats'abuyser ach'ets'nel; **to grow up** ach'el

guard *noun* t'iknapah; *verb* pashtpanel

guerrilla partizan

guest hyur

guesthouse hyuranots'

guide *noun* gid; *verb* ughekts'el

guidebook ughets'uyts' girk'

gum lind

gun hërats'an; **gun barrel** p'ogh

gunman avtomatavor

gust porrt'kum

gut aghik'

gynecologist ginekolog

H

hail *noun* karkut

hair mazer

hairbrush mazeri khozanak

haircut sanërvatsk'; **I want a haircut please. Yes uzum em**

him

mazerës këtrem.
hairdresser varsavir
hairdryer fen
half kes; **half year** kestari
half-brother khort' yeghbayr
half-hour keszham
half-sister khort' k'uyr
hammer *noun* murch'
hand *noun* dzerr; **to hand over** handznel
handbag payusak
handful burr
handicraft arhest
handkerchief t'ashkinak
handle *noun* bërrnak
hang kakhel
hangar ot'anavashenk'
hanger *clothes* kakharan
happen patahel
happy yerjanik
hard *difficult* dëzhvar; *not soft* kosht
hardware store yerkat'eghen ireri khanut'
hare napastak
harmful vënasatu
harvest berk'
hashish hashish
hat boloragëlkhark; **fur hat** mort'e boloragëlkhark
hate *verb* atel; *noun* atelut'yun
have unenal; **to have to** stipvats linel
hawk shahen
hay chor khot
he na
head gëlukh; *boss* ghekavar; **head clerk** gëlkhavor klerk; **head of state** petut'yan ghekavar
headache gëlkhats'av
headman ghekavar
headmaster tënoren
headquarters shtab
headscarf sharf
heal buzhel
health arrokhchut'yun

healthcare arrokhchapahut'yun
healthy arrokhch
hear lësel
heart sirt; **heart attack** sërti harvats; **heart condition** sërti vich'ak
heat *noun* tap'; *verb* tak'ats'nel
heat wave yerasht
heaven yerkink'
heavy tsanr
hedgehog vozni
heel kërunk
height bardzrut'yun
helicopter ughghat'irr
hell dëzhokhk'
hello! barev
help *noun* ok'nut'yun; *verb* ok'nel; **help!** Ok'nets'ek'!; **Can you help me?** Duk' karogh ek' indz ok'nel?
hem yezër
hen hav
hepatitis lyart'i borbok'um
her nëran; **I told her.** Yes nëran asats'i.; **her book** nëra girk'ë
herb buys
herd hot
here aystegh
hero heros
hers nëra
herself na ink'ë
hidden t'aknëvats
hide t'aknëvel
high bardzër; **high blood pressure** aryan bardëzr ch'ënshum
high school bardzraguyn dëprots
highway khëch'ughi
hijack arrevangel
hijacker ahabekich
hijacking ahabekchut'yun
hike *verb* k'aylel
hill bëlur
hillside lanj
him nëran; **I told him.** Yes nëran asats'i.

himself

himself na ink'ë
Hindi hindi
Hindu hëndik
Hinduism hinduizm
hip azdër
hire *verb* varts'el
his nëra
historian patmaban
history patmut'yun
hit *verb* harvatsel
hold pahel
hole tsak
holiday ton
holidays arts'akurt
holy sërp'azan; **holy man** sërp'azan mart'
homeland hayrenik'
homeless anot'evan
homework tënayin ashkhatank'
honey meghër
honor pativ
hood *of car* tsatskots'
hook *noun* kart'
hookah nargile
hope huys
horn yeghjyur; *car* shëchak
hornet dziastats'
horse dzi; **horses** dzier; **horse racing** dziarshav
horseback riding dziagënats'ut'yun
hospitable hyurënkal
hospital hivandanots'
host ter
hostage patand; **to take hostage** patand verts'nel
hostel hanrakats'aran
hot tak'; **hot water** tak' jur; **I am hot.** Yes shogum em.; **It is hot.** Shog e.
hotel hyuranots'
hound vorskan shun
hour zham
house tun
how? inchpes?; **how far?** vork'an herru?; **How far is the next village?** vork'an herru e hajord gjughë?; **how many?** inchk'an?; **how much?** inchk'an?; **how much is it?** Sa inch arje?; **How much does this cost?** Sa inch arje?

however hamenayndepës
human (being) *noun* mart'; *adjective* mart'kayin; **human rights** mart'kayin iravunk'ner
humanitarian humanitar; **humanitarian aid** humanitar ok'nut'yun
humid khonav
humor humor
humorous zaveshtakan
hundred haryur
hunger sov
hungry k'aghts'ats; **I'm hungry.** Yes sovats em.
hunt *noun* vors
hunting vorsordut'yun
hurry shtapoghakanut'yun; **I'm in a hurry.** Yes shtapum em.; **hurry up!** Aragats'rek'!
hurt *noun* ts'av; *verb* ts'aval; **It hurts here.** Aystegh ts'avum e.; **My back hurts.** Mejk'ës ts'avum e.
husband amusin
hygiene higiyena

I

I yes
ice sarruyts'
ice cream pakhpaghak
icy sarrts'akalats
I.D. nuynakanats'um
idea gaghap'ar
identification nuynakanats'um
if yet'e; **if not** yet'e voch; **if only** yet'e miayn; **if possible** yet'e hënaravor e
ill hivand; **to be ill** hivand linel; **I am ill.** Yes hivand em.

intestine

illegal aporini
illiterate angëraget
illness hivandut'yun
image patker
imagination yerevakayut'yun
imam imam
immediately anmijapes
immigrant emigrant
immigration nergaght'
impolite ank'aghak'avari
import *verb* nerkërel
importance karevorut'yun
important karevor
impossible anhënarin
improve lavats'nel
in *see pages 11-14.*; **in addition to** i havelumn; **in front of** dimats'ë; **in the country** gyughum
included nerarryal
incomplete anavart
indeed irok'
independence ankakhut'yun
independent ankakh; **independent state** ankakh petut'yun
index finger ts'uts'amat
India Hëndkastan
Indian *person* hëndik; *thing* hëndkakan
indicator light *blinker* lusayin indikator
indigestion anmarsoghut'yun
industry ardyunaberut'yun
infant derrhas
infected: It is infected. Varakvats: Sa varakvats e.
infection infekts'ia
inflammable anbërrënkeli
influenza grip
information teghekatvut'yun; **information office** teghekatvakan grasenyak
infuse nershënchel
injure vënasel
injured vënasvats
injury vënasvatsk'

ink t'anak'
inner-tube ot'apahpanich
innocent anmegh
inquiry harst'um
insane khelagarrvats
inscription makagrut'yun
insect bëjij; **insects** bëjijner
insecticide insektits'id
inside mejë
insignificant annëshan
instance: for instance orinak
instead p'okharen
institute institut
instruction *teaching* usuts'um
instructions *on use* dzerrnark
insurance apahovagrut'yun; I have medical insurance. Yes unem bëjëshkakan apahovagrut'yun.
insured: My possessions are insured. Apahovagrvats: Im unets'vatsk'ë apahovagërvats e.
intelligent khelamit
intend mëtadrvel
intention mëtadrut'yun
interest *noun* hetak'ërk'rut'yun; *financial* tokosadruyk'; *verb* hetak'ërk'ërel
interesting hetak'ërk'ir
interior *adjective* nerk'in; *noun* yent'aka; **ministry of the interior** nerk'in gortseri nakhararutyun
internal nerk'in
international mijazgayin; **international operator** mijazgayin karravarich; **international code** mijazgayin kod; **international flight** mijazgayin tërrichk'
internet internet
interpret t'argmanel
interpreter t'argmanich
intersection khachmeruk
interval interval
interview harts'azruyts
intestine aghik'

into

into *see pages 11-14.*
introduce nerkayats'nel
invade nerkhuzhel
invasion nerkhuzhum
investigate hetak'ënnel
investigation hetak'ënnum
invitation hëraver
invite hëravirel
Iran Iran
Iranian *person* iranats'i; *thing* iranakan
Iraq Irak'
Iraqi *person* irak'ts'i; *thing* irak'akan
Ireland Irlandia
Irish *person* irlandats'i; *thing* irlandakan; *language* irlanderen
iron *for clothes* art'uk
Islam islam
Islamic mahmedakan
Israel Isrrayel
Israeli *person* israelats'i; *thing* israelakan
it na
Italian *person* italats'i; *thing* italakan; *language* italeren
Italy Italia
itch *noun* k'os
item hodvats
its nëra

J

jackal shënagayl
jacket bach'kon
jam hërmështuk'
jelly dondoghak
janitor dërrnapan
January hunvar
Japan Ch'aponiya
Japanese *person* ch'aponats'i; *thing* ch'aponakan; *language* ch'aponeren
jaw dunch
jazz jaz
Jew hrea
jeweler voskerich

jewelry voskerchut'yun
Jewish hreakan
jihad jihad
job ashkhatank'
joiner ataghdzagorts
joint hod
joke *noun* katak
journalist lëragrogh
Judaism hreakanut'yun
judge *noun* datavor
jug kuzh
juice hyut'; **fruit juice** mërk'ayin hyut'
July hulis
jumper ts'atkotan
June hunis
junior kërtser
just now hents' hima
justice art'arut'yun

K

kebab k'yabab
keep pahel
ketchup kechup
kettle t'eynik
key banali
khaki khaki
kid *goat* ul
kidnap arrevangel
kidnapper arrevangich
kidnapping arrevangum
kidney yerekam; **kidneys** yerekamner
kill spanel
killer mardaspan
killing mardaspanut'yun
kilogram kilogram
kilometer kilometr
kind *adjective* bari; *noun* tesak
king t'agavor
kiosk kiosk
kiss *verb* hamburel
kitchen khohanots'
kite t'ëkht'e ot'aparuk
knead tërorel
knee tsunk

kneel tsunk chok'el
knife danak
knit gortsel
knock t'akel
know imanal; **I know.** Yes gitem.; **I don't know.** Yes chëgitem.; **Do you know him/her?** Du nëran gites?
knowledge gitelik'
known ch'anachvats
Koran K'oran
Kurd k'urd
Kurdish *thing* k'ërdakan; *language* k'ërderen

l

laboratory laboratoria
lack *noun* pakasut'yun
ladder sandukhk'
ladle sherep'
lake lich'
lamb garr; *meat* garri mis
lamp lamp
land *noun* ts'amak'; *verb (airplane)* vayrechk' katarel
landlord tënater
landslide soghvatsk'
language lezu
lantern lapter
laptop *computer* lep't'op'
large mets
last verchin; **last night** ants'ats gisher; **last week** ants'ats shap'at'; **last year** ants'ats tari
late ush; **I am late.** Yes ushats'a.
laugh *verb* tsistaghal
laughter tsistagh
laundry lëvats'k'atun; **laundry person** lëvats'k'arar
law orenk'; **law court** dataran
lawyer iravaban
lay (down) zeteghel
Laz *person* laz; *thing* lazakan; *language* lazeren
laziness alarkutut'yun
lazy alarkot

lead *noun: metal* arch'ich'
lead *verb* varel
leader lider
leaf terev
leak t'ap'vel
lean *adjective* vëtit; *verb* henvel
leap ts'aytkum; **leap year** nahanj tari
learn sovorel; **to learn by heart** angir sovorel
leather kashi
leave meknel
Lebanon Libanan
Lebanese *person* libanats'i; *thing* libananakan
lecture *noun* dasakhosut'yun
left *side* dzakh; **to the left** depi dzakh
left-handed dzakhlik
left-wing dzakh
leg vot
legal iravakan; **the legal profession** iravakan masnagitut'yun
legend arraspel
lemon kit'ron
lend partk'ov tal
length yerkarut'yun
lengthen yerkarats'nel
lens linza
Lent pas
lentils vosp
leopard ëndzarryuts
less k'ich; **-less** an-
lesson das
let t'uylatrel; **Let's go!** Yekek' gënank'!
letter namak; *of alphabet* tarr; **letters** *of alphabet* tarrer
lettuce salat'
level *adjective* hart'; *noun* makardak
lever lëtsak
liberate azatagrel
liberty azatut'yun

library

library gëradaran
lice vochil
lick lëpëstel
lie *noun* sut
lie down parrkel
life kyank'
lifeless ankent'an
lift *elevator* verelak; *verb* bardzrats'nel
light *noun* luys; *electric* luys; *torch* lapter; *adjective: bright* paytsarr; *color* bats'; *not heavy* t'et'ev; *verb* lusavorel; **to light a fire** kërakë varrel; **Do you have a light?** Duk' luts'ki unek'?
lightbulb elektralamp
lighter kërakayrich
lightning kaytsak; *bolt* kaytsak
like *preposition* nëman; *verb* dur gal; **I like...** Yes sirum em...; **I don't like...** Yes chem sirum...
likely: to be likely kartses: t'ëvum e, t'e...
limbs *of body* verjavorut'yunner
limit sahman; **limits** sahmanner
line gits
linguist lezvaban
linguistics lezvabanut'yun
lining *of clothes* astarr
lion arryuts
lip shërt'unk'
lipstick shërt'nak'suk'
liquid heghuk
liquor ëmpelik'
list ts'uts'ak
listen lësel
listener unkëndrogh
liter litër
literature gërakanut'yun
little *small* p'ok'ër; *less* aveli k'ich; **little finger** ch'ëkuyt; **little by little** kamats'-kamats'
live: live broadcast ughigh yet'er; **live wire** larvatsut'yan tak lar

live *verb* aprel; *to dwell* bënakvel
liver lyard
livestock gëlkhak'anak
lizard moghes
load berr
loaf hats'
local teghakan; **a local shop for local people** teghamasayin khanut'
location vayr
lock *noun* koghp'ek'; *verb* p'akel
locomotive gënats'k'asharzh
locust morekh
loft dzeghnahark
loins gotkategh
long yerkar
look nayel; **to look for** p'ëntrel
loot *verb* hap'shtakel
lorry berrnatar mek'ena
lose *to mislay* korts'nel; *to be defeated* tarvel; **I have lost my key.** Yes banalis korts'rel em.
lost: I am lost. korats: Yes molorvets'i.
lot vich'ak; **a lot** shat
lottery vich'akakhagh
loud bardzër
loudly bardzër
louse vochil
love *noun* ser; *verb* sirel
low ts'atsër; **low blood pressure** aryan ts'atsër chënshum
lower *verb* ts'atsrats'nel
luck bakht
luggage berr
lumps *of earth* metsabekorner
lunch lanch
lung t'ok'

M

machete machet'e
machine mek'ena
machine gun avtomat
magazine *printed* amsagir; *gun* pahestatup'

magnetic magnisayin
mail p'ost
mailbox p'ostarkëgh
main gëlkhavor
main square kentronakan hëraparak
maintain pahpanel
maize yegiptats'oren
majority metsamasnut'yun
make anel
make-up *cosmetics* kosmetika
malaria dogherots'k'
male *noun* tëghamard; *adjective* arakan
mammal kat'nasun
man tëghamart'
manager karravarich
manner *mode* dzev
manual *book* dasagirk'
manure gomaghb
many shat
map k'artez; **map of Yerevan** Yerevani k'artez
March mart
mare zambik
mark nëshel
market shuka
marriage amusnut'yun
married: I am married. Yes amusnats'ats em.
marrow *of bone* voskratsuts
marry *see* **married** amusnanal
marsh ch'ahich'
martyr tarrapyal
mascara sevanerk
match *football* mërts'akhagh
matches *for fire* luts'ki
material nyut'; *cloth* gortsvatsk'
mathematics mat'ematika
matter *subject* arrarka; **It doesn't matter!** Da nëshanakut'yun ch'uni!
mattress matras
May mayis
maybe hënaravor e

me yes, indz
meadow mark'agetin
meal utelik'
mean *verb* nëshanakel; **What does this mean?** Inch e sa nëshanakum?
meaning nëshanakut'yun
measure *verb* chap'el
meat mis
mechanic mekhanikakan
media mijots'; **mass media** zangvatsayin lëratvut'yan mijots'ner
medical *adjective* bëzhëshkakan; **medical insurance** bëzhëshkakan apahovagrut'yun
medication buzhum
medicine deghorayk'
meet handipel
meeting handipum
melon sekh
member ant'am
memory hishoghut'yun
men tëghamart'ik
menu menyu
mercenary varts'kan
message haghort'agrut'yun
metal *noun* metagh; *adjective* metaghya
meter hashvich; *measure* metër
metro metro
mid mechteghi
midday kesor
middle mechtegh
midnight kesgisher
midwife mankabardzuhi
mile mëghon
military *adjective* rrazmakan
military service rrazmakan tsarrajut'yun
milk kat'; **cow's milk** kovi kat'; **goat's milk** aytsi kat'; **powdered milk** kat'i p'oshi
mill aghats'
millennium hazaramyak

miller jëraghats'pan
millet korek
million milion
millstone jëraghats'ak'ar
mind *noun* banakanut'yun
mine *adjective* im; *mineral* hank'aran; *explosive* akan; anti-personnel mine hakahetevakayin akan; anti-tank mine hakatankayin akan
minefield akanadasht
miner hank'ap'or
mineral hank'; mineral water hank'ayin jur
minister nakharar
ministry nakhararutyun
minority p'ok'ramasnut'yun
mint daghdz
minute *noun* rope
miracle hërashk'
mirror hayeli
mislead apakoghmnoroshel
miss *verb: not hit* vripel
missile hërtirr
mission arrak'elut'yun
mist marrakhogh
mistake sëkhal; to make a mistake sëkhal tuyl tal
mix kharrnel
mixture kharrnurd
mobile phone bëjëjayin herrakhos
mode dzev
model *example* nëmush
modem modem
modern zhamanakakits'
modest hamest
mole khal
moment pah
monarch miapet
monarchy miaputut'yun
monastery vank'
Monday yerkushap't'i
money dram
monkey kapik
month amis

monthly amsekan
monument arts'an
moon lusin
more aveli shat; more or less k'ich t'e shat; more than that aveli shat k'an
morning arravot; this morning ays arravot
mortgage gërav
mosque mëzkit'
mosquito motsak; mosquito net motsakneri ts'ants'
most mets masë
mother mayr; mothers mayrer
mother-in-law skisur
motorbike motots'iklet
motorcycle motots'iklet
motorway khëch'ughi
mount bardzranal; *a horse* dzi nëstel
mountain sar; mountain pass lerrnants'k'; mountain stream lerrnakhbyur
mouse muk
mouth beran
move sharjvel
movie kinonëkar; movie theater kinot'atron
much shat; not much voch shat
mud ts'ekh
muffler *of car* khëlarar
mug *noun* gavat'
mulberry t'ut'
mule jori
multiplication bazmapatkum
multiply bazmapatkel
munitions handerts'ank'
murder *noun* mart'aspanut'yun; *verb* spanel
murderer mart'aspan
muscle mëkan; muscles mëkanner
museum t'angaran
music yerazhështut'yun; music festival yerazhështakan p'arrat'on

Muslim *person* mahmedakan; *thing* mahmedakan
must borbos
mustache bekh
mutton vochkhari mis
my im
myself yes ink'ës
mystic *person* mistik

Ո

nail *of finger/toe* yeghung; *metal* mekh
naked merk
name anun; **What is your name?** Inchpes e dzer anunë?; **My name is Fred.** Im anunë Fred e.
nape *of neck* tsotsrak
napkin andzerrots'ik
nappy votnalat'; **I need to change my baby's nappy.** Yes petk' e p'okhem yerekhayis taki shorë.
narrow negh
nation azg
national azgayin
nationality azgut'yun
natural bënakan; **natural disaster** bënakan aghet; **natural resources** bënakan pasharner
nature *the natural world* bënut'yun
navel port
near mot
nearby shërjakayk'
nearly hamarya
necessary anhrazhesht; **it's necessary** da anhrazhesht e
necessity anhrazheshtut'yun
neck viz
necklace manyak
necktie vëzkap
need *noun* pahanj; **to need** *verb* karik' unenal; **I need...** indz

petk' e...
needle asegh; **Do you have a needle and thread?** Duk' unek' t'el yev asegh?
negotiator banakts'ogh
neighbor harevan
neither ... nor voch ... voch
nephew zarmik
nerve nyart'
net: fishing net ts'ants': dzëknorsayin ts'ants'; **mosquito net** motsakneri ts'ants'
never yerp'ek'
new nor; **new moon** noralusin; **new year** nor tari; **New Year festival** Amanorya p'arraton
New Zealand Nor Zelandia
newborn child noratsin yerekha
news norut'yun
newspaper t'ert'; *daily* orat'ert'; **newspaper in English** t'ert' anglerenov
newsstand kiosk
next hajord; **next week** hajord shap'at'
nice hach'eli
nickname makanun
niece zarmikuhi
night gisher
nightclub gisherayin akumb
nightingale sokhak
nightmare mëghdzavanj
nine inë
nineteen tasnëinë
ninety inësun
no voch; **no entry** mutk' chëka; **no problem!** khënt'ir chëka!; **no smoking** tsëkheln ark'elvum e; **no sugar** arrants' shak'ar
nobody vochmek
noise aghmuk
nomad k'ochvor
none voch mi; vochmekë

noon kesor
normal normal
normally sovorabar
north *noun* hyusis
north(ern) *adjective* hyusisayin
Northern Ireland Hyusisayin Irlandia
Norway Norvegia
nose k'it'
not voch; **not yet** derr voch
note: banknote t'ëght'adram
notebook not'atetër
nothing vochinch
nought zëro
noun goyakan
novel *noun* patmëvatsk'
November noyember
now hima
nowhere vochmitegh
nuclear power atomayin energia
nuclear power station atomayin elektrakayan
nuclear reactor atomayin rreaktor
number t'iv
nurse dayak
nut popok

O

o'clock zham; **It is six o'clock.** Zhamë vets'ën e.
objective nëpatak
observer ditord
occasionally yerbemën
occupation *job* ashkhatank'
occupy a country gëravel yerkir
occupying forces gëravogh uzher
occur patahel
ocean ovkianos
October hoktember
of *see pages 11-12;* **the plays of Shakespeare** Shek'spiri piesnerë

office gërasenyak; **office worker** gërasenyaki ashkhatogh
officer *military* spa
official *adjective* pashtonakan; *noun* pashtonya; **officials** pashtonyaner
often hach'akh
oil *cooking* yugh; *engine* naft'; **oil pipeline** naft'amugh; **oil refinery** naft'amëshakogh gortsaran; **oil tanker** tanker; **oil well** naft'ahor
oilcan yughamas
oilfield naft'ahank'
ointment k'suk'
old tser; **old man** tser mard; **old woman** tser kin; **old city** hin k'aghak'; **How old are you?** K'ani tarekan ek' duk'?; **I am … years old.** Yes … tarekan em.
on vra; **on foot** votk'ov
once mi ank'am
one mek
oneself ink'n iren
one-way: one-way street miakoghmani: miakoghmani p'oghots'; **one-way ticket** toms mek ughghut'yamb
onion(s) sokh
only *alone* miaynak; *adverb* miayn
onto *preposition* vëra
open *adjective* bats'; *verb* bats'el
opera opera
opera house operayin t'atron
operating theater/room virabuzhakan dahlich'
operation *surgical* virahatut'yun
operator operator; **telephone operator** herrakhosavar
opium ap'ion
opponent hakarrakord
opposite hakadir

opposition ënddimut'yun

or kam

orange *fruit* narinj; *color* narënjaguyn

orchard pëtghatu aygi

order *command* hëraman; *arrangement* kark'; *to command* hëramayel; **to order a meal** utelik patvirel

ordinary sovorakan

organ *of body* organ

origin tsak'um

original iskakan

orphan vorp'

orphanage vorp'anots'

other urish

ounce unts'ia

our mer

ourselves menk' ink'neres

out: to go out durs gal

outside dursë

oven varraran

over verin

overcoat verarku

overcome haght'aharel

overtake *by car* hasnel

overturn vayr gëlorvel

owl bu

own *adjective* sep'akan; *verb* tirel

owner ter; *of building* sep'akanater

ownership *of property* sep'akanut'yun

ox ts'ul

oxygen t'ët'vatsin

P

pace k'aylvatsk'

package p'ak'et'

packet p'ak'et'

packhorse berrnakir dzi

padlock koghpek'

page ej

pain ts'av

painkiller ts'avazërkogh

paint *noun* nerk; *verb* nerkel

painter nëkarich

painting nëkar

palace dëghyak

pale sëpërt'nats

palm *of hand* ap'

pamphlet parsavagir

pancreas yent'astamok'sayin geghdz

pantyhose zuk'agulpaner

paper *substance* t'ught'; *newspaper* t'ert'; *article* hodvats

parachute parashyut

paradise dërakht

paralyze kat'vatsel

paralyzed kat'vatsahar

parcel tsanrots'

parents tsënoghner

park *noun* zbosaygi

parliament khorërdaran; *Armenian National Assembly* Hayastani Azgayin Zhoghov

parrot t'ut'ak

part mas

participate masnakts'el

partridge chil kak'av

party *celebration* yerekuyt'; *political* kusakts'ut'yun

pass *noun: I.D.* ants'at'ught'; **mountain pass** kirch'; *verb* ants'nel; **to pass an exam** k'ënnut'yunë handznel; **to pass time** zhamanak ants'kats'nel

passable: Is the road passable? ënt'anali: Ays ch'anaparë ënt'anali e.

passenger ughevor

passer-by ants'ord

passport andznagir; **passport number** andznagri hamar

past *adjective* ants'ats; *noun* ants'yalë; **some years past** mi k'ani tari arraj; **the past century** ants'ats dar

pasta

pasta pasta
path arahet
patient *adjective* hamp'eratar; **Be patient!** hamp'erek'!; *medical* pats'ient
patrol parek
paunchy hastap'or
pay *noun* vëch'ar; *verb* vëch'arel
payment vëch'ar
pay-phone vëch'arovi herrakhos
peace khaghaghut'yun; **peace talks** khaghagh banakts'ut'yunner; **to make peace** khaghagut'yan hasnel; **to bring peace** khaghaghut'yun berel
peace-keeping troops khaghaghapah zork'er
peach(es) deghdz
peacock siramarg
peak gagat'
pear tandz
pearl margarit
pebble kopich'
pedestrian hetiotën
pediatrician mankabuyzh
pediatrics mankabuzhut'yun
pelvis konk'
pen gërich
pencil matit
penicillin penits'ilin
penknife gërchahat
penname keghtsanun
people mart'ik
pepper tak'degh
perfect kataryal
perform katarel
performance katarum
perfume otsanelik'
perhaps hënaravor e
period *of time* shërjan; *class* das; *menstrual* dashtanashërjan
Persian *person* parsik; *language* parskeren
person andz
petition hanragir

petrol benzin; **I have run out of petrol.** Im benzinë verjats'el e.
pharmacy deghatun
pheasant p'asian
phone *noun* herrakhos; *verb* herradzaynel; **Please phone me.** Khënt'rum em zangaharek' indz.
photo lusanëkar
photocopier patch'ena-hanman mek'ena
photocopy *noun* patch'en; *verb* patch'enahanel
photographer lusanëkarich
photography lusanëkarum
physical fizikakan
physics fizika
physiotherapy fiziot'erapia
piano dashnamur
pickax k'ëlung
picnic zbosakhënjuyk'
picture nëkar
piece këtor
pig khoz
pigeon aghavni
pilgrim ukhtagënats'
pilgrimage ukhtagënats'ut'yun; **to go on pilgrimage** ukhtagënats'ut'yan gënal
pill hab
pillow bardz
pilot ot'achu
pin dëndasegh
pink mekhak
pipe khoghovak; tsëkhamorch'
pistol atërch'anak
pitch *football* gëndaki netum
place *noun* tegh; *verb* teghadrel; **place of birth** tsënëndavayr
placenta ënkerk'
plain *noun* hart'avayr
plane hart'ut'yun
plank dzoghik
plant *noun* buys; *verb* tënkel
planting tënkum

plaster *medical* speghani

plastic plastik

plate ap'se

platform *railway* platforma; **platform number** platformai hamar

platoon dasak

play *noun: theater* pies; *verb* khaghal; *a musical instrument* nëvagel

please! khënt'rum em!

pleasure hach'uyk'

plow *noun* gut'an; *verb* herkel

plug *bath* khëts'an; *electric* vart'ak

plum bal

p.m. kesorits' heto

poach *animals/game* vorsagoghut'yamb zbaghvel

pocket gërpan

poem poem

poet banasteghts

poetry poezia

point ket

poison t'uyn

police vostikanut'yun; **police station** vostikanatun

policeman vostikan

polite k'aghak'avari

political k'aghak'akan

politician k'aghak'akan gortsich

politics k'aghak'akanut'yun

polo polo

pomegranate(s) nurr

pond lëch'ak

pony poni

pool jërp'os

poor aghk'at

pope k'ahana

population bënakchut'yun

porcupine khozuk

pork khozi mis

port navahangist

portion bazhin

portrait dimanëkar

position dirk'

possess tirapetel

possibility hënaravorut'yun

possibly hënaravor

post office p'ost

postcard bats'ik

pot anot'; **cooking pot** kerakrakat'sa

potatoes kartofil

pottery kavagortsut'yun

poultry tënayin t'ërrchun

pound *weight/sterling* funt

pour lëts'nel

poverty aghk'atut'yun

powder p'oshi

power uzh

praise govergank'

pray aghot'el

prayer aghot'k'; **funeral prayer** hogehangëstyan

prefer geradasel

pregnant hëghi; **I'm pregnant.** Yes hëghi em.

preparation patrastum; **preparations** patrastut'yunner

prepare patrastvel

present *adjective: time* nerka; *noun: time* nerka; *gift* nëver

president *of country* nakhagah; *of organization* nakhagah

presidential guard nakhagahakan t'iknazor

press: the press mamul; **the free press** azat mamul; *verb* ch'ënshel

pressure chënshum

pretty lavik

prevent kankhel

previously nakhorok'

price gin

pride hëpartut'yun

priest k'ahana

prime minister varchapet

prince ark'ayazn

principal *adjective* skëzbunk'ayin;
  noun: school tënoren
print tëpel
printer *company* tëparan;
  computer tëpich
prison bant
prisoner bantarkyal; **to take**
  prisoner dzerp'akalel
prisoner-of-war rrazmageri
prize mërts'anak
probability havanakanut'yun
probable havanakan; **It is**
  probable. Da havanakan e.
probably havanabar
problem khënt'ir
product artadrank'
profession masnagitut'yun
professional *person*
  arhestavarzh
professor profesor
program: radio program
  haghordum: radio
  haghordum; **computer**
  program hamakark'chayin
  tsëragir
progress arrajënt'ats'
projector proyektor
pronounce artasanel
pronunciation artasanut'yun
proof apats'uyts'
proper patshach'
prophet mark'are
proposal arrajark
prosthesis prot'ez
protect pashtpanel
protection pashtpanut'yun
protest *noun* boghok'arkum;
  verb boghok'arkel
proud hëpart
prove apats'uts'el
proverb asats'vatsk'
province gavarr
provisions parenayin
  aprank'ner
publish hëratarakel
publisher hëratarakich
pull dzëk'el; **to pull out** durs

hanel
pump *noun* pomp; **water pump**
  jërapomp; *verb* parpel; **to**
  pump water jurë pompov
  k'ashel
pumpkin dët'um
puncture khots'um; **I have a**
  puncture. Im anvadogherë
  tsakvel en.
punish patzhel
pupil *school* ashakert; *of eye* bib
puppy lakot
purple tsirani
pursue hetapëndel
push hërel
put dënel; **to put down** tsa'ts
  dënel; **to put in** mëts'ënel; **to**
  put on *clothes* hak'nëvel
puzzled shëp'ot'vats

Q

quarrel vich'el
quarter k'arrord; *area*
  t'aghamas; **quarter of an**
  hour k'arrord jam
quarterly yerramsya
queen t'aguhi
question harts'
queue *noun* hert'
quick arag
quickly aragoren
quiet *adjective* handart
quietly handartoren
quilt mëgdakats' vermak
quit dadarets'nel
Quran K'oran

R

rabbit ch'agar
rabies: to catch rabies
  divaharut'yun: divaharvel
radar radiolokator
radiator rradiator
radio rradio; **radio broadcast**

rradio yet'er; **radio program** rradio haghordum; **radio station** rradiokayan

radish amsakan bokhk

raid martarshav; **air-raid** ot'ayin harts'akum

railway yerkat'ughi

railway station yerkat'u-ghayin kayaran

rain andzrev; **rain shower** amprop'; **rainstorm** p'ot'orik; **It is raining.** Andzrev e galis.

rainbow tsiatsan

raisins chamich

ram khoy

Ramadan Rramadan

range sharan

rape *noun* kanch'rak

rapid sërënt'ats'

rapidly arag

rat arrnet

rate *speed* aragut'yun

ravine kirch'

raw hum

razor sap'rich

razor blade sheghp'

reach *arrive at* zhamanel

read kart'al

reading ënt'erts'um

ready patrast; **I am ready.** Yes patrast em.

real irakan

reality irakanut'yun

realize gitakts'el

reaping hëndzum

reason patch'arr; **reason for travel** ch'anaparort'ut'yan nëpatak

rebel *noun* apstamb

receipt andorragir

receive stanal

recent *adjective* t'arm

recently vercherës

reception (desk/area) ëndunaran

recess *break* ëndmijum

recognize ch'anachel

reconciliation hashtets'um; **national reconciliation** azgayin hashtut'yun

record *verb* dzaynagrel

recreation kazdurum

red karmir

Red Crescent Karmir Mahik

Red Cross Karmir Khach

referee mërts'avar

refinery: oil refinery naft'amëshakogh gortsaran

refrigerator sarrnaran

refugee p'akhëstakan; **refugees** p'akhëstakanner; **refugee camp** p'akhëstakanneri ch'ambar

regime rrejim

region taratsashërjan

regulation kanonakark'um

reign *noun* t'agavorum

reinforcements hamalërum

relationship haraberut'yun; *blood* azgakts'ut'yun

relative barekam

relatives barekamner

relax hangëstanal

release arts'akel

relief aid humanitar ok'nut'yun

religion kron

religious kronakan; **religious sect** kronakan aghand

remain mënal

remaining mënats'ogh

remember hishel

rent *for oneself* varts'el; *to someone* varts'ov tal

repair *noun* veranorok'um; *verb* veranorok'el

repeat kërknel

replace p'okharinel

reply *noun* pataskhan; *verb* pataskhanel

report *noun: news* haghorda-grut'yun; *verb* haghordel

reporter t'ëght'akits'

represent nerkayats'nel

representation narkayats'uts'chut'yun

representative nerkayats'uts'ich

republic hanrapetut'yun

research *noun* hetazotum; *verb* usumnasirel

reservation *ticket* patviratoms

reserve *verb* amragrel; **Can I reserve a place/seat?** Yes karogh em tegh amragrel?

reside bënakvel

resist dimadrel

respect hargank'

rest *remainder* mënatsordë; *relaxation* hangist; *verb* hangëstanal

restaurant rrestoran

result art'yunk'

retreat *verb* nahanjel

return *verb* veradarts'nel

reverse *verb* shërjel

revolution heghap'okhut'yun

rib(s) koghoskër

rice *raw* brindz; *hulled* mak'tars brindz; *cooked* yep'ats brindz

rich harust

ride *a horse* dzi nëstel

riding dziagënats'ut'yun

rifle hërats'an

right *correct* chisht; *side* ach; *legal right* orinakan iravunk'; **to the right** depi ach; **right hand** ach dzerrk'; **You are right.** Duk' iravats'i ek'.; **right now** hents' hima

rights iravunk'ner; *civil rights* k'aghak'ats'iakan iravunk'ner; **human rights** mardu iravunk'ner; **women's rights** kanats' iravunk'ner

right-wing ach

ring *noun* ogh; *verb: bell* zang; *to phone someone* zangaharel; **I want to ring Emma.** Yes uzum em Emmayin zangaharel.

riot *noun* apstambut'yun

ripe hasun

rise *verb: prices etc.* ach'el

risk *noun* rrisk; *verb* rriski dimel

river get; **riverbank** geti ap'

road ch'anapar; **tarmac road** gudronapatats khëch'ughi; **road map** khëch'ughineri k'artez; **road sign** ch'anaparayin nëshan

roadblock ughekal

roast tapakel

rob koghoptel; **I've been robbed!** Indz t'alanel en!

robber koghoptich

robbery koghoput

rock zhayrr

rocket hërt'irr

rocket-launcher hërt'irrayin ardzakich

roll up p'at'at'el

roof tanik'

room senyak

rooster ak'aghagh

root armat

rope paran

rose vart'

rotten nekhats

rough *coarse* kosht

round këlor

roundabout *road* zartughi

route ch'anapar

row *argument* vech'

row *line* shark'

royal t'ak'avorakan

rub tërorel

rubber *eraser* rretin

rubbish aghp'

rubble getak'ar

rude kopit

rug gorg

rugby rregbi

ruins p'ëlataknerer

rule *government* tirapetut'yun; *regulation* kanon

ruler *instrument* k'anon; *person* tirakal
run vazel; **to run out (of)** sparrvel
Russia Rrusastan
Russian *person* rrus; *thing* rrusakan; *language* rruseren
rust *noun* zhang
rye ashora

S

sack *noun* park; *verb: dismiss* azatel
sacred sërp'azan
sad tëkhur
safe anvëtang
safety anvëtangut'yun; **safety pin** dëndasegh
saffron shafran
saint surp'
salad aghts'an
salesman vach'arrogh
saleswoman vach'arroghuhi
saliva t'uk'
salt agh
saltless alani
salty aghi
same nuyn
sand avaz
sandals sandalner
sandwich sendvich
sanitary towel sërp'ich
satchel payusak
satellite arbanyak; **satellite phone** arbanyakayin herrakhos
satisfactory bavarar
satisfied bavararvats
Saturday shap'at'or
sauce sous
saucer t'eyaman
sausage yershik
save *rescue* p'ërkel; *money* dizel
saw *noun* sëghots'
say asel

scarf sharf
scatter sëp'rrel
school dëprots'; **school pupil** dëprots'i ashakert; **school teacher** dëprots'i usuts'ich
science gitut'un
scientific gitakan
scientist gitnakan
scissors mëkrat
score *noun: sports* hashiv; *verb: sports* gëndak khëp'el; **What's the score?** Inchk'an e hashivë?; **Who scored?** Ov khëpets' gëndak'ë?
scorpion karich'
Scot shotlandats'i
Scotland Shotlandia
Scottish *person* shotlandats'i; *thing* shotlandakan
screw *noun* pëtutak
screwdriver pëtutakich
scythe gerandi
sea tsov
search (for) p'ëntrel; **to search a person** andz p'ntrel; **to search a house** tun p'ntrel
season yeghanak
seat nëstelategh; *in vehicle* nëstots'; *political* pashton
seated nëstats
second *adjective* yerkrord; *noun* ok'nakan
secondhand ok'tagortsats
secret *adjective* gakhtni; *noun* gakhtnik'; **secrets** gaghtnik'ner; **secret police** gakhtni vostikanut'yun
secretary k'artughar
security anvëtangut'yun
see tesnel
seedling tënki
seeds sermer
seek p'ntrel
seem t'ëval
seize zavt'el
select ëntrel

self yes
sell vach'arrel
seminary seminaria
send ugharkel
senior *adjective* avak'
sense *meaning* nëshanakut'yun
sentence *of words* nakhadasut'yun
separate *adjective* arrandzin
separate *verb* taranjatel
separation tërohum
September september
septic septik
series: radio series serial; **TV series** serial
serious lurj; **The situation is serious.** Iravich'akë lurj e.
servant tsarra
service tsarrayut'yun
session nëstashërjan
set: television set herrustats'uyts'
seven yot'
seventeen tasnëyot'
seventy yot'anasun
several mi k'ani
severe dazhan; **severe heat** dazhan shok'
sew karel
sewing machine kari mek'ena
sex *gender* serr; *act* serrakan akt
shade *noun* stver
shake t'ap'aharel
shame *noun* amot'; *verb* amachets'nel
shampoo shampun
shape dzev
share *verb* bazhanel
sharp sur
sharpen sërats'nel
shave sap'ërvel
shaving cream sap'ërvelu k'suk'
shawl shal
she na

shear khuzel
sheep vochkhar
sheepdog gamp'ërr
sheet savan; *of paper* t'ert'
shelf darak
shell *military* ark; *snail/sea* khëkhunj
shelter apastan
shepherd hoviv
shine p'aylel
ship nav
shirt shapik
shock *medical* shok
shoe *noun* koshik; **shoes** koshikner; *verb: a horse* paytel
shoeshop koshiki khanut'
shoot kërakel; **Don't shoot!** Mi kërakek'!
shop khanut'
shopkeeper khanut'i ter
shopping gënumner
shore ap'
short karch
shortage pakasut'yun
shoulder us; **shoulder blade** t'iak
shout *verb* bëghavel
shovel bah
show *noun: fair* tonavach'arr; **trade show** tonavach'arr; *verb* ts'uts'adrel
shower *bath* ts'ënts'ugh; *of rain* amprop'
shrapnel shrapnel
shut *verb* tsatskel
sick hivand; **I am sick.** Yes hivand em.
sickle mangagh
side *direction* koghm; *of body* koghm
sidestreet nërp'ants'k'
siege *blockade* pasharum
sight *eyesight* tesoghut'yun
sign *noun* nëshan; *verb* storagrel
signature storagrut'yun
sign language nëshanneri

sore

lezu
silence lërrut'yun
silencer *of car* khëlats'uts'ich
silent lërrelyayn
silk metak's; **silk worms** sheram
silken metak'se
silly himar
silver artsat'
similar nëman
simple hasarak
since skësats; **since Monday** yerkushap'tiorvanits'
sing yerk'el
single miaynak; *not married* chamusnats'ats; **single room** mek hok'u senyak
sink *noun* konk'; ts'atsradasht; *verb* suzvel
sister k'uyr; **sisters** k'uyrer
sister-in-law *brother's/ husband's brother's wife* hars; *husband's sister* tal; *wife's sister* k'eni
sit nëstel
sitting nist
situated teghakayvats
situation iravich'ak
six vets'
sixteen tasnëvets'
sixth vets'erord
sixty vatsun
size chap's
ski *verb* dahuknerov sahel
skill hëmtut'yun
skilled hëmut
skin mashk
skull gang
sky yerkink'
slaughter *an animal* spand
slave struk
sleep *verb* k'ënel; **to go to sleep** gënal k'ënelu
sleeping bag nënjapark
sleeping pill(s) kënaber degh
sleepy kënkokh
sleeve t'evk'
slippery sayt'ak'un

slope t'ek'vatsk'
slow dandagh
slowly! Dandagh!
small p'ok'ër
smell *noun* hot
smoke *noun* tsukh; *verb* tsëkhel
smoker tsëkhogh
smoking tsëkhelë
smooth hart'
smuggler mak'saneng
snack akrat
snail khëkhunj
snake ots'
snakebite ots'i khayt'um
sneeze *noun* p'ërrështum; *verb* p'ërrështal
snore khërrëmp'ots'
snow dzyun; **snowflakes** dzyan p'at'ilner; **It is snowing.** Dzyun e galis.
so aytpes; **so much/many** aytk'an shat
soap och'arr
soccer futbol; **soccer match** futboli mërts'akhagh
social hasarakakan
society hasarakut'yun
socks gulpaner
soft p'ap'uk
soil hogh
soldier zinvor
sole t'at'
solve lutsel
some mi k'ani
somebody inchvor mekë
somehow inchvor kerp
someone inchvor mekë
something inchvor ban
sometimes yerp'emn
somewhere inchvor tegh
son vort'i; **sons** vort'iner
son-in-law p'esa
song yerk'; **love song** siro yerk'
soon shutov
sore verk'; **sore throat** mërrsats kokord

sorrow visht
sorry! kënerek'!
sort *noun* tesak
soul vok'i
sound dzayn
soup sup
sour t'ët'u
source aghbyur
south *noun* haraf
south(ern) *adjective* harafayin
sow ts'anel
space taratsk'
spade bah
Spaniard ispanats'i
Spanish *language* ispaneren; *thing* ispanakan
spanner *wrench* pëtutakabanali
spare tëntesel
spare tire pahestayin aniv
sparrow ch'ënch'ghuk
speak khosal; **Do you speak English?** Duk' khosum ek' angleren?; **I speak English.** Yes khosum em angleren.
speaker barts'rakhos; *on radio, etc.* haghort'avar; *of parliament* nakhagah
specialist masnaget
spectacles aknots'
speed aragut'yun
spell: How do you spell that? Inchpes e sa gërvum?
spend *money* tsakhsel; **to spend time** zhamanak znts'kats'nel
spice hamemunk'
spicy *hot* këtsu
spider sard
spill *verb* t'ap'el
spin *noun* pëtëtum
spinach spanakh
spinal column voghnashar
spine voghnashar
spit *verb* t'ëk'el
splint *medical* bekakal
split *verb* ch'ekhk'el
spoil p'ëchats'nel
sponge spung

spoon gët'al
sports sport
sportsman sportsmen
spread taratsel
spring *metal* zëspanak; *of water* aghp'yur; *season* garun
sprout *noun* sharravigh
spy lërtes
square k'arrakusi; **town square** hëraparak
squeeze seghmel
squirrel skyurrik
stadium stadion
staff andznakazm
stag yeghjeru
stage *theater* bem
stairs astich'anner
stale chor
stallion hovatak
stamp *postal* namakanish; *official* droshmakënik'; **to stamp a document** p'astat'ught'ë droshmel
stand *verb* kangnel
star astëgh; **stars** astgher
start *verb* skësel
state *noun: condition* vich'ak; *federal* petut'yun; *nation* azg; *verb* p'astel
station kayaran
stationer's shop gërasenyakayin pituk'neri khanut'
stationery gërasenyakayin pituk'ner
statue arts'an
stay mënal
steak steik'
steal goghanal
steam *food* yep'el
steel yerkat'
steering wheel ghek
stem bun
stepbrother khort' yekhpayr
stepfather khort' hayr
stepmother khort' mayr
sterling sterling
stethoscope lësap'oghak

stick *noun* p'ayt; **walking stick** k'aylelu p'ayt; *verb* khërel

still *yet* minchderr

sting *verb* khayt'el

stink *verb* zhantahotel

stir kharrnel

stitch *in one's side* ts'avi bërrnkum

stitches *surgical* karer

stomach stamok's

stomachache stamok'si ts'av

stone k'ar

stool at'orrak

stop kangnel; **stop!** kangnek'!; **don't stop!** mi kangnek'!

store *shop* khanut'; *for storage* pahest

storm p'ot'orik; **rainstorm** p'ot'orik; **thunderstorm** p'ot'orik

story *tale* patmëvatsk'; *news* norut'yun; *floor* hark

stove varraran; **heating stove** jerruts'ogh varraran

straight ughigh

straightness ughighut'yun

strange tarorinak

stranger antsanot'

straw tseghik

strawberry yelak

stream hosk'; **mountain stream** lerrnayin vëtak

street p'oghots'

strength uzh

stretcher *hospital* patgarak

strike *noun: from work* gortsadul; *verb: hit* harvatsel; *from work* gortsadul anel

string t'el

strong uzhegh

structure karruts'vatsk'

struggle payk'ar

stuck taghvats; **Our car is stuck.** Mer mek'enan t'aghvel e.

student *university* usanogh

study *noun* usumnasirum; *verb* sovorel; *academic* usutsum

subject arrarka

submachine gun avtomat

submit handznel

subtract hanel

subtraction hanum

suburb arvarts'an

success hajoghut'yun

such aytpisi

suck tsëtsel

suddenly hankartsaki

sufficient bavarar

sugar shak'ar; **sugar bowl** shak'araman

suit *of clothes* kostyum

suitable harmar

suitcase ch'ampruk

sultan sult'an

sum gumar

summer amarr

summit gagat'nazhoghov

sun arev

sunblock arevapashtpan k'ësuk'

sunburn arevayruk

Sunday kiraki

sunglasses arevapashtpan aknots'

sunny arevot; **It is sunny.** Arevot e.

sunrise arevatsak'

sunset arevamut

supermarket supermarket

supper ënt'rik'

supplies matakararumner

supply *verb* matakararel

sure *adjective* hamozvats; *adverb* ankaskats

surgeon virabuyzh

surgery *subject* virabuzhut'yun; *operation* virahatut'yun

surname *family name* azganun

surprised zarmats'ats

surprising: to be surprising zarmanali: zarmanali linel

surrender andznatur linel

surround shërjapatel

survey *noun* usumnasirut'yun;
verb usumnasirel

surveyor usumnasirogh

suspicion kaskats

swallow *bird* tsitserrnak; *verb*
kul tal

swamp ch'ahich'

swear *to curse* anitsel; **to swear
an oath** yert'um tal

sweat *noun* k'ërtink'

sweater sviter

sweep avlel

sweeper avlets'uts'ich

sweet *adjective* k'akhëts'r; *noun*
k'akhts'reghen

swell urrchel

swim loghal

swimming logh; **swimming
pool** loghavazan

swimsuit loghazgest

switch *noun: electric* anjatich;
verb **to switch off** anjatel; **to
switch on** miats'nel

syce shesh

symbol simbol

symptom *medical* akhtanish

synagogue sinagoga

syntax sharahyusut'yun

Syria Siria

Syrian *person* siriats'i; *thing*
siriakan

syringe nerarkots'

syrup mërk'ahyut'

system hamakark'

T

table seghan

tablecloth sëp'rrots'

tablet hab

tactic patshach'; **tactics** taktika

tailor derts'ak

take verts'nel; **to take away**
khëlel; **to take off** *something*
khëlel; **to take out** hanel; **to
take shelter** patsparvel;

**What time does the plane
take off?** Ink'nat'irrë vor
zhamin e tërchum?

talk *verb* zëruts'el

tall barts'rahasak

tame sandzel

tank *military* tank; *petrol/water*
ts'isterrn

tanker lëts'anav

tap *faucet* tsorak

tape zhapaven; *cassette* kaset;
tape recorder magnitofon

tarmac *road* gudronapatats
khëch'ughi

taste *noun* ch'ashak; *verb*
hamtesel

tasteless anham

tasty hamegh

tax *noun* hark; *verb* harkel

tax-free harkerits' azatvats

taxi tak'si

tea t'ey; **black tea** sev t'ey;
green tea kanach t'ey; **tea
with milk** kat'ov t'ey; **tea
house** t'eyaran

teach usuts'anel

teacher usuts'ich; *primary
school* mankavarzh

team t'im

teapot t'eynik

tear *noun* arts'unk'

tear *verb* patrrel

teaspoon t'eyi gët'al

technical tekhnikakan

technique tekhnika

teenager *boy* patani; *girl*
p'armani

teeth atamner

telecommunications herrahaghordagrut'yun

telegram herragir

telephone *noun* herrakhos;
telephone operator
herrakhosavar; *verb*
herradzaynel

telescope astghaditak

television herrustats'uyts'

telex telek's

tell asel

temperature jermut'yun; The temperature in summer is high. Amrranë jermut'yunë bardzr e.; The temperature in winter is low. Dzëmrranë jermut'yunë ts'atsr e.; I have a temperature. Yes jermut'yun unem.

temple *religious* tach'ar

ten tas

tenant bënakich

tend *to the sick* khënamel

tender mërts'uyt'; k'ënk'ush

tennis tenis

tent tent

tenth taserort'

termite termit

terrible ahavor

territory taratsk'

test *noun* test; *academic* stugoghakan ashkhatank'; **blood test** aryan analiz; *verb* stugel; *academic* k'ënnel

testify vëkayel

text tek'st

than k'an; This book is better than that one. Ays girk'ë aveli lavn e k'an ayn.

thank *verb* shnorakalut'yun haytnel; **thank you!** shnorakalut'yun!; **thanks** shnorakalut'yun

that ayn; *conjunction* vor

theater t'atron

theft goghut'yun

their nërants'

theirs nërants'

them nërants'

themselves nërank' inknerë

then heto

theoretical tesakan

theory tesut'yun

there ayntegh; there is/are ... ka ...

therefore hetevapes

thermometer jermachap'

these ays

they nërank'

thick *wide* ger; **thick cloth** hast shorer; **thick forest** khit antarr; **thick soup** t'andzër sup

thief gogh; **thieves** gogher

thigh azdër

thimble matnots'

thin nihar

thing ir

think mtatsel; I think that... Yes kartsum em vor...

thinness barakut'yun

third yerrord

thirst tsarav

thirsty tsarav; I'm thirsty. Yes tsarav em.

thirteen tasnerek'

thirty yerresun

this ays; **this (very)** hents' ays; **this afternoon** ays kesor; **this morning** ays arravot; **this much** aysk'an; **this week** ays shabat

thorax kërtsk'avandak

thorn p'ush

those ayn

thought mitk'

thoughtless anmit

thousand hazar

thread t'el

three yerek'

throat kokord

thrombosis t'romboz

throne gah

through mijev; *by means of* mijots'ov

throw netel; **to throw out** durs netel

thumb bët'amat

thunder vorot

thunderstorm amprop

Thursday hingshabti

tibia mets sërunk'oskër

ticket

ticket toms; **ticket office**
dramarkëgh
tie *necktie* vëzkap; *verb* kapel
tight pind
tights zugagulpaner
time zhamanak; *an instance*
akënt'art; **at the same time**
nuyn zhamanakin; **for a long
time** yerkar zhamanakov; **on
time** zhamanakin; **I don't
have time.** Yes zhamanak
chunem.; **What time is it?**
Zhamë k'anisn e?; **Has the
bus arrived on time?**
Avtobusë zhamanakin yekav?
timetable ts'uts'ak; **travel
timetable** chëvats'uts'ak
tire *noun* anvadogh; *verb* hognel
tired hognats; **to get tired**
hognel
tissues andzerots'ikner
to *see pages 11-14*; **I gave it to
her.** Yes tëvets'i da nëran.;
This is superior to that. Sa
nëranits' bardzr e.
toast *bread* tost
tobacco tsëkhakhot
today aysor
toe mat
together miasin
toilet(s) zuk'aran; **toilet paper**
zuk'arani t'ught'
tomato lolik
tomb gerezman
tomorrow vaghë; **the day after
tomorrow** vaghë che myus
orë
ton; tonne tonna
tongue lezu
tonight ays gisher
too *also* nuynpes; *very* shat; **too
little** shat k'ich; **too many**
shat; **too much** shat
tools gortsik'ner
tooth atam; **teeth** atamner
toothache atamnats'av
toothbrush atami khozanak

toothpaste atami matsuk
toothpick atamnak'ëchp'orik
top gagat'
torrent teghatarap'
torture *noun* tanjank'; *verb*
tanjel
tough *meat* pind; **This meat is
tough.** Ays misë pind e.
tourism zbosashërjikut'yun
tourist zbosashërjik; **tourists**
zbosashërjikner; **tourist
office** zbosashërjikayin
grasenyak
tow buk'sirel; **tow rope**
buk'sirayin ch'opan; **Can you
tow us?** Karogh ek' mez
buk'sirov k'ashel?
towel sërp'ich
tower ashtarak
town k'aghak'; **town center**
k'aghak'i kentron; **town hall**
k'aghak'apetaran; **town
square** k'aghak'i hëraparak
tracer bullet lusatsërogh
gëndak
trachea shënchap'ogh
track hetk'
tractor traktor
trade union armoiut'yun
trader arrevtrakan
tradition avanduyt'
traditional avandakan
traffic *noun* yert'evekut'yun;
traffic lights lusakir; **traffic
police** ch'anaparayin
vostikanut'yun
train *noun* gënats'k'; **train
station** yerkat'ughayin kayan
tranquilizer hangëstats'uts'ich
deghamijots'
transfer flights tarants'ik
t'errichk'
transformer p'okharkich
**transfusion: blood trans-
fusion** aryan p'okhnerarkum
translate t'argmanel
translation t'argmanut'yun

106 · Eastern Armenian Dictionary & Phrasebook

translator t'argmanich
transmit haghordel
transmitter haghordich
transport *noun* transport; *verb* p'okhadrel
trap *noun* tsughak
trash aghb
trauma vënasvatsk'
travel *noun* ch'anaparordut'yun; *verb* ch'anaparordel; **travel agency** ch'anaparordakan gortsakalut'yun
traveler ch'amp'ord; **travelers** ch'amp'ordner
traveler's checks ch'amp'ord cheker
tray skutegh
treacherous nengali
treasury *ministry* gandzapetaran
treaty paymanagir
tree tsarr; **trees** tsarrer
trench khëramat
trial *legal* datavarut'yun; *test* p'ordzarkum
trolleybus troleibus
troops zork'er
trouble *inconvenience* anhangëstut'yun; *problems* khëndir; **What's the trouble?** Inchumn e khëndirë
trousers andravartik'
truce zinadat'ar
truck berrnatar mek'ena
true ch'ëshgërit
trunk *box* ch'ampruk; *of car* bagazhategh; *of tree* bun
truth ch'ëshmartut'yun
try p'ordzel
tube khoghovak
tuberculosis tuberkulyoz
Tuesday yerek'shabt'i
tunnel tunel
turban chalma
Turk t'urk'
Turkish *thing* t'urk'akan; *language* t'urk'eren
turkey hëndkahav

Turkey T'urk'ia
turn *noun* pëtuyt; *verb* shërjel; **turn left!** shërjek' dzakh; **turn right!** shërjek' aj
turnip shaghgam
twelve tasnerku
twenty k'san
twice yerku angam
twins yerkvoryakner
twist volork'
twisted khëch'ëch'vats
two yerku
type *noun* tesak; *verb* tëpel
typewriter gëramek'ena
tyre *noun* anvadogh

U

ulcer khots'; **stomach ulcer** stamok'si khots'
umbilical cord portalar
umbrella hovanots'
unbeliever anhavat
uncle *father's brother* horekhbayr; *mother's brother* k'erri
uncomfortable anharmar
uncooked anep'
under *adverb* nerk'evi; *preposition* tak; **under the table** seghani tak
underground *adjective/adverb* storgetnya /getni tak; *subway* metro
understand haskanal; **Do you understand?** Duk' haskanum ek'?; **I understand.** Yes haskanum em.; **I don't understand.** Yes chem haskanum.
underwear nerk'nazgest
undress: to get undressed hanvel: hanvel
unemployed gortsazurk
unemployment gortsazërkut'yun

unexploded bomb chëpayt'ats rumb
unfortunate dëzhbakht
unfortunately dëzhbakhtabar
unfriendly anbaryats'akam
unhappy tëkhur
uniform *clothing* hamazgest
uninformed anteghyak
union miut'yun; **trade union** armiut'yun
unique unikal
unit *military* zoramas
United Nations Miavorvats Azger
United States of America Amerikayi Miats'yal Nahangner
university hamalsaran
unknown anhayt
unless minchev vor ch...
unsuccessful anhajogh
until minchev
unwise anmit
up verev
upright ughigh
urgent anhetadzëgeli
urine mez
us pron.pers. mez
U.S.A. AMëNë
use *noun* gortsatsut'yun; *verb* ok'tagortsel
useful ok'takar
usefulness ok'takarut'yun
usual sovorakan
usually sovorabar
uterus vorovayn
utility ogtavetut'yun

U

vacation arts'akurd
vaccinate patvastel; **I have been vaccinated.** Indz vakts'inayov patvastel en.
vaccination vakts'inayov patvastum
valley hovit
value *verb* gënahatel

veal hort'i mis
vegetable shop banjaregheni khanut'
vegetables *fresh* banjaregheni; *ready to eat* mëshakats banjaregheni
vegetarian busaker mard; **I am a vegetarian.** Yes busaker mard em.
vein yerak
venereal disease venerakan hivandut'yun
veranda veranda
verb bay
vertebra voghnoskër
very shat
veto *noun* ark'elk'; *verb* ark'elk' dënel
vice-president *of country* p'okhnakhagah
victim zoh; **victims** zoher; **the victims of the earthquake** yerkrasharzhi zoher
victory haght'anak
video cassette tesazhapaven
video player tesamagnitofon
view *noun* tesaran
village gyugh; **village elder** gyughapet
villager gyughats'i
vine vort'
vinegar k'ats'akh
violence bërrnut'yun
viper izh
virus virus
visa viza
visit *verb* ayts'elel
visitor ayts'elu
vitamins vitaminner
voice dzayn
volume *size* tsaval; *book* hator
vomit p'ëskhel; **I have been vomiting.** Yes p'ëskhum ei.
vote *noun* k've; *verb* k'vearkel; **to cast a vote** dzayn tal
voter ëntrogh
vulture angëgh

W

wage war paterazm varel
waist iran
waistband iranakal
waistcoat *vest* zhilet; *jacket* bach'kon
wait spasel; **to wait for** spasel; **wait a moment!** Spasets'ek'!
waiter matuts'ogh
waiting spasum
waitress matuts'oghuhi
wake up art'nanal; **Please wake me up at ...** Khëndrum em, art'nats'rek' indz zhamë ...
walk k'aylel
walking stick dzerrnap'ayt
wall pat
wallet dramapanak
want ts'ankanal; **What do you want?** Inch ek' ts'ankanum?; **I want ...** Yes uzum em ...; **I don't want ...** Yes chem uzum ...
war paterazm
warm tak'
warmonger paterazmi hërdzig
wash lëvanal
washbowl lëvatsaran
washed lëvats'ats
washing powder lëvats'k'i p'oshi
wasp kret
watch *clock* zhamats'uyts'; **to watch** ditel
water jur; **Is there drinking water?** Khëmelu jur ka?
water bottle jëri shish
waterfall jërvezh
watermelon dzëmeruk
watermill jëraghats'
way ch'anapar; *manner* varveladzev; **way of life** aprelakerp
we menk'
weak t'uyl
weapon zenk'
wear hak'nel

weasel ak'is
weather yeghanak
weave hyusel
wedding harsanik'
Wednesday chorek'shap't'i
week shabat'
weekend uik-end
weekly shap'at'akan
weep lats' linel
weight k'ash
welcome! Bari galust
well *adjective/adverb* lav; *noun: of water* jërhor
well-known ch'anachvats
west *noun* arevmutk'
west(ern) arevmëtyan
wet t'ats'
what? inch?; **what's that?** inch e da?; **what kind?** inchpisi?
whatever inch vor; **Take whatever you want.** Verts'rek' inch vor uzum ek'.
wheat ts'oren; **wheat bin** ts'oreni hatik
wheel aniv
wheelchair hashmandami bazkat'orr
when? yerb?
where? vortegh?; **where is?** vortegh e?; **where are?** vortegh en?; **where from?** vorteghits'?
whether art'yok'
which vor; **which (one)?** vor mekë?
while minch derr
whistle *noun* sulots'
white spitak
whitish spitakavun
who? ov?
whole amboghj
why? inchu?
wide layn
widow ayri
widower ayri tghamard
wife kin
wild *animal* vayri

wild goose vayri sag

win haght'el; **Who won?** Ov e haght'el?

wind *noun* k'ami

wind *verb* volorvel; **to wind thread** pat'at'el t'elë

window patuhan; **window pane** apaku shërjanak

windpipe shënchap'ogh

windscreen; windshield avtomek'enayi dimats'i apaki

windy k'amot

wine gini

winter dzëmerr

wire lar

wisdom imastut'yun; **wisdom tooth** imastut'yan atam

wise imastun

wish *verb* ts'ankanal

with het; **I went with him.** Yes gnats'i nëra het.; **They fought with courage.** Nërank' k'ajut'ymb kërrvum ein.

without arrants'; **without work** arrants' ashkhatank'i

witness akanates

wolf gayl

woman kin

womb argand

women kanayk'

wood *substance* p'ayt; *forest* antarr

wool burd

woolen bërt'ya

word barr

work *noun* ashkhatank'; *verb* ashkhatel; **I work in a bank.** Yes ashkhatum em bankum.; **The phone doesn't work.** Herrakhosë chi ashkhatum.

worker ashkhatogh

world ashkharh

worms vorder

worried anhangëstats'ats; **to be worried** anhangëstats'ats linel

worse aveli vat; **I feel worse.** Yes aveli vat em zgum.

worth: to be worth gin: arzhel

wound *noun* verk'; *verb* viravorel

wrap p'at'at'el

wrench *tool* pëtutakabanali

wrestling ëmbshamart

wrist dastak

wristwatch dzerrk'i jamats'uyts'

write gërel

writer gërogh

writing gir

wrong sëkhal

X

X-rays rrentgenyan ch'arragayt'ner

Y

yard *courtyard* bak; *garden* aygi; *distance* yard

year tari; **this year** ays tari

yearly tarekan

yellow deghin

yes ayo

yesterday yerek; **the day before yesterday** nakhants'yal orë; **yesterday's** yerekva

yet derr

yogurt matsun

you *singular* du; *plural* duk'

young yeritasard; **young person** yeritasard mard; **young girl** parmanuhi; **youngest child** amenap'ok'ër erekha

your *singular* k'o; *plural* dzer

yours *singular* k'onë; *plural* dzerë

yourself du ink'ëd

yourselves duk' ink'nerëd

Z

zero zëro

zipper kaytsakach'armand

zoo gazananots'

ARMENIAN
Phrasebook

1. ETIQUETTE

Hello!
   Response:
	Vokhjuyn!
	   Vokhjuyn!

See you tomorrow!
   Response:
	Vaghë këtesnëvenk'!
	   **Arrayzhëm,
	   minch vaghë!**

Good-bye!
   Response:
	Ts'ëtesut'yun!
	   Ts'ëtesut'yun!

Welcome!
   Response:
	Bari galust!
	   Shnorakalut'yun!

Please eat!	**Hamtes arek', khënt'rum em!**
Please sit down!	**Nëstek' khënt'rem!**
Congratulations!	**Shnorhavorank'nerës!**
Excuse me!	**Nerets'ek' indz!**
Sorry!	**Kënerek'!**
yes	**ayo**
no	**voch**
please	**khënt'rem** *or* **khënt'rum em**
thank you	**shnorakalut'yun**

2. QUICK REFERENCE

I	**yes**
you *singular*	**du**
you *formal/plural*	**duk'**
he/she/it	**na/na/na**
we	**menk'**
they	**nërank'**
this	**ays**
that	**ayn**
these	**ays**
those	**ayn**
here	**aystegh**
there	**ayntegh**
where?	**vortegh**
who?	**ov**
what?	**inch**
when?	**yerp'**
which?	**vor**
how?	**inchpes**
why?	**inchu**
how much?	**vork'an**
how many?	**vork'an**
what's that?	**inch e sa?**
is/are there . . . ?	**ka ayntegh ...?**
where is . . . ?	**vortegh e ... ?**
where are . . . ?	**vortegh en ...?**
here is . . .	**aha ...**
here are . . .	**aha ...**

what must I do?	**yes inch petk' e anem?**
what do you want?	**inch ek' ts'ankanum?**
very	**shat**
and	**yev**
or	**kam**
but	**bayts'**
more or less	**k'ich t'e shat**
I like . . .	**Yes sirum em ...**
I don't like . . .	**Yes ch'em sirum ...**
I want . . .	**Yes uzum em ...**
I don't want . . .	**Yes ch'em uzum ...**
I know.	**Yes gitem.**
I don't know.	**Yes ch'ëgitem.**
Do you understand?	**Duk' haskanum ek'?**
I understand.	**Yes haskanum em.**
I don't understand.	**Yes ch'em haskanum.**
Sorry!	**Ts'avum em!**
My condolences. *if someone dies*	**Ts'avakts'um em.**
I am grateful.	**Yes yerakhtapart em.**
It's important.	**Sa karevor e.**
It doesn't matter.	**Da nëshanakut'yun chuni.**
You're welcome!	**Khënt'rem!**
No problem!	**Khënt'ir ch'ëka!**
Is everything OK?	**Amen inch lav e?**
Danger!	**Vëtangavor e!**

Could you repeat that?	**Cheik' kërkëni da?**
How do you spell that?	**Inchpes e da gërvum?**

—Feelings

I am hot.	**Yes shok'um em.**
I am right.	**Yes chisht em.**
I am sleepy.	**Yes uzum em k'ënel.**
I am hungry.	**K'akhts'ats em.**
I am thirsty.	**Tsarav em.**
I am angry.	**Zayrats'ats em.**
I am happy.	**Yerjanik em.**
I am sad.	**Tëkhur em.**
I am tired.	**Hok'nats em.**
I am well.	**Lav em.**
I am cold.	**Mërrsum em.**

—Colors

black	**sev**
blue	**kapuyt**
sky blue	**yerknaguyn**
brown	**shaganakaguyn**
khaki; grey	**mokhraguyn**
green	**kanach**
pink	**vart'aguyn**
red	**karmir**
white	**spitak**
yellow	**deghin**

3. INTRODUCTIONS

What is your name?	**Inchpes e dzer anunnë?**
My name is . . .	**Im anunnë ...**
May I introduce you to . . .	**T'uyl tëvek' nerkayats'nel ...**
This is my . . .	**Sa im ...**
friend	**ënkern e**
companion	**kompanionn e**
colleague	**gortsënkern e**
relative	**barekamn e**

> **TITLES** — "Mr." is **Paron** and "Mrs." is **Tikin**, used in much the same way as in English. Use **Oriard** for Ms. and **Miss** for "Miss". Especially when you don't know someone's name, these can also be used to mean "Sir", "Madam" etc.

—Nationality

Armenia	**Hayastan**
—Armenian *person*	**—hay**

Where are you from?	**Duk' vorteghits'* ek?**
I am from . . .	**Yes . . . em.**
America	**Amerika-yits'***
Australia	**Avtsralia-yits'**
Britain	**Britania-yits'**
Canada	**Kanada-yits'**
China	**Chinastan-its'**
Cyprus	**Kipros-its'**
England	**Anglia-yits'**
Europe	**Yevropa-yits'**
France	**Fransia-yits'**
Germany	**Germania-yits'**
Greece	**Hunastan-its'**
India	**Hëndkastan-its'**
Iran	**Iran-its'**

* -(y)its' means "from". The hyphen is there to make it clearer.

Ireland	**Irlandia-yits'**
Italy	**Italia-yits'**
Japan	**Ch'aponia-yits'**
Lebanon	**Libanan-its'**
the Netherlands	**Niderlandner-its'**
New Zealand	**Nor Zelandia-yits'**
Northern Ireland	**Hyusisayin Irlandia-yits'**
Pakistan	**Pakistan-its'**
Scotland	**Shotlandia-yits'**
Spain	**Ispania-yits'**
Syria	**Siria-yits'**
the USA	**Miats'yal Nahangner-its'**
Wales	**Uels-its'**
I am . . .	**Yes . . . em.**
American	**Amerikats'i**
Australian	**Afstralats'i**
British	**Britanast'i**
Canadian	**Kanadats'i**
Chinese	**Chinats'i**
Cypriot	**Kipriot**
Dutch	**Holandats'i**
English	**Angliats'i**
French	**Angliats'i**
German	**Germanats'i**
Greek	**Huyn**
Indian	**Hëndik**
Iranian	**Iranats'i**
Irish	**Irlandats'i**
Israeli	**Israelats'i**
Japanese	**Ch'aponats'i**
Lebanese	**Libanats'i**
Pakistani	**Pakistants'i**
Scottish	**Shotlandats'i**
Spanish	**Ispaniats'i**
Syrian	**Siriats'i**
Welsh	**Uelsts'i**

INTRODUCTIONS

| Where were you born? | **Vortegh ek' tsënvel?** |
| I was born in . . . | **Yes tsënvel em ...** |

— Regional nationalities

Caucasus	**Kovkas**
—Caucasian	**—kovkasyan**
Azerbaijan	**Adërbejan**
—Azerbaijani	**—adërbejants'i**
Georgia	**Vërastan**
—Georgian	**—vërats'i**
Armenia	**Hayastan**
—Armenian	**—hay**
Iraq	**Irak'**
—Iraqi	**—irak'ts'i**
Russia	**Rrusastan**
—Russian	**—rrus**
Turkey	**T'urk'ia**
—Turkish	**—t'urk'**
Ukraine	**Ukraina**
—Ukrainian	**—ukraynats'i**
Uzbekistan	**Uzbekistan**
—Uzbek	**—Uzbek**

Kurd	**k'urd**
Arab	**arab**
Assyrian	**aysor**
Laz	**laz**
Hemshin	**hamzhents'i**

— Occupations

What do you do?	**Inchov ek' zbaghvum?**
I am a/an ...	**Yes ... em.**
accountant	**hashvapah**
administrator	**administrator**
agronomist	**gyughatëntesaget**
aid worker	**ok'nakan**

architect	**ch'artarapet**
artist	**nëkarich**
blacksmith	**darp'in**
business person	**gortsarar**
carpenter	**atakhdzagorts**
consultant	**khorhërt'atu**
dentist	**atamnabuyzh**
diplomat	**divanaget**
doctor	**bëzhishk**
economist	**tëntesaget**
engineer	**inzhener**
farmer	**fermer**
film-maker	**kinonëkarich**
joiner	**atakhtsagorts**
journalist	**lëragrogh**
judge	**datavor**
lawyer	**iravaban**
mechanic	**mek'enaget**
negotiator	**banagënats'**
nurse	**dayak**
observer	**ditord**
office worker	**gërasenyaki ashkhatogh**
pilot	**ot'achu**
political scientist	**k'aghak'akanaget**
scientist	**gitnakan**
secretary	**k'artughar**
soldier	**zinvor**
student *school*	**ashakert**
university	**usanogh**
surgeon	**virabuyzh**
tailor	**derts'ak**
teacher	**usuts'ich**
specialist	**masnaget**
tourist	**zbosashërjik**
trader	**arreftrakan**
writer	**gërogh**

INTRODUCTIONS

I work in . . .	**Yes ... ashkhatum em.**
an aid agency	**baregortsakan gortsakalut'yun**
the hotel industry	**hyuranots'ayin biznesum**
industry	**ardyunaberut'yunum**
I.T.	**barts'ër tekhnologianeri volortum**
the media	**zangvatsayin lëratvut'yan michots'nerum**
telecommunications	**herrahaghordakts'u-t'yan volortum**
the tourist industry	**zbosashërjikut'yan biznesum**

— Age

How old are you?	**Duk' k'ani tarekan ek'?**
I am . . . years old.	**Yes ... tarekan em.**

— Family

Are you married?	**Duk' amusnats'ats ek'?**
I am not married.	**Yes amusnats'ats ch'em.**
I am married.	**Yes amusnats'ats em.**
I am divorced.	**Yes bazhanvats em.**
I am a widow.	**Yes ayri em.**
Do you have a boyfriend?	**Duk' unek' ënker?**
Do you have a girlfriend?	**Duk' unek' ënkeruhi?**
What is his/her name?	**Inch e nëra anunë?**

How many children do you have?	**Duk' vork'an yerekha unek'?**
I don't have any children.	**Yes yerekha chunem.**
I have a daughter.	**Yes unem dustër.**
I have a son.	**Yes unem vordi.**
How many brothers do you have?	**Duk' k'ani yeghpayr unek'?**
How many sisters do you have?	**Duk' k'ani k'uyr unek'?**
How many brothers and sisters do you have?	**Duk' k'ani yeghpayr ev k'uyr unek'?**

RELATIVES — Armenians have a highly developed sense of family ties and there is therefore a wide range of special words for relatives — distant as well as close. Only immediate family are outlined below. For details of aunts, cousins and in-laws, look up the relevant English term in the dictionary section.

---

father	**hayr**
mother	**mayr**
parents	**tsënoghner**
grandfather	**pap**
grandmother	**tat**
granddaughter	**t'orr**
grandson	**t'orr**
brother	**yeghpayr**
sister	**k'uyr**
daughter	**dustër**
son	**vort'i**
twins	**yerkvoryakner**
husband	**amusin**
wife	**kin**
family	**ëntanik'**
man	**tëghamard**

woman	**kin**
boy	**tëgha**
girl	**akhchik**
baby; child	**yerekha**
children	**yerekhaner**
teenager	**derrahas**
elder *old person*	**tseruni**
person	**andznavorut'yun**
people	**mart'ik**
orphan	**vorp'**

— Religion

The Armenians are mostly Orthodox Christians with their own autocephalous church. (For more, see "Religious Heritage" on page 168).

What is your religion?	**Vorne dzer kronë?**
I am (a) . . .	**Yes ... em.**
Muslim	**mahmedakan**
Buddhist	**budayakan**
Orthodox	**ughghap'arr**
Christian	**k'ristonya**
Catholic	**kat'oghik**
Hindu	**hinduistakan**
Jewish	**hreakan**

| I am not religious. | **Yes havatats'yal chem.** |

4. LANGUAGE

Aside from other indigenous languages spoken in the Caucasus, most Armenians will speak Russian. Many will also know at least one or more European languages like German and English, while the older generations will tend to know French. In addition, you will find many speakers of regional languages such as Georgian, Kurdish, Azerbaijani, Turkish, and Farsi.

Do you know/speak Armenian?	**Duk' khosum ek' hayeren?**
Do you know English?	**Duk' khosum ek' angleren?**
Do you know Russian?	**Duk' khosum ek' rruseren?**
Do you know German?	**Duk' khosum ek' germaneren?**
Do you know Georgian?	**Duk' khosum ek' vrats'eren?**
Do you know French?	**Duk' khosum ek' franseren?**
Do you know Farsi?	**Duk' khosum ek' farsi?**
Do you know Spanish?	**Duk' khosum ek' ispaneren?**
Do you know Turkish?	**Duk' khosum ek' t'urk'eren?**
Do you know Arabic?	**Duk' khosum ek' araberen?**
Does anyone know English?	**Vorevits'e mekë giti angleren?**
I know a little . . .	**Yes mi kich gitem ...**
I don't know any . . .	**Yes ëndhanrapes chëgitem ...**

I understand.	**Yes haskanum em.**
I don't understand.	**Yes ch'em haskanum em.**
Please point to the word in the book.	**Khëndrum em ts'uts' tëvek' ays barrë barraranum.**
Please wait while I look up the word.	**Khëndrum em spasek' minch yes nayem aus barrë barraranum.**
Could you speak more slowly, please?	**Duk' karogheik' aveli dandagh khosal?**
Could you repeat that?	**Cheik' kërkni?**
How do you say . . . in Armenian?	**Inchpes ek' asum ... hayeren?**
What does . . . mean?	**Inch e nëshanakum ... ?**
How do you pronounce this word?	**Inchpes ek' artasanum ays khoskhë?**
I know . . .	**Yes gitem ...**
Arabic	**araberen**
Chinese	**chineren**
Danish	**danieren**
Dutch	**holanderen**
English	**angleren**
Farsi	**farsi**
French	**franseren**
Georgian	**germaneren**
German	**germaneren**

Greek	**huneren**
Hindi	**hëndkeren**
Italian	**italeren**
Japanese	**ch'aponeren**
Kurdish	**k'ërderen**
Russian	**rruseren**
Spanish	**ispaneren**
Turkish	**t'urk'eren**

Some common expressions ...

Here are a few expressions you'll hear in everyday conversation:

lav!; bari!	all right!; okay!
kets'es!	bravo!
avagh!; akh!	alas!
aysinkën ...	I mean...; that's to say...
ap'sos!	what a pity!
bavakan e!	enough!; well now!
charzhi!	not at all!
ha!	yes!
art'yok'?	really?
inchu che?	why not?
lav!	well!
khënt'ir ch'ëka!	no problem!
apa!	hey!
hapa!	come on!; hey!
pah!	wow!
vakh!	ow!
urra!	hooray!

5. BUREAUCRACY

> Note that many forms you encounter may also be written in Russian or English.

name	**anun**
surname	**azganun**
middle name	**hayranun**
address	**hasts'e**
date of birth	**tsënëndyan**
place of birth	**tsënëndyan vayrë**
nationality	**azgut'yun**
citizenship	**k'aghak'ats'iut'yun**
age	**tarik'**
sex: female	**igakan**
male	**arakan**
religion	**kron**
reason for travel:	**ch'anaparordut'yan nëpatakë**
business	**gorts**
tourism	**zbosashërjikut'yun**
work	**ashkhatank'**
personal	**andznakan**
profession	**masnagitut'yun**
marital status	**ëntanekan kargavich'ak**
single *male*	**chamusnats'ats**
female	**chamusnats'ats**
married *male*	**amusnats'ats**
female	**amusnats'ats**
divorced	**bazhanvats**
date	**amsat'iv**
date of arrival	**zhamanman amsat'ivë**
date of departure	**meknelu amsat'ivë**
passport	**andznagir**
passport number	**andznagri hamar**
visa	**viza**
currency	**artarzhuyt'**

—Inquiries

Is this the correct form?	**Sa chisht dzevn e?**
What does this mean?	**Inch e sa nëshanakum?**
Where is . . . 's office?	**Vortegh e .... grasenyakë?**
Which floor is it on?	**Ayn vor harkum e?**
Does the lift/elevator work?	**Verelakë ashkhatum e?**
Is Mr./Ms. . . . in?	**Paron/Tikin ... aystegh e?**
Please tell him/her that I am here.	**Khëndrum em asats'ek' nëran vor yes aystegh em.**
I can't wait, I have an appointment.	**Yes ch'em karogh spasel, yes zhamadërvats em.**
Tell him/her that I was here.	**Asats'ek' nëran vor yes aystegh ei.**

—Ministries

Ministry of Defense	**Pashtapanut'yan nakhararut'yun**
Ministry of Agriculture	**Gyughatëntesut'yan nakhararut'yun**
Ministry of Home Affairs	**Nerk'in gortseti nakhararut'yun**
Ministry of Foreign Affairs	**Artak'in gortseri nakhararut'yun**
Ministry of Health	**Arrokhchapahut'yan nakhararut'yun**
Ministry of Education	**Kërt'ut'yan nakhararut'yun**
Ministry of Justice	**Art'aradatut'yan nakhararut'yun**

6. TRAVEL

PUBLIC TRANSPORT — Buses or trolley buses can often be too packed for comfort, and Yerevan's metro (see below) is being swiftly outpaced by the growth of new suburbs. Far more practical are the numerous privately run minibuses (called **yertughayin tak'si**) which stop at predetermined pick-up points. You pay the driver's assistant when you get out. Longer distance travel out of town offers you the usual variety of means. There are now many car rental firms, offering you vehicles with or without drivers. Rates vary. Buses are reliable and leave from specially designated areas. Travel by rail can be slow and subject to long delays mid-journey. Note that all public announcements, particularly for trains and planes, are also made in Russian. Bicycles and motorbikes are difficult to find and, in view of the mountainous terrain in most of the country, often impractical.

METRO — Yerevan's metro system was opened in 1981 and is a clean, fast and easy way to get around. At the moment, there is only one main line in operation, and ten stops. Trains are relatively frequent and stop running at 11pm.

What time does . . . leave/arrive?	**Zhamë k'anisin e zhamanum/ meknum ...?**
the airplane	**ink'nat'irrë**
the boat	**navë**
the bus	**aftobusë**
the train	**gënatsk'ë**
The plane is delayed.	**T'ërrichk'ë het adzëk'vum e.**
The plane is canceled.	**T'ërrichk'ë cheghyal e hamarvel.**
The train is delayed.	**Gënats'kë hetadzëk'vum e.**
The train is canceled.	**Gënats'kë cheghyal e hamarvel.**
How long will it be delayed?	**Vork'anov e ayn hetadzëk'vum?**
There is a delay of . . . minutes.	**Ayn hetadzëk'vum e ... ropeov.**

There is a delay of . . . hours.	**Ayn hetadzëk'vum e ... zhamov.**
Excuse me, where is the ticket office?	**Nerets'ek, vortegh e tomsarkghë?**
Where can I buy a ticket?	**Vortegh karogh em toms gënel?**
I want to go to . . .	**Yes uzum em gënal ...**
I want a ticket to . . .	**Yes uzum em toms depi ...**
I would like . . .	**Yes këts'ankanayi ...**
a one-way ticket	**mek ughut'yamb toms**
a return ticket	**yetadarts' toms**
first class	**arrajin das**
second class	**yerkrord das**
Do I pay in dollars or in drams?	**Yes vëch'arelu em dolarov t'e haykakan dramov?**
You must pay in dollars.	**Duk' petk' e vëch'arek' dolarov.**
You must pay in drams.	**Duk' petk' e vëch'arek' dramov.**
You can pay in either.	**Duk' karogh ek' vëch'arel ts'ankats'ats artarzhuyt'ov.**
Can I reserve a place?	**Karogh em tegh patvirel?**
How long does the trip take?	**Inchk'an e tevum ughevorut'yunë?**
Is it a direct route?	**Sa ughigh yert'ughi e?**

—Air

Is there a flight to . . . ?	**Ka t'ërrichk' depi ... ?**
When is the next flight to . . . ?	**Yerp' e hajort' t'ërrichk'ë ... ?**

How long is the flight?	**Vork'an e tevum t'ërrichk'ë?**
What is the flight number?	**Inchpes e t'ërrichk'i hamarë?**
You must check in at . . .	**Duk' petk' e gërants'vek' ...**
Is the flight delayed?	**T'ërrichk'ë hetadzëk'vum e?**
How many hours is the flight delayed?	**K'ani zhamov e tërrichk'ë hetadzëkvum?**
Is this the flight for . . . ?	**Sa ... chëvert'n e?**
Is that the flight from . . . ?	**Sa ...-its' chëvert'n e?**
When is the London flight arriving?	**Yerp' e zhamanelu Londoni chëvert'ë?**
Is it on time?	**Ayn chi oshanum?**
Is it late?	**Ayn ushanum e?**
Do I have to change planes?	**Yes petk' e ink'natirrë p'okhem?**
Has the plane left London yet?	**Ink'natirrë arden meknel e Londonits'?**
What time does the plane take off?	**Zhamë k'anisin e ink'natirrë meknum?**
What time do we arrive in Yerevan?	**Zhamë k'anisin enk' menk' zhamanelu Yerevan?**
excess baggage	**avelort' berr**
international flight	**michazgayin chëvert'**
internal flight	**nerk'in chëvert'**

—Bus

bus stop	**aftokangarr**
bus station	**aftokayan**
Where is the bus stop?	**Vortegh e aftokangarrë?**

Where is the bus station?	**Vortegh e aftokayanë?**
Please take me to the bus station.	**Khënt'rum em indz tanel depi aftokayan.**
Which bus goes to . . . ?	**Vor aftobusn e gënum depi ...?**
Does this bus go to . . . ?	**Ays aftobusë gënum e depi ...?**
How often do buses pass by?	**Vork'an hach'akh en aftobusnerë ants'num?**
What time is the . . . bus?	**Yerp' e ... aftobusë?**
next	**hajort'**
first	**arrachin**
last	**verchin**
Where can I get a bus to . . . ?	**Vortegh yes karogh em nëstel aftobus depi ...?**
When is the first bus to . . . ?	**Yerp' e arrachin aftobusë depi ...?**
When is the last bus to . . . ?	**Yerp' e verchin aftobusë depi ...?**
When is the next bus to . . . ?	**Yerp' e hajort' aftobusë depi ...?**
Do I have to change buses?	**Yes petk' e p'okhem aftobusë?**
Will you let me know when we get to . . . ?	**Duk' indz këzgushats'nek' yerp' menk këhasnenk' ...?**
I want to get off at . . .	**Yes uzum em ichnel ...**
Please let me off at the next stop.	**Khënt'rum em, kangnek' hajort' kangarrin.**
Stop, I want to get off!	**Kangnek', yes uzum em ichnel.**

Please let me off here.	**Khënt'rum em, kangnek' aystegh.**
How long is the journey?	**Vork'an e tevum ughevorut'yunë?**
What is the fare?	**Vork'an e vardzë?**
I need my luggage, please.	**Indz petk' e im berrë.**
That's my bag.	**Aha im payusakë.**

— Rail

Please take me to the railway station.	**Khënt'rum em indz tanel yerkat'gits kayan.**
Is this the right platform for . . . ?	**Aysteghits e meknum gënats'kë depi ...?**
Is there a timetable?	**Ka chëvats'uts'akë?**
Where can I buy tickets?	**Vortegh yes karogh em tomser gënel?**
Which platform should I go to?	**Vor platformayin petk'e yes gënam?**
platform one	**arrachin platformayin**
platform two	**yerkrort' platformayin**
The train leaves from platform . . .	**Gënats'kë meknum e ... platformayits'.**
Passengers must . . .	**Ughevornerë petk' e ...**
change trains.	**p'okhen gënats'knerë.**
change platforms.	**p'okhen platforman.**
You must change trains at . . .	**Duk' petk'e gnats'k'ë p'okhek' ...**
Will the train leave on time?	**Gënats'kë zhamanakin e sharzhvelu?**

There will be a delay of . . . minutes.	**Ayn kushana ... ropeov.**
There will be a delay of . . . hours.	**Ayn kushana ... zhamov.**

– Taxi

> Some taxis are marked, while others are not. To avoid unpleasant surprises, agree to fares in advance. It is useful to be able to tell the driver your destination in Armenian or Russian too (or have it written down on a piece of paper). Be warned, however, that some drivers will have as little idea as you as to the precise whereabouts of your destination. A reliable option is to call up one of the growing number of radio taxi (**radio tak'si**) companies.

Taxi!	**Tak'si!**
Where can I get a taxi?	**Vortegh karogh em tak'si patvirel?**
Please could you get me a taxi?	**Duk' karogh eik' indz tak'si gëtnel?**
Can you take me to . . . ?	**Duk' karogh ek' indz tanel depi ...?**
Please take me to . . .	**Khëndrum em indz tarek' ...**
How much will it cost to . . . ?	**Vork'an karzhena gënal depi ...?**
How much?	**Inchk'an petk' e vëch'arem?**
To this address, please.	**Ays hasts'eov, khënt'rum em.**
Turn left.	**T'ek'vek' dzakh.**
Turn right.	**T'ek'vek' ach.**
Go straight ahead.	**Ughigh gënats'ek'.**
Stop!	**Kangnek'!**
Don't stop!	**Mi kangnek'!**

I'm in a hurry.	**Yes shtapum em!**
Please drive more slowly!	**Khënt'rum em aveli dandagh varek'!**
Here is fine, thank you.	**Aystegh lav e, shnorakalut'yun.**
The next corner, please.	**Hajort' ankyunë, khëntrum em.**
The next street to the left.	**Hajord p'oghots'ë depi dzakh.**
The next street to the right.	**Hajord p'oghots'ë depi ach.**
Stop here!	**Aystegh kangnek'!**
Stop the car, I want to get out.	**Kangnets'rek' mek'enan, yes uzum em durs gal.**
Please wait here.	**Khënt'rum em aystegh spasel.**
Please take me to the airport.	**Khënt'rum em indz tanel depi ot'anavakayan.**

– General phrases

I want to get off at . . .	**Yes uzum em ichnel ...**
Excuse me!	**Nerets'ek'!**
I want to get out (of the bus).	**Yes uzum em idurs gal ...**
These are my bags.	**Srank' en im payusaknerë.**
Please put them there.	**Khënt'rum em aystegh dërek'.**
Is this seat free?	**Ays nëstateghë azat e?**

I think that's my seat. | **Yes kartsum em, sa im nëstateghn e.**

—Extra words

airport	**ot'anavakayan**
airport tax	**ot'anavakayani tak'si**
ambulance	**shtap ok'nut'yun**
arrivals	**zhamanumner**
bag	**payusak**
baggage	**ugheberr**
baggage counter	**berri ksherrk'**
bicycle	**hetsaniv**
boarding pass	**nëstakëtron**
boat	**nav**
border	**sahman**
bus stop	**avtobusi kangarr**
camel	**ukht**
car	**avtomek'ena; mek'ena**
cart *horse-drawn*	**sayl**
check-in	**gërants'um**
check-in counter	**gërants'man vayr**
closed	**p'ak e**
customs	**mak'satun**
delay	**hetadzëk'um**
departures	**meknumner**
donkey	**avanak**
emergency exit	**pahustayin yelk'**
entrance	**mutk'**
exit	**yelk'**
express	**ch'epënt'ats'**
ferry	**lastanav**
foot: on foot	**votk'ov**
frontier	**sahman**
4-wheel drive	**jip**

TRAVEL

helicopter	**ughat'irr**
horse	**dzi**
information	**teghekatvut'yun**
ladies/gents	**tiknayk'/paronayk'**
local	**teghakan**
lorry	**berrnatar mek'ena**
luggage	**ugheberr**
motorbike	**motots'iklet**
mule	**jori**
no entry	**mutk'n ark'elvum e**
no smoking	**tsëkheln ark'elvum e**
open	**bats' e**
path	**ants'k'**
platform number	**platformayi hamar**
railway	**yerkat'gits**
reserved	**patvirvats e**
radio taxi	**radio tak'si**
road	**ch'anapar**
tarmac road	**gudronapatats khëch'ughi**
sign	**nëshan**
sleeping car	**nënjavagon**
station	**kayaran**
bus station	**aftokayan**
train station	**kayaran**
subway; underground	**metro**
telephone	**herrakhos**
ticket office	**tomsarkëgh**
timetable	**ts'uts'ak**
toilet(s)	**zuk'aran**
town center	**k'aghak'i kentron**
trolleybus	**troleibus**
truck	**berrnatar mek'ena**
van	**furgon**

7. ACCOMMODATION

The hotel and guesthouse network in Armenia is rapidly being developed. Should adequate accommodation be found away from the major towns, you will find that room service is not available, and breakfast or other meals will have to be negotiated and paid for separately. An excellent option in more rural areas is to have your accommodation arranged at a private house, where traditional hospitality will guarantee that you are well looked after and, as always in Armenia, well fed. More and more places are starting to offer details of their services and location on the internet, as well as offering facilities for payment by credit card.

Where can I find a hotel?	**Vortegh e hyuranots'ë?**
I am looking for a hotel.	**Yes hyuranots' em p'ëntrum.**
Is there anywhere I can stay for the night?	**Ka vorev e tegh, vortegh yes karoghem gisher ants'kats'nel?**
Where is . . .	**Vortegh e ...**
a cheap hotel	**ezhan hyuranots'**
a good hotel	**lav hyuranots'**
a nearby hotel	**motaka hyuranots'**
a clean hotel	**mak'ur hyuranots'**
What is the address?	**Inchpes e hasts'en?**
Could you write the address please?	**Duk' karogh ek' gërel hasts'en?**

– At the hotel

Do you have any rooms free?	**Duk' unek' azat hamar?**
I would like . . .	**Yes kuzenayi ...**
a single room	**mek andzi hamar**
a double room	**yerku andzi hamar**

ACCOMMODATION

We'd like a room.	**Menk' uzum enk' hamar patvireink'.**
We'd like two rooms.	**Mez petk' e yerku hamar.**
I want a room with . . .	**Yes uzum em hamar ...**
a bathroom	**logaran-ov**
a shower	**ts'ënts'ugh-ov**
a television	**herrustats'uyts'-ov**
a window	**patuhan-ov**
a double bed	**yerkteghani mahch'akal-ov**
a balcony	**patshgamb-ov**
a view	**tesaran-ov**
I want a room that's quiet.	**Yes uzum em hangist senyak.**
How long will you be staying?	**Inchk'an zhamanak ek' duk' mënalu?**
How many nights?	**K'ani gisher?**
I'm going to stay for . . .	**Yes mënalu em ...**
one day	**mek or**
two days	**yerku or**
one week	**mek shap'at**
Do you have any I.D.?	**Duk' unek' p'astat'ught?**
Sorry, we're full.	**Nerets'ek, bayts' menk' azat tegh ch'unenk'.**
I have a reservation.	**Yes patvirel em.**
We have a reservation.	**Menk' patvirel enk'.**
My name is . . .	**Im anunë ... e.**
May I speak to the manager please?	**Karogh em zëruts'el karravarchi het?**
I have to meet someone here.	**Yes aystegh zhamadërvats em.**

ACCOMMODATION

How much is it per night?	**Inchk'an e mek orva arzhek'ë?**
How much is it per week?	**Vork'an e kazmum arzhek'ë mek shap'atva hamar?**
How much is it per person?	**Inchk'an e mek andzi hamar?**
It's . . . per day.	**... mek orva hamar.**
It's . . . per week.	**... mek shabatva hamar.**
It's . . . per person.	**... mek andzi hamar.**
Can I see the room?	**Karogh em hamarë tesnel?**
Are there any others?	**Kan urish hamarner?**
Is there . . . ?	**Ka ...?**
air conditioning	**odarakum**
a telephone	**herrakhos**
hot water	**tak' jur**
laundry service	**lëvats'k'atun**
room service	**hamarneri spasarkum**
No, I don't like it.	**Voch, sa im durë ch'i galis.**
It's too . . .	**Ayn shat ... e.**
cold	**sarrn**
hot	**tak'**
big	**mets**
dark	**mut'**
small	**p'ok'r**
noisy	**aghmëkot**
dirty	**keghtot**
It's fine, I'll take it.	**Hoyakap e, yes verts'num em ayn.**
Where is the bathroom?	**Vortegh e logaranë?**
Is there hot water all day?	**Tak' jurë shurjorya e?**
Do you have a safe?	**Duk' unek' seif?**

ACCOMMODATION

Is there anywhere to wash clothes?	**Ka voreve tegh shorerë lëvanalu hamar?**
Can I use the telephone?	**Karogh em ogtëvel herrakhosits'?**

—Needs

I need candles.	**Indz petk' en momer.**
I need toilet paper.	**Indz petk' e zuk'arani t'ught'.**
I need soap.	**Indz petk' e och'arr.**
I need clean sheets.	**Indz petk' en mak'ur savanner.**
I need an extra blanket.	**Indz petk' e avelord vermak.**
I need drinking water.	**Indz petk' e khëmelu jur.**
I need a light bulb.	**Indz petk' e elektralamp.**
Please change the sheets.	**Khënt'rum em savannerë p'okhel.**
I can't open the window.	**Yes ch'em karogh patuhanë bats'el.**
I can't close the window.	**Yes ch'em karogh patuhanë tsatskel.**
I have lost my key.	**Yes korts'rel em im banalinerë.**
Can I have the key to my room?	**Karogh em stanal im senyaki banalin?**
The toilet won't flush.	**Zuk'arani jurë ch'i hosum.**
The water has been cut off.	**Jurë këtërvel e.**
The electricity has been cut off.	**Eletrakanut'yunë anjatvel e.**

The gas has been cut off.	**Gazë anjatvel e.**
The heating has been cut off.	**Jerruts'umë anjatvel e.**
The heater doesn't work.	**Varraranë ch'i ashkhatum.**
The air conditioning doesn't work.	**Ot'arakumë ch'i ashkhatum.**
The phone doesn't work.	**Herrakhosë ch'i ashkhatum.**
I can't flush the toilet.	**Yes ch'em karogh zuk'aranum jurë k'ashel.**
The toilet is blocked.	**Zuk'aranë p'ak e.**
I can't switch off the tap.	**Yes ch'em karogh tsorakë p'akem.**
Where is the plug socket?	**Vortegh e vart'akë?**
wake-up call	**art'nats'nelu zang**
Could you please wake me up at . . . o'clock.	**Duk' karogh ek' indz art'nats'nel zhamë ...-in?**
I am leaving now.	**Yes hima meknum em.**
We are leaving now.	**Mek hima meknum enk'.**
May I pay the bill now?	**Karogh em hima vëch'arel?**

—Extra words

bathroom	**logaran**
bed	**mahch'akal**
blanket	**vermak**
candle	**mom**
candles	**momer**
chair	**at'orr**
cold water	**sarrë jur**
cupboard	**paharan**

ACCOMMODATION

door	**durr**
door lock	**koghp'ek'**
electricity	**elektrakanut'yun**
excluded	**chëhashvats**
floor *story*	**hark**
fridge	**sarrnaran**
hot water	**tak' jur**
included	**hashvats**
key	**banali**
lamp	**lamp**
laundry service	**lëvats'k'atun**
light *electric*	**luys**
mattress	**matras**
meals	**utelik'**
mirror	**hayeli**
name	**anun**
noisy	**aghmëkot**
padlock	**koghp'ek'**
pillow	**barts'**
plug *bath*	**khëts'an**
electric	**vart'ak**
quiet	**hangist**
quilt	**mëgdakats' vermak**
roof	**këtur**
room	**senyak**
room number	**sanyaki hamar**
sheet	**savan**
shelf	**darak**
shower	**ts'ënts'ugh**
stairs	**astich'an**
suitcase	**ch'ampruk**
surname	**azganun**
table	**seghan**
towel	**sërp'ich**
veranda	**tsatskapatëshgamb**
wall	**pat**
water	**jur**
window	**patuhan**

8. FOOD & DRINK

Food plays an important part of Armenian life, and important events in all aspects of life and the year are marked with a feast of one form or another. Food is a very important part of hospitality — it is both the host's duty to make sure his guests are eating and the guest's duty to partake of what is offered. Armenian cuisine is one of the world's wonders and in normal times, at homes or in restaurants, you will be offered a dazzling variety of dishes, delicacies and drinks, which vary from area to area and from season to season. Any menu you may encounter may be written in Armenian, Russian or English.

breakfast	**nakhach'ash**
lunch	**lanch**
dinner, supper	**ch'ash, ënt'rik'**
dessert	**desert**

— Restaurants

I'm hungry.	**Yes sovats em.**
I'm thirsty.	**Yes tsarav em.**
Have you eaten yet?	**Duk' art'en ch'ashel ek'?**
Do you know a good restaurant?	**Duk' gitek' lav restoran?**
Do you have a table, please?	**Duk' unek' azat seghan?**
I would like a table for . . . people, please.	**Yes uzum em seghan ... andzi hamar.**
Can I see the menu please?	**Karogh em menyun tesnel?**
I'm still looking at the menu.	**Yes der nayum em menyun.**
I would like to order now.	**Yes uzum em hima patvirel.**

What's this?	**Inch e sa?**
Is it spicy?	**Sa këtsu e?**
Does it have meat in it?	**Ayntegh ka mis?**
Do you have . . . ?	**Duk' unek' ...?**
We don't have . . .	**Menk' ch'unenk' ...**
What would you recommend?	**Duk' inch khorurt' këtayik'?**
Do you want . . . ?	**Duk' uzum ek' ...?**
Can I order some more . . . ?	**Yes karogh em kërkin patvirel ...?**
That's all, thank you.	**Aysk'anë, shnorakalut'yun.**
That's enough, thanks.	**Bavakan e, shnorakalut'yun.**
I haven't finished yet.	**Yes derr ch'em avartel.**
I have finished eating.	**Yes avartets'i utelë.**
I am full up!	**Yes kusht em!**
Where are the toilets?	**Vortegh en zuk'arannerë?**
I am a vegetarian.	**Yes busaker em.**
I don't eat meat.	**Yes mis ch'em utum.**
I don't eat chicken or fish.	**Yes ch'em utum dzuk kam hav.**
I don't drink alcohol.	**Yes alkohol ch'em oktagortsum.**
I don't smoke.	**Yes ch'em tsëkhum.**
I would like . . .	**Yes këts'ankanayi ...**
an ashtray	**mokhraman**
the bill	**hashivë**
a glass of water	**mi bazhak jur**
a bottle of water	**mi shish jur**
another bottle	**yevës mek shish**

a bottle-opener	**bats'ich**
a corkscrew	**khëts'anahan**
dessert	**desert**
a drink	**ëmpelik'**
a chair	**at'orr**
a plate	**ap'se**
a bowl	**ap'se**
a glass	**bazhak**
a cup	**gavat'**
a napkin	**andzerrots'ik**
a fork	**patarrak'agh**
a knife	**danak**
a spoon	**gët'al**
the menu	**menyu**
a jug	**kuzh**
a table	**seghan**
a teaspoon	**t'eyi gët'al**
a toothpick	**atamnak'ëchp'orik**
the sugar bowl	**shak'araman**
a washbowl	**lëvats'aran**

—Tastes & textures

fresh	**t'arm**
raw	**hum**
uncooked	**chep'ats**
cooked	**yep'ats**
ripe	**hasun**
tender	**p'ap'uk**
tough *meat*	**pind**
spicy (hot)	**tak'**
stale	**chor**
sour	**t'ët'u**
sweet	**k'aghts'ër**
bitter	**darrë**
hot	**tak'**
cold	**sarrë**

salty	**aghi**
taste	**ham**
tasteless	**anham**
tasty	**hamegh**
bad/spoiled	**anorak**
too much	**shat**
too little	**shat k'ich**
not enough	**anbavarar**
empty	**datark**
full	**li**
good	**lav**

– General food words

burger	**burger**
butter	**karag**
bread *flat*	**hats'**
loaf	**bok'on**
cake	**t'ëkhvatsk'**
candy	**konfet**
cheese	**panir**
cottage cheese	**kat'nashorr**
chewing gum	**tsamon**
coriander	**gindz**
egg	**dzu**
fat *animal*	**yugh**
flour	**alyur**
french fries	**fri**
garlic	**sëkhtor**
ginger	**zenjefil**
gravy	**t'andzramokank'**
honey	**meghër**
ice-cream	**paghpaghak**
jam; jelly	**dondoghak**
ketchup	**ketchup**
mint	**dakhdz**

mustard	**mananegh**
nut	**ënkuyz**
almond	**nush**
hazel	**pënduk**
pistachio	**pistak**
walnut	**ënkuyz**
oil	**yugh**
pasta	**pasta**
pepper *black*	**sev pëghpegh**
pepper *hot*	**tak'degh**
pizza	**pits'a**
provisions	**sënëdamët'erk'**
rice	**brindz**
salad	**aghts'an**
salt	**agh**
sandwich	**sendvich**
sauce	**sous**
shopping	**gënumner**
soup	**apur**
spice	**hamemunk'**
sugar	**shak'ar**
syrup	**mërk'ahyut'**
tablecloth	**sëp'rrots'**
tray	**skutegh**
teapot	**t'eynik**
vinegar	**k'ats'akh**
yogurt	**matsun**

—Vegetables

aubergine	**sëmbuk**
beans	**p'och'ok**
green beans	**lobi**
beetroot	**ch'akndegh**
cabbage	**kaghamb**
carrot	**gazar**

FOOD & DRINK

cauliflower	**tsakhkakaghamb**
chickpeas	**siserr**
cucumber	**varung**
eggplant	**sëmbuk**
lentils	**vosp**
lettuce	**salat'**
okra	**bamia**
onion	**sokh**
peas	**siserr**
pepper	**pëkhpegh**
potatoes	**kartofil**
pumpkin	**dët'um**
radish	**bokhk**
salad	**akhts'an**
spinach	**spanakh**
tomato	**lolik**
turnip	**shaghgam**
vegetables *ready to eat*	**banjareghen**

—Fruit

almond	**nush**
apple	**khëndzor**
apricot	**tsiran**
banana	**banan**
cherry	**bal**
date	**khurma**
fruit	**pëtugh**
grapefruit	**greip'frut'**
grapes	**khaghogh**
lemon; lime	**kit'ron**
melon	**sekh**
mulberry	**t'ut'**
orange	**narinj**
peach	**deghdz**
pear	**tandz**
plum	**bal**

pomegranate	**nurr**
raisins	**chamich**
watermelon	**dzëmeruk**

– Meat

beef	**tavar**
chicken	**hav**
egg	**havkit'**
boiled egg	**yepats havkit'**
fat *noun*	**yugh**
fish	**dzuk**
goat *meat*	**aytsi mis**
kebab	**k'yabab**
lamb *meat*	**garri mis**
meat	**mis**
mutton	**vochkhari mis**
veal	**hort'i mis**

– Drinks

> Remember to ask for modern soft drinks by brand name.

alcohol	**alkohol**
alcoholic drinks	**alkoholayin khëmichk'ner**
beer	**garejur**
bottle	**shish**
can	**anot'**
coffee	**surch'**
coffee with milk	**kat'ov surch'**
fruit juice	**mërk'ayin hyut'**
ice	**sarruyts'**
milk	**kat'**
mineral water	**hank'ayin jur**
tea	**t'ey**
black tea	**sev t'ey**

FOOD & DRINK

green tea	**kanach t'ey**
tea with milk	**kat'ov t'ey**
no sugar, please!	**arrants' shak'ar, khëndrum em!**
water	**jur**
wine	**gini**

More on food & drink ...

Armenian cuisine worldwide is an incredibly varied range of tastes and styles. The Republic has a bustling café and restaurant culture, while weddings are a frequent opportunity to enjoy a feast. The many **khoravadz** (barbecue) restaurants in Yerevan are to be recommended, but the best is always a feast prepared in a private home the traditional way. Armenians place great emphasis on lamb which is served in a variety of ways, either grilled or in soups and stews. Hors d'oeuvres are usually served at meal times and can include a wide range of foods such peppers and vine leaves stuffed with meat and rice, pickled vegetables, sheep's cheese, bread, and cured meats. Some common specialities include:

bozbash — lamb soup.

shashlik — grilled lamb served with flat bread.

dolma — meat wrapped in vine or cabbage leaves, and served with yogurt and garlic.

"summer" dolma — meat stuffed into aubergines, pepper and tomatoes.

kufte — ground beef with onion, green pepper, garlic and salt.

gavar kufte — ground meat spiced with onions and rolled into balls then boiled in water.

khashlama — boiled meat and potatoes.

kebab — grilled spiced ground meat.

harisa — wheat and chicken dish traditionally eaten at Easter.

spas — soup made of egg and flour stirred into yogurt.

basturma — dried slices of lean beef soaked in spicy marinade.

khash — beef shins boiled in unsalted water and served hot with crushed garlic and **lavash** bread.
brinzov pilaf — classic Armenian pilaf rice with spices.
bulghur pilaf — cracked wheat.

There are also many different types of fish in Armenia, and **ishkan** (trout) is considered to be especially good. Armenian cuisine is also rich in seasonal vegetable dishes, including lentils, beans and eggplants, and salads, which may be served with nuts, mint or yogurt (**matsun**, e.g. **jajukh**, yogurt with cucumbers). Yogurts are used also in soups and drinks as well as in side dishes that depend from season. Other side dishes include **turshi** (mixed pickles), **sujukh** (highly spiced dried sausage), **panir** (cheese) and pizzas.

—Bread is always on the Armenian table, and the two traditional types of bread in Armenia are **matnakash** and **lavash**. The wafer-thin oven-baked **lavash** is a particular favorite — it is used to wrap Armenian cheese or meat spiced with onions and salads, and marinated before barbecuing or baking in a clay oven (**tonir**). Rolls called **khoravadz** are served with fried tomatoes, aubergines and sweet peppers.

—Desserts can include various filos, strudels and cakes as well as the ever popular dried apricots, or grapes dried into flat sheets (**pastegh**) and rolled around nuts such as walnuts. Depending on the season there will always be fruit such as apricots, peaches, apples, pears, quinces, cherries, mulberries, pomegranates, figs, strawberries and water melons. In winter you'll find many of these offered as delicious compotes or sweet preserves (**muraba**), including slightly more unusual offerings such as walnuts, rose petals and sweet eggplants. Often you'll be given these as an accompaniment to tea.

—Armenians are proud of their mineral waters, which come in a variety of bottled brands. Served strong and black in small cups, coffee marks the end of every Armenian meal. It is usually served with a delicious assortment of sweet pastries and cakes including **gata** and **pakhlava** (flaky layers of nut filled pastry). **Anukh** or mint tea is a gentler alternative. Beer and vodka are produced locally, but Armenians are proudest of their wine and brandies. **Raki** is a very strong spirit distilled from raisins and flavored with anise, and which should be approached with care! Those being entertained in Armenian homes should be warned that Armenian hospitality traditionally involves a ready supply of alcohol and endless toasts!

9. DIRECTIONS

Where is . . . ?	**Vortegh e ...?**
the academy	**akademian**
the airport	**odanavakayanë**
the art gallery	**patkerasrahë**
a bank	**bankë**
the church	**yekeghets'in**
the city center	**k'aghak'i kentronë**
the consulate	**hyupatosut'yunë**
the . . . embassy	**... despanatunë**
the . . . faculty	**fakultetë**
the hotel	**hyuranots'ë**
the information office	**teghekatvakan kentronë**
the main square	**kentronakan hëraparakë**
the market	**shukan**
the Ministry of . . .	**... nakhararut'yunë**
the mosque	**mëzkit'ë**
the museum	**t'angaranë**
parliament	**khorhërdaranë**
lower house	**storin palatë**
upper house	**verin palatë**
the police station	**vostikanatunë**
the post office	**postë**
the railway station	**yerkat'ughayin kayaranë**
the telephone center	**kapi kentronë**
the toilet(s)	**zuk'aranë**
the university	**hamalsaranë**
What . . . is this?	**Inch ... e sa?**
bridge	**kamurj**

building	**shenk'**
city	**k'aghak'**
district	**shërjan**
river	**get**
road	**ch'anapar**
street	**p'oghots'**
town	**k'aghak'**
village	**gyugh**

What is this building?	**Inch shenk e sa?**
What is that building?	**Inch shenk e na?**
What time does it open?	**Zhamë k'anisin e ayn bats'vum?**
What time does it close?	**Zhamë k'anisin e ayn?**
Can I park here?	**Karogh em aystegh mek'enan kangnets'nel?**
Are we on the right road for . . . ?	**Sa e ch'anaparë depi ...?**
How many kilometers is it to . . . ?	**Inchk'an kilometr e aysteghits' depi ...?**
It is . . . kilometers away.	**Ayn ... kilometr e.**
How far is the next village?	**Vork'an herru e hajord gyughë?**
Where can I find this address?	**Vortegh karogh em gëtnel ays hasts'en?**
Can you show me on the map?	**Karogh ek' indz k'artezov ts'uyts' tal?**
How do I get to . . . ?	**Inchpes karogh em hasnel ...?**
I want to go to . . .	**Yes uzum em gënal ...**
Can I walk there?	**Yes karogh em ayntegh votk'ov gënal?**

DIRECTIONS

Is it far?	**Da herru e?**
Is it near?	**Da motik e?**
Is it far from here?	**Da herru e aysteghits'?**
Is it near here?	**Da motik e aysteghits'?**
It is not far.	**Da herru ch'e.**
Go straight ahead.	**Ughigh gënats'ek'.**
Turn left.	**T'ek'vek' dzakh.**
Turn right.	**T'ek'vek' aj.**
to the left	**depi dzakh**
to the right	**depi aj**
to one side	**nuyn koghmn e**
at the next corner	**hajord ankyunin**
at the traffic lights	**lusakiri mot**

behind	**yetevum**
far	**herru**
in front	**dimats'ë**
left	**dzakh**
near	**mot**
opposite	**dimats'ë**
outside	**dursë**
right	**aj**
straight on	**ughigh**
under	**tak**

bridge	**kamurj**
corner	**ankyun**
crossroads	**khachmeruk**
one-way street	**miakoghmani p'oghots'**

north	**hyusis**
south	**harav**
east	**arevelk'**
west	**arevmutk'**

10. SHOPPING

WHEN TO SHOP — Shops open around 10.00 am and close around 5.30 pm. New private shops tend not to break for lunch, while older state shops do. Markets are open every day except Easter Sunday and Christmas (by the Orthodox calendar).

HOW TO PAY — Everything is best paid for in cash. Credit cards are increasingly acceptable in the cities but traveler's checks are still difficult to cash. Many shops now have price tags attached to items but in most places you will have to ask.

FOOD AND WINE — As well as the main streets of stores in the town centers, every street seems to have its own small produce kiosk or store. There is also a growing number of specialty shops, including supermarkets where you can buy western products – and some truly excellent winesellers.

MARKETS — For fresh produce go to a **tonavach'arr**, or big market. Prices and availability of goods are seasonal. As a foreigner, you may occasionally find yourself paying a little more here – but not much! The best time is early morning when everything is at its freshest, particularly for meat and fish. Many local delicacies can be found here, including smoked sturgeon, caviar, smoked and dried meats, and a veritable plethora of spices, nuts and berries. In Yerevan, visit the colorful Hayastan market near Barekamut'yun metro station or the Hrazdan market near the stadium of the same name – places where you can buy all the usual produce and consumer products at a bargain, from cigarettes to CD-players, from clothing to pirate DVDs.

Where can I find a . . . ?	**Vortegh karogh em gëtnel ...?**
Where can I buy . . . ?	**Vortegh karogh em gënel ...?**
Where's the market?	**Vortegh e shukan?**
Where's the nearest . . . ?	**Vortegh e motaka ...?**
Can you help me?	**Karogh ek' indz ognel?**
Can I help you?	**Yes karogh em dzez ognel?**

I'm just looking.	**Yes ëndamenë nayum em.**
I'd like to buy . . .	**Yes uzum em ... gënel.**
Could you show me some . . . ?	**Karogh ek' indz ts'uts' tal ...?**
Can I look at it?	**Karogh em nayel sa?**
Do you have any . . . ?	**Duk' unek' voreve ...?**
This.	**Ays.**
That.	**Ayn.**
I don't like it.	**Da im durë ch'i galis.**
I like it.	**Da im durë galis e.**
Do you have anything cheaper?	**Isk duk' unek' aveli ezhan?**
cheaper/better	**aveli ezhan/aveli lav**
larger/smaller	**aveli mets/ aveli p'ok'ër**
Do you have anything else?	**Unek' yevs?**
Sorry, this is the only one.	**Kënerek', bayts' sa miakn e.**
I'll take it.	**Yes këgënem sa.**
How much/many do you want?	**Inchk'an ek' ts'ankanum?**
How much is it?	**Inchk'an e sa?**
Can you write down the price?	**Karogh ek' ginë gërel?**
Could you lower the price?	**Karogh eik' ginë ijets'nel?**
I don't have much money.	**Yes shat p'ogh chunem.**
Do you take credit cards?	**Duk' ëndunum ek' kredit k'arter?**
Would you like it wrapped?	**Ts'ankanum ek' sa p'at'atenk'?**

Will that be all?	**Aysk'anë?**
Thank you, goodbye.	**Shnorakalut'yun, ts'ëtesut'yun.**
I want to return this.	**Yes uzum em sa ver adardznel.**

– Outlets

auto spares shop	**avtopahestamaseri khanut'**
baker's	**hats'i p'urr**
bank	**bank**
barber's	**varsaviranots'**
I'd like a haircut please.	**Yes uzum e mazerës këtrem.**
bookshop	**gërk'eri khanut'**
butcher's	**mësi khanut'**
pharmacy	**deghatun**
clothes shop	**shoregheni khanut'**
dairy goods store	**kat'naran**
dentist	**atamnabuyzh**
department store	**hanrakhanut'**
dressmaker	**derts'ak**
electrical goods store	**elektrakan aprank'neri khanut'**
florist	**tsaghkabuyts**
greengrocer	**nëparavach'arr**
hairdresser	**varsavir**
hospital	**hivandanots'**
kiosk	**kërpak**
laundry *place*	**lëvats'k'atun**
market	**shuka**
newsstand	**kiosk**
shoeshop	**koshiki khanut'**
shop	**khanut'**
souvenir shop/salon	**hushanëverneri khanut'**

stationer's	**gërasenyakayin pituk'neri khanut'**
supermarket	**supermarket**
travel agent	**ch'anaparordayin gortsakal**
vegetable shop	**banjareghenneri khanut'**
watchmaker's	**zhamagorts**

– Gifts

> **ARTS & CRAFTS** — Armenia boasts numerous artists of varying quality and there are a number of antique shops, notably on Abovyan Avenue in Yerevan. Remember that there are restrictions on what you can take out of the country. Buying art is not a problem as every Armenian seems to have a friend who is an artist. So you can spend many a pleasant afternoon as you are taken round various houses to examine mini collections. Quality art is also sold in the street and parks. The best places still to buy gifts, souvenirs and carpets are the "salons," or handicrafts galleries.
>
> **ANTIQUES** — Depending on what you've bought, it is illegal to take out of the country certain Armenian antiques unless accompanied by the relevant paperwork. Check with the dealer beforehand.

boots		**koshikner**
box		**arkëgh**
bracelet		**aparanjan**
candlestick		**momakal**
carpet	*felt*	**karpet t'aghik'e**
	knotted	**hyusats**
	woven	**gortsats gorg**
chain		**shëght'a**
chest *box*		**arkëgh**
clock		**zhamats'uyts'**
copper		**pëghindz**
crystal		**byureghapaki**
curtain		**varak'uyr**
cushion		**barts'**

earrings	**akanjogher**
emerald	**zëmrukht**
gold	**voski**
handicraft	**dzerragorts**
headscarf	**shal**
iron	**yerkat'**
jewelry	**voskerchakan irer**
leather	**kashi**
metal	**metagh**
modern	**zhamanakakits'**
necklace	**manyak**
pottery	**kave irer**
ring	**ogh**
rosary	**vart'aran**
silver	**artsat'**
steel	**poghpat**
stone	**k'ar**
traditional	**avandakan**
turban	**chalma**
vase	**skahak**
watch	**zhamats'uts'**
wood	**p'ait**

— Clothes

bag	**payusak**
belt	**goti**
boot	**koshik**
boots	**koshikner**
rubber boots	**rretine koshikner**
bra; brassiere	**kërtskal**
bracelet	**aparanjan**
button	**koch'ak**
buttonhole	**koch'kamer**
cloth	**gortsvatsk'**
clothes	**hagust**
coat	**verarku**

collar	**odzik'**
cotton	**bambak**
dress	**shor**
fabric	**gortsvatsk'**
gloves	**dzerrnots'ner**
handbag	**zerrk'i payusak**
handkerchief	**t'ashkinak**
heel	**kërunk**
jacket	**bach'kon**
jumper	**jemper**
leather	**kashi**
material	**nyut'**
necktie	**vëzkap**
overcoat	**vararku**
pin	**dëndasegh**
pocket	**gërpan**
sandals	**sandalner**
scarf	**sharf**
scissors	**mëkrat**
shawl	**shal**
shirt	**shapik**
shoes	**koshikner**
silk	**metak's**
silken	**metak'se**
socks	**gulpaner**
sole *of shoe*	**koshkatak**
stick: walking stick	**k'aylelu p'ayt**
suit *of clothes*	**kostyum**
sweater	**sviter**
thimble	**matnots'**
thread	**t'el**
tie *necktie*	**vëzkap**
tights	**zugagulpaner**
trousers	**andravartik'**
umbrella	**hovanots'**
underwear	**hagnelu spitakeghen**
waistcoat	**bach'kon**

walking stick	**k'aylelu p'ayt**
wool	**burd**
zipper	**kaytsakach'armand**

– Toiletries

aspirin	**aspirin**
brush	**khozanak**
comb	**sanër**
condom	**pahpanak**
cotton wool	**bambak**
deodorant	**hotazertsich**
hairbrush	**mazeri khozanak**
lipstick	**shërt'nak'suk'**
mascara	**sevanerk**
mouthwash	**beran voghoghelu heghuk**
nail-clippers	**yeghung këtrelu sark'**
nail-polish	**lak'**
perfume	**otsanelik'**
powder	**p'oshi**
razor *electric*	**sap'rich**
razorblade	**shekhp**
safety pin	**dëndasegh**
shampoo	**shampun**
shaving cream	**sap'ërvelu k'ësuk'**
sleeping pills	**k'ënaber haber**
soap	**och'arr**
sponge	**spung**
sunblock cream	**arevapashtpan k'suk'**
thermometer	**jermachap'**
tissues	**andzerrots'ikner**
toilet paper	**zugarani t'ught'**
toothbrush	**atami khozanak**
toothpaste	**atami matsuk**
toothpick	**atamnak'ëchp'orik**

—Stationery

ballpoint	**ink'nahos gërich**
book	**girk'**
dictionary	**barraran**
envelope	**tsërar**
guidebook	**ughets'uyts' girk'**
ink	**t'anak'**
magazine	**amsagir**
map	**k'artez**
road map	**chanaparneri k'artez**
a map of Yerevan	**Yerevani k'artez**
newspaper	**orat'ert'**
a newspaper in English	**orat'ert' anglerenov**
notebook	**not'atetër**
novel	**vep**
a novel in English	**vep anglerenov**
paper	**t'ught'**
a piece of paper	**t'ert'**
pen	**gërich**
pencil	**matit**
postcard	**bats'ik**
scissors	**mëkrat**
writing paper	**gërelu t'ukht'**

Do you have any foreign publications?	**Duk' unek' voreve otar lezvov t'ert'er?**

—Photography

How much is it to process (and print) this film?	**Inchk'an zhamanak ktevi ays zhapavenë yerevats'nel ev tëpel?**
When will it be ready?	**Yerp' patrast këlini?**

I'd like film for this camera.	**Yes uzum em zhapaven ays kamerayi hamar.**
black and white film	**sev u spitak zhapaven**
camera	**kamera**
color film	**gunavor zhapaven**
film	**zhapaven**
flash	**p'aylatakum**
lens	**linzaner**
light meter	**lusakayats'uyts'**

—Electrical equipment

> **BUYING TIP** — For hi-tech stuff like cassettes, videos/ video-players or transformers, CD-players and DVD you are more likely to be understood if you use the English terms.

adapter	**adapter**
battery	**martkots'**
cassette	**kaseta**
CD	**kompakt disk**
CD player	**kompakt disk**
fan	**odap'okhich**
hairdrier	**fen**
heating coil	**elektrasaliki parurak**
iron (for clothing)	**art'uk**
kettle	**t'eynik**
plug *electric*	**vart'ak**
portable T.V.	**dyurakir herrustats'uyts'**
radio	**rradio**
record	**dzaynagrum**
tape (cassette)	**zhapaven**
tape recorder	**magnitofom**
television	**herrustats'uyts'**

transformer	p'okharkich
video (player)	tesamagnitofon
videotape	tesazhapaven

– Sizes

small	p'ok'ër
big	mets
heavy	tsanër
light	t'et'ev
more	aveli shat
less	aveli k'ich
many	shat
too much/many	chap'its' durs shat
enough	bavarar
That's enough.	Bavakan e.
also	nuynpes
a little bit	mi k'ich

| Do you have a carrier bag? | Duk' unek' mets payusak? |

11. WHAT'S TO SEE

Do you have a guidebook?	**Duk' unek' ughets'uyts' girk'?**
Do you have a local map?	**Duk' unek' teghakan k'artez?**
Is there a guide who speaks English?	**Ka ardyok' angleren imats'ogh gid?**
What are the main attractions?	**Voronk' en himnakan hetak'ërk'ërakan tegherë?**
What is that?	**Inch e sa?**
How old is it?	**Vork'an hin e ayn?**
May I take a photograph?	**Yes karogh em sa lusanëkarel?**
What time does it open?	**Zhamë k'anisin e ayn bats'vum?**
What time does it close?	**Zhamë k'anisin e ayn p'akvum?**
Is there an entrance fee?	**Mutk'ë vëch'arovi e?**
How much?	**Inchk'an?**
What is this monument/ statue?	**Inch e ays ardzanë/ hushardzanë?**
Who is that statue of?	**Sa um ardzanne?**
What's there to do in the evening?	**Inchov karelie zbaghvel yerekoyan?**
Are there any night clubs/ discos?	**Inch gisherayin akumbner/ diskotekner kan?**

Is there a concert?	**Ka voreve hamerg?**
How much does it cost to get in?	**Vork'an arzhe mutk'ë?**
When is the wedding?	**Yerb e harsanik'ë?**
What time does it begin?	**Zhamë k'anisin e ays skësvum?**
Can we swim here?	**Menk' karogh enk' aystegh loghanal?**
classical music	**dasakan yerazhështut'yun**
concert	**hamerg**
dancing	**parer**
disco	**diskotek**
disk-jockey	**disk-zhokey**
elevator	**verelak**
escalator	**eskalator**
exhibition	**ts'uts'ahandes**
folk dancing	**zhoghovërdakan par**
folk music	**zhoghovërdakan yerazhështut'yun**
jazz	**jazz**
lift	**verelak**
nightclub	**gisherayin akumb**
opera	**opera**
party	**ts'erekuyt'**
pop music	**p'op' yerazhështut'yun**
pub	**bar**

– Buildings

academy of sciences	**gitut'yunneri akademia**
apartment	**bënakaran**

apartment building	**bnënakeli shenk'**
archaeological	**hënagitakan**
art gallery	**patkerasërah**
bakery	**p'urr**
bar	**bar**
(apartment) block	**t'aghamas**
building	**shenk'**
casino	**kazino**
castle	**dëghyak**
cathedral	**tach'ar**
cemetery	**gerezmanatun**
church	**yekeghets'i**
cinema	**kinot'atron**
city map	**k'aghak'i k'artez**
college	**k'olej**
concert hall	**hamergayin srah**
convent	**yekeghets'i**
embassy	**despanatun**
hospital	**hivandanots'**
house	**tun**
housing estate/project	**bënakeli t'aghamas**
library	**gëradaran**
main square	**kentronakan**
	hëraparak
market	**shuka**
monastery	**vank'**
monument	**hushardzan**
mosque	**mëzkit'**
museum	**t'angaran**
old city	**hin k'aghak'**
opera house	**operayi t'atron**
park	**zbosaygi**
parliament (building)	**khorërt'aran**
restaurant	**rrestoran**
ruins	**p'ëlatakner**
school	**dëprots'**
seminary	**seminaria**

shop	**khanut'**
shrine	**dambaran**
stadium	**marzadasht**
statue	**arts'an**
store	**khanut'**
street	**p'oghots'**
tea house	**t'eyaran**
temple	**tach'ar**
theater	**t'atron**
tomb	**gerezman**
tower	**ashtarak**
university	**hamalsaran**
zoo	**kent'anabanakan aygi**

—Occasions

birth	**tsënund**
death	**vakhch'an**
funeral	**hugharkavorut'yun**
wedding	**harsanik'**

Religious heritage ...

Christianity has played a fundamental role in the formation of Armenia's national identity. Armenia was was the first country to adopt Christianity as its state religion. The guiding force behind this was St Gregory the Illuminator who converted the Armenian king, Trdat the Great, at the start of the fourth century A.D. One of the Church's Founding Fathers was St. Mesrop Mashtots (c. 360-440), a monk, theologian, and linguist who invented the Armenian alphabet and helped establish Armenia's Golden Age of Christian literature.

The Armenian Church has since developed independently from the other Christian Churches, spurred on by the driving sense of national identity and unity that exists up to today. It is this Church that has constantly stood as a bedrock throughout Armenia's turbulent history, in the process acting as custodian of the nation's culture and forming an essential part of the growing Diaspora.

The head of the Armenian Orthodox Church is referred to as the supreme catholicos. For the majority of Armenian Christians this is the catholicos whose seat is in Armenia's holy city of Echmiadzin. There is also a minority which recognizes as their head the Cilician Catholicos in Antilyas, Lebanon. Although the overwhelming majority of the Republic's population are members of the Armenian Church, there are also smaller Armenian communities who are Roman Catholic, Protestant or Russian Orthodox. Within the Republic too there are significant numbers of Christians from other ethnic groups plus many Muslims, most of whom are Kurdish.

Armenia's longstanding history of Christianity means that wherever you are you'll never be far from one of Armenia's splendid churches. Echmiadzin is the seat of the Armenian Church, and it is therefore here that you can see its most important cathedral, founded by St. Gregory. The city is also home to the ruins of the seventh-century Church of St. Gregory, and the still preserved Church of St. Hripsime dating from the same century.

Holidays & festivals

There are a wide variety of traditional festivals celebrated in every village and area that strongly reflect Armenian culture and history. Major Armenian holidays commemorate both religious and historical events. Besides Christmas (January 6) and Easter (March/April), the most important holidays are Vartanants, marking the fifth-century defense of Christianity against the Persians, and Genocide Memorial Day (April 24), which commemorates the 1915 Genocide of the Armenians in Turkey. Other national holidays include: Women's Day (March 8), Motherhood & Beauty Day (April 7), Victory Day (May 9, commemorating those who fought in World War II), Resoration of Statehood Day (May 28, commemorating the Republic of Armenia regaining its statehood in 1918 after half a millennium of lost sovereignty), Constitution Day (July 5), Independence Day or Referendum Day (September 21, when the Republic of Armenia announced the results of a national referendum on secession from the Soviet Union), Memorial Day for Victims of the 1988 Earthquake (December 7).

Other festivals — Erebuni or "Yerevan Day" (late September/early October), celebrated with concerts, traditional dancing and music and concluded by the huge "Golden Fall" festival; Grape Blessing Day (second Sunday of August), when the Supreme Catholicos of the Armenian Church blesses the grape harvest; and Vardavar (second Sunday of June), a day celebrating the ancient Armenian goddess of beauty, Anahit.

12. FINANCE

CURRENCIES — Everything is best paid for in cash. Credit cards are increasingly acceptable in cities as are traveler's checks which are best purchased in U.S. dollars. The national currency is the **dram** which comes in bills of various denominations between 10 and 10,000. However, U.S. dollars are used throughout the country and euros are also accepted in many places. Bills may be refused it they are creased, torn, old or simply a low denomination. Be prepared to accept change in drams. Also, if you're paying with drams, avoid taking large bills as you might have difficulty getting them changed when out shopping.

CHANGING MONEY — Banks are open between 9 am and 12.30 pm every day from Monday to Friday but you can change money in the bureaux de change which are open until late in the evening seven days a week. The cashiers will often know a European language or two, and almost all will show the workings of the exchange on a calculator for you and give you a receipt. Many shops and kiosks will also be happy to change money for you.

TIPPING — If you're happy with the service you receive in restaurants then 10 per cent of the check is the norm (but always doublecheck with friends when you get to Armenia!). If you're only having a coffee in a café simply round up the total.

I want to change some dollars.	**Yes uzum em dollarner p'okhel.**
I want to change some euros.	**Yes uzum em yevro p'okhel.**
I want to change some pounds.	**Yes uzum em funter p'okhel.**
Where can I change some money?	**Vortegh karogh em p'ogh p'okhel?**
What is the exchange rate?	**Vork'an e p'okhanakman p'okharzjek'ë?**

What is the commission?	**Vork'an e p'okhanakman tokosë?**
Could you please check that again?	**Karogh eyk' sa kërkin stugel?**
Could you write that down for me?	**Karogh eyk' sa gëri arrnel indz hamar?**
Can I use your calculator?	**Karogh em ok'tëvel dzer hashvich mek'enayits'?**
dollar	**dolar**
euro	**yevro**
ruble	**rubli**
pound (sterling)	**funt sterrling**
bank notes	**t'ëkht'adram**
calculator	**hashvarkich**
cashier	**gandzapah**
coins	**metaghadram**
credit card	**k'redit k'art**
commission	**pahum**
exchange	**p'okhanakum**
foreign exchange	**artarzhuyt'i p'okhanakum**
(loose) change	**manër dram**
receipt	**andorragir**
signature	**storagrut'yun**

13. COMMUNICATIONS

Where is the post office?	**Vortegh e p'ostatunë?**
When does the post office open?	**Yerb e bats'vum p'ostatunë?**
When does the post office close?	**Zhamë k'anisin e p'akvum p'ostatunë?**
Where is the mail box?	**Vortegh e p'ostarkghë?**
Is there any mail for me?	**Kan namakner indz hamar?**
How long will it take for this to get there?	**Inchk'an zhamanakum sa tegh këhasni?**
How much does it cost to send this to . . . ?	**Inchk'an karzhena sa ugharkel ...?**
I need some stamps.	**Indz petk' en namakanishner.**
I would like to send . . .	**Yes uzum em ugharkel ...**
a letter	**namak**
a postcard	**bats'ik**
a parcel	**tsërar**
a telegram	**herragir**
air mail	**ot'ayin p'ost**
envelope	**tsërar**
mailbox	**p'ostarkëgh**
to parcel up	**p'at'etavorel**
registered mail	**gërants'vats p'ost**
stamp	**namakanish**

—Tele-etiquette

I would like to make a phone call.	**Yes uzum em zangaharel.**
I would like to send a fax.	**Yes uzum em fak's ugharkel.**
I would like to fax this letter.	**Yes kuzenayi ays namakë fak'sov ugharkel.**
Where is the telephone?	**Vortegh e herrakhosë?**
May I use your phone?	**Karogh em dzer herrakhosits' ok'tëvel?**
Can I telephone from here?	**Karogh em aysteghits' zangaharel?**
Can you help me get this number?	**Kok'nek' indz ays hamarov kapnëvel?**
Can I dial direct?	**Karogh em ughigh zangaharel?**
May I speak to . . . ?	**Karogh em zëruts'el ... het?**
Can I leave a message?	**Karogh em haghordagrut'yun t'oghnel?**
Who is calling?	**Ov e zangaharum?**
Who are you calling?	**Um ek' zangaharum?**
Can I take your name?	**Karogh em dzer anunë gërants'el?**
Which number are you dialing?	**Vor hamarov ek' duk' zangaharum?**
He/She is not here at the moment — would you like to leave a message?	**Na ays pahin aysteg che. Ts'ankanum ek' haghordagrut'yun t'oghnel?**

This is not . . .	**Sa . . . ch'e.**
You are mistaken.	**Duk' sëkhalvum ek'.**
This is the . . . office.	**Sa . . . gërasenyakn e.**
Hello, I need to speak to . . .	**Baredzez, karogh em zruts'el . . . het.**
I am calling this number . . .	**Yes zangaharu em ays hamarov . . .**
Please phone me.	**Khëndrum em indz zangaharek'.**
Send me a text message!	**Indz tek'stayin haghort'agrut'yun ugharkek'!**
The telephone is switched off.	**Herrakosë anjatvats e.**
I want to call . . .	**Yes uzum em zangaharel . . .**
What is the code for . . . ?	**Vorn e . . . kodë?**
What is the international code?	**Vorn e mijazgayin kodë?**
The number is . . .	**Hamarë . . . e**
The extension is . . .	**Nerk'in hamarë . . .**
It's busy.	**Zbaghvats' e.**
I've been cut off.	**Anjatvets'.**
The lines have been cut.	**Gitsë anjatvets'.**
Where is the nearest public phone?	**Vortegh e amenamotik herrakhosë?**
digital	**t'ëvaynats'vats**
e-mail	**elektronayin p'ost**
fax	**fak's**
fax machine	**fak'si mek'ena**
international operator	**mijazgayin karravrich**

internet	**internet**
internet cafe	**internet kafe**
line	**gits**
mobile phone; cell phone	**bëjëjayin herrakhos**
modem	**modem**
pager	**p'eyjer**
operator *male*	**herrakhosavar**
female	**herrakhosavar**
satellite phone	**arbanyakayin herrakhos**
sim card	**sim k'art**
Where can I buy a sim card for my mobile phone?	**Vortegh yes karogh em gënel sim kart' im bëjëjayin herrakhosi hamar?**
telephone center	**herrakhosayin kentron**
telex	**telek's**
to transfer/put through	**haghordel**

More on tele-etiquette ...
When answering the phone, you say **barev** or **barev dzez**. If the caller knows you, they will generally respond with **barev** or **barev dzez**, prompting your response **inchpes es?** or **inchpesek'?** Now you are ready to start the conversation.

—Faxing & e-mailing

Where can I send a fax from?	**Vorteghits' kareli e fak's ugharkel?**
Can I fax from here?	**Karogh em aysteghits' fak's ugharkel?**

How much is it to fax?	**Inchk'an karzhena fak's ugharkel?**
Where can I find a place to e-mail from?	**Vorteghits' kareli e imeyl ugharkel?**
Is there an internet café near here?	**Motakayk'um ka internet-kafe?**
Can I e-mail from here?	**Karogh em aysteghits' imeyl iygharkel?**
How much is it to use a computer?	**Inchk'an arzhe hamakargchits' ogtvelë?**
How do you turn on this computer?	**Inchpes ek' miats'num ays hamakargichë?**
The computer has crashed.	**Hamakargichë ch'i ashkhatum.**
I need help with this computer.	**Ognek' indz ays hamakargchits' ogtvel.**
I don't know how to use this program.	**Yes ch'ëgitem t'e inchpes ogtëvel ays tsëragrits'.**
I know how to use this program.	**Yes karogh em ogtëvel ays tsëragrits'.**
I want to print.	**Yes uzum em tëpel.**

14. THE OFFICE

chair		**at'orr**
computer		**hamakargich**
desk		**seghan**
drawer		**darak**
fax		**fak's**
file	*paper*	**tëkht'apanak**
	computer	**fayl**
meeting		**handipum**
paper		**t'ught'**
pen		**gërich**
pencil		**matit**
photocopier		**k'serok's**
photocopy		**patch'en**
printer *computer*		**tëpich**
program *computer*		**tsëragir**
report		**zekuyts'**
ruler		**k'anon**
telephone		**herrakhos**
telex		**telek's**
typewriter		**tëpich mek'ena**

15. THE CONFERENCE

article	**hodvats**
a break for refreshments	**sërch'i ëndmijum**
conference room	**konferents'-dahlich'**
copy	**patch'en**
discussion	**k'ënnarkum**
forum	**forum**
guest speaker	**hëravirvats**
	zekuts'ogh
a paper	**t'ught'**
podium	**bemahart'ak**
projector	**proyektor**
session	**nëstashërjan**
a session chaired by . . .	**nëstashërjanin**
	nakhagahum e ...
speaker	**zekuts'ogh**
subject	**arrarka**

16. EDUCATION

to add	**avelats'nel**
addition	**avelats'um**
bench	**nëstaran**
blackboard	**gëratakhtak**
book	**girk'**
calculation	**hashvarkum**
to calculate	**hashvarkel**
chalk	**kavich'**
class	**dasaran**
to copy	**patch'enahanel**
to count	**hashvel**
crayon	**gunavor matit**
difficult	**dëzhvar**
to divide	**bazhanel**
division	**bazhanum**
easy	**hesht**
eraser	**rretin**
exam	**k'ënnut'yun**
exercise book	**tetër**
to explain	**bats'atrel**
felt-tip pen	**flomaster**
geography	**ashkharagrut'yun**
glue	**sosindz**
grammar	**k'erakanut'yun**
history	**patmut'yun**
holiday(s)	**ardzakurt**
homework	**tënayin ashkhatank'**
illiterate	**angëraget**
language	**lezu**
laziness	**alarkotut'yun**
to learn by heart	**angir sovorel**
lesson	**das**
library	**gëradaran**

literature	**gërakanut'yun**
math	**mat'ematika**
memory	**hishoghut'yun**
multiplication	**bazmapatkum**
to multiply	**bazmapatkel**
notebook	**not'atetër**
page	**ej**
paper	**t'ught'**
to pass *an exam*	**k'ënnut'yun**
	handznel
pen	**gërich**
pencil	**matit**
progress	**arrajënt'ats'**
to punish	**patzhel**
pupil	**ashakert**
to read	**kardal**
to repeat	**kërknel**
rubber *eraser*	**rretin**
ruler *instrument*	**k'anon**
satchel	**payusak**
school	**dëprots**
seminary	**seminaria**
sheet *of paper*	**t'ert'**
student *university*	**usanogh**
to subtract	**hanel**
subtraction	**hanum**
sum	**gumar**
table	**seghan**
teacher	**usuts'its'**
to test *academic*	**k'ënnel**
time	**zhamanak**

17. AGRICULTURE

agriculture	**gyughatëntesut'yun**
barley	**gari**
barn	**shtemaran**
cattle	**khoshor anasun**
combine harvester	**kombayn**
corn	**hats'ahatik**
cotton	**bambak**
crops	**hats'ahatikayin**
	mëshakabuyser
to cultivate	**ach'ets'nel**
earth *land*	**ts'amak'**
soil	**hogh**
fallowland	**haros t'oghats**
	varelahogh
farm	**ferma**
farmer	**fermer**
farming	**gyughatëntesut'yun**
to feed an animal	**anasun kerakrel**
fertilizer	**parartanyut'**
field	**dasht**
fruit	**pëtugh**
furrow	**akos**
garden	**partez**
grass	**khot**
to grind	**aghal**
to grow *crops*	**ach'ets'nel**
harvest	**berk'**
hay	**chor khot**
haystack	**dez**
irrigation	**irigats'ia**
leaf	**terev**
livestock	**gëlkhak'anak**
maize	**yegiptats'oren**

AGRICULTURE

manure	**gomaghb**
marsh	**ch'ahich'**
meadow	**margagetin**
to milk *an animal*	**kët'el**
mill	**aghats'**
miller	**jëraghats'pan**
millstone	**jëraghats'ak'ar**
orchard	**pëtghatu aygi**
to plant	**tënkel**
plow	**gut'an**
to plow	**herkel**
potato	**kartofil**
poultry	**tënayin t'ërrchun**
to reap	**hëndzel**
rice	**brindz**
root	**armat**
rye	**ashora**
season	**yeghanak**
seeds	**sermer**
to shoe *a horse*	**paytel**
sickle	**mangagh**
silkworms	**sheram**
to sow	**ts'anel**
straw	**tseghik**
tractor	**traktor**
tree	**tsarr**
trunk *of tree*	**bun**
vine	**vort'**
wheat	**ts'oren**
well *of water*	**jërhos**

18. ANIMALS

bat	**chëghjik**
bear	**arj**
boar	**krrtats khoz**
bull	**ts'ul**
calf	**hort'**
camel	**ught**
cat	**katu**
cow	**kov**
deer	**yeghjeru**
dog	**shun**
donkey	**avanak**
ewe	**vochkar**
fish	**dzuk**
flock *of sheep*	**yeram**
fox	**aghves**
gazelle	**gazel**
goat	**nokhaz**
hare	**napastak**
herd	**hot**
hound	**vorskan shun**
horse	**dzi**
hyena	**boreni**
jackal	**shnagayl**
lamb	**garr**
leopard	**ëndzarryuts**
lion	**aryuts**
mare	**zambik**
mole	**khlurd**
monkey	**kapik**
mouse	**muk**
mule	**jori**
ox	**ts'ul**
pig	**khoz**

pony	**poni**
rabbit	**ch'agar**
ram	**khoy**
rat	**arrnet**
sheep	**vochkhar**
sheepdog	**gamp'ërr**
squirrel	**skyurrik**
stag	**yeghjeru**
stallion	**hovatak**
wolf	**gayl**

—Birds

bird	**tsit**
chicken	**hav**
crow	**agrrav**
dove	**aghavni**
duck	**bad**
eagle	**artsiv**
falcon	**baze**
goose	**sag**
hawk	**shahen**
hen	**hav**
nightingale	**sokhak**
owl	**bu**
parrot	**t'ut'ak**
partridge	**chil kak'av**
peacock	**siramarg**
pheasant	**p'asian**
pigeon	**aghavni**
quail	**lor**
rooster	**ak'aghagh**
sparrow	**ch'ënch'ghuk**
turkey	**hëndkahav**
vulture	**angëgh**

— Insects & amphibians

ant	**mërjyun**
bee	**meghu**
butterfly	**t'it'err**
caterpillar	**t'ërt'ur**
cicada	**kënch'it'avor ch'pur**
cobra	**kobra**
cockroach	**tarakan**
crab	**tsovakhets'getin**
cricket	**tsëghrid**
dragonfly	**ch'purr**
fish	**dzuk**
flea(s)	**lu**
fly	**ch'anj**
frog	**gort**
grasshopper	**tsëgrid**
hedgehog	**vozni**
hornet	**dziastats'**
insect	**bëjij**
lizard	**moghes**
louse	**vojil**
mosquito	**motsak**
scorpion	**karich'**
snail	**khëkhunj**
snake	**odz**
grass snake	**lortu**
spider	**sard**
termite	**termit**
tick	**tiz**
viper	**izh**
wasp	**kret**
worms	**vorder**

19. COUNTRYSIDE

avalanche	**heghegh**
canal	**khoghovak**
cave	**k'arandzav**
dam	**ambartak**
earth	**yerkragund**
earthquake	**yerkrasharzh**
fire	**bots'**
flood	**jërheghegh**
foothills	**nakhalerrnashërjan**
footpath	**mayt'**
forest	**antarr**
hill	**bëlur**
lake	**lich'**
landslide	**soghvatsk'**
marsh	**ch'ahich'**
mountain	**sar**
mountain pass	**lerrnants'k'**
mountain range	**lerrnashëght'a**
peak	**gagat'**
plain	**hart'avayr**
plant	**buys**
pond	**lëch'ak**
ravine	**kirch'**
river	**get**
riverbank	**getap'**
rock	**zhayrr**
sand	**avaz**
soil	**hogh**
slope	**t'ek'vatsk'**
spring *of water*	**aghbyur**
stone	**k'ar**

stream	**hosk'**
mountain stream	**lerrnayin vëtak**
summit	**gagat'**
swamp	**ch'ahich'**
torrent	**teghatarap'**
tree	**tsarr**
valley	**hovit**
waterfall	**jërvezh**
a wood	**p'ayt**

READING ARMENIAN

Referring back to the Armenian alphabet table on page 26, work out these commonly found words and signs:

ռատիօ	գինի
Երեւան	թէյ
թաքսի	օփերա
Հայաստան	քաղաք
մեքենայ	մեթրո
Ամերիկա	հարսնիք
Բրիտանիա	փողոց
հեռախոս	համալսարան

Լոս-Անճելես

20. WEATHER

Armenian winters can be long and snowy followed by summers which get extremely hot, particularly in the low areas such as the Ararat Valley. Certainly a good time to go to Armenia is in autumn, between September and October when day-time temperatures are pleasant and the nights not too cold. The mountainous nature of Armenia ensures that there the country has great opportunities for skiing, especially between January and February.

What's the weather like?	**Inchpisin e yeghanakë?**
The weather is . . . today.	**Yeghanakë aysor ... e.**
cold	**sarrn**
cool; fresh	**zov**
cloudy	**ampamats**
foggy	**marrakhlapat**
hot	**shog**
misty	**mëshushot**
very hot	**shat shog**
very cold	**shat sarrn**
windy	**k'amot**

It's going to rain.	**Andzrev e galu.**
It is raining.	**Andzrev e galis.**
It is snowing.	**Dzyun e galis.**
It's becoming very cold.	**Shat ts'urt e darrnum.**
It is sunny.	**Arevot e.**

– Climate words

air	**od**
climate	**kilma**
cloud	**amp**
dew	**ts'ogh**

drought	**yerasht**
famine	**sov**
fog	**marrakhugh**
to freeze	**mërrsel**
frost	**sarrnamanikʻ**
hail	**karkut**
heat wave	**yerasht**
ice	**sarruytsʻ**
lightning	**kaytsak**
mist	**mëshush**
moon	**lusin**
new moon	**noralusin**
full moon	**lëriv lusin**
rain	**andzrev**
rainbow	**tsiatsan**
shower *of rain*	**ampropʻ**
sky	**amp**
snow	**dzyun**
snowflakes	**dzyan pʻatʻilner**
star	**astëgh**
stars	**astgher**
storm	**pʻotʻorik**
rainstorm	**pʻotʻorik**
thunderstorm	**amprop**
sun	**arev**
to thaw	**halvel**
thawed	**halats**
thunder	**vorot**
weather	**yeghanak**
wind	**kʻami**

—Seasons

summer	**amarr**
autumn	**ashoun**
winter	**dzmerr**
spring	**garoun**

21. CAMPING

Where can we camp?	**Vortegh karogh enk' menk' ch'ambar dënel?**
Can we camp here?	**Menk' karogh enk' aystegh ch'ambar dënel?**
Is it safe to camp here?	**Aystegh ch'ambar dënelë anvëtang e?**
Is there drinking water?	**Ka khëmelu jur?**
May we light a fire?	**Karogh enk' mank' kharuyk varrel?**

—Equipment

ax	**tapar**
backpack	**t'iknapayusak**
bucket	**duyl**
campsite	**ch'ambar**
can opener	**bats'ich**
compass	**koghmnats'uyts'**
firewood	**varrelap'ayt**
flashlight	**lapter**
gas canister	**balon**
hammer	**murch'**
ice-pick	**sarrts'atapar**
ice-box	**sarrts'aman**
lamp	**lamp**
mattress	**matras**
penknife	**gërchahat**
rope	**paran**
sleeping bag	**nënjapark**
stove	**varraran**
tent	**tent**
tent pegs	**ts'ëts'ikner**
water bottle	**jërov shish**

22. EMERGENCY

COMPLAINING — If you really feel you have been cheated or misled, raise the matter first with your host or the proprietor of the establishment in question, preferably with a smile. Armenians are proud but courteous, with a deeply felt tradition of hospitality, and consider it their duty to help any guest. Angry glares and shouting will get you nowhere.

CRIME — Armenians are law-abiding people, but petty theft does occur. Without undue paranoia, take usual precautions: watch your wallet or purse, securely lock your equipment and baggage before handing it over to railway or airline porters, and don't leave valuables on display in your hotel room. On buses, look out for pickpockets – keep valuables in front pockets and your bag close to your side. If you are robbed, contact the police. Of course in the more remote areas, sensible precautions should be taken, and always ensure that you go with a guide. In general, follow the same rules as you would in your own country and you will run little risk of encountering crime.

LOST PROPERTY — If you lose something, save time and energy by appealing only to senior members of staff or officials. If you have lost items in the street or left anything in public transport, the police may be able to help.

DISABLED FACILITIES — The terrain and conditions throughout most of Armenia do not make it easy for any visitor to get around in a wheelchair even at the best of times. Access to most buildings in the cities is difficult, particularly since the majority of lifts function irregularly. Facilities are rarely available in hotels, airports or other public areas. See the vocabulary section at the end of this chapter, on pages 194 and 196, for useful expressions and vocabulary.

TOILETS — You will find public utilities located in any important or official building. You may use those in hotels or restaurants. You may sometimes encounter failed plumbing and absence of toilet paper.

Help!	**Ognut'yun!**
Could you help me, please?	**Du karogh eik' indz ognel?**
Do you have a telephone?	**Duk' unek' herrakhos?**
Where is the nearest telephone?	**Vortegh e amenamotik herrakhosë?**

Does the phone work?	**Herrakhosë ashkhatum e?**
Get help quickly!	**Shtap ognut'yun kanchek'!**
Call the police!	**Kanchek' vostikanut'yun!**
I'll call the police.	**Yes këzangaharem vostikanut'yun.**
Is there a doctor near here?	**Motakayk'um ka bëzhishk?**
Call a doctor!	**Bëzhishk kanchek'!**
Call an ambulance!	**Kanchek' shtap ok'nut'yun!**
I'll get medical help!	**Yes bëzhishk këkanchem!**
Where is the doctor?	**Vortegh e bëzhishkë?**
Is there a doctor?	**Ka aystegh bëzhishk?**
Where is the hospital?	**Vortegh e hivandanotsë?**
Where is the pharmacy?	**Vortegh e deghatunë?**
Where is the dentist?	**Vortegh e atamnabuyzhë?**
Where is the police station?	**Vortegh e vostikanatunë?**
Take me to a doctor!	**Tarek' indz bëzhishki!**
There's been an accident.	**Aystegh patahar e teghi unets'el.**
Is anyone hurt?	**Voreve mekë viravorvele?**
This person is hurt.	**Ays mard viravorvele.**
There are people injured.	**Kan tuzhatsner.**

Don't move!	**Mi sharzhvek'!**
Go away!	**Herrats'ek'!**
Stand back!	**Yet kangnek!**
I am lost.	**Yes molorvets'i.**
I am ill.	**Yes hivand em.**
I've been robbed.	**Indz koghoptel en.**
Stop, thief!	**Bërrnek' goghin!**
My . . . has been stolen.	**Im ... goghats'el en.**
I have lost . . .	**Yes korts'rel em ...**
my bags	**im payusaknerë**
my camera equipment	**im kamerayi sark'avorumnerë**
my handbag	**im dzerrk'i payusakë**
my laptop computer	**im lep'top' hamakargichë**
my money	**im p'oghë**
my passport	**im andznagirë**
my sound equipment	**im dzaynayin sark**
my traveler's checks	**im chanaparordakan chek'erë**
my wallet	**im dramapanakë**
My possessions are insured.	**Im unets'vatsk'ë apahovagërvats e.**
I have a problem.	**Yes mi khënt'ir unem.**
I didn't do it.	**Yes ayt ch'em arel.**
I'm sorry.	**Nerets'ek'.**
I apologize.	**Yes nereghut'yun em khënt'rum.**
I didn't realize anything was wrong.	**Yes ch'ei haskanu vor inch vor bane teghi unenum.**

I want to contact my embassy.	**Yes uzum em kapnëvel im despanatan het.**
I speak English.	**Yes khosum em angleren.**
I need an interpreter.	**Indz petk' e t'ark'manich.**
Where are the toilets?	**Vortegh en zuk'arannerë?**

—Disabilities

wheelchair	**hashmandami bazkat'orr**
disabled	**hashmandam**
Do you have seats for the disabled?	**Dzez mot kan tegher hashmandamneri hamar?**
Do you have access for the disabled?	**Dzez mot ka mutk' hashmandamneri hamar?**
Do you have facilities for the disabled?	**Dzez mot kan harmarut'yunner hashmandamneri hamar?**

23. HEALTHCARE

> **INSURANCE** — Make sure any insurance policy you take out covers Armenia, although this will only help in flying you out in case of a serious accident or illness. Consult your doctor for any shots required or recommended when making any trip outside of North America and Western Europe.

What's the trouble?	**Inchumn e khënt'irë?**
I am sick.	**Yes hivand em.**
My companion is sick.	**Im gortsënkerë hivand e.**
May I see a female doctor?	**Yes karogh em tesnel kin-bëzhishk?**
I have medical insurance.	**Yes unem bëzhëshkakan apahovagrut'yun.**
Please take off your shirt.	**Khënt'rum em, hanek' dzer shapikë.**
Please take off your clothes.	**Khënt'rum em, hanek' dzer shorerë.**
How long have you had this problem?	**Vork'an zhamanak duk' unek' ays khënt'irë?**
How long have you been feeling sick?	**Inchk'an zhamanak ek dzez vat zgum?**
Where does it hurt?	**Vortegh e ts'avum?**
It hurts here.	**Aystegh ts'avum e.**
I have been vomiting.	**Yes p'ëskhum ei.**
I feel dizzy.	**Glukhës pëtëtvum e.**
I can't eat.	**Yes ch'em karogh utel.**
I can't sleep.	**Yes ch'em karogh k'ënel.**

HEALTHCARE

I feel worse.		**Yes aveli vat em zgum.**
I feel better.		**Yes avei lav em zgum.**
Do you have diabetes?		**Duk' shak'arakht unek'?**
Do you have epilepsy?		**Duk' ënknavorut'yun unek'?**
Do you have asthma?		**Duk' ast'ma unek'?**
I'm pregnant.		**Yes hëghi em.**
I have . . .		**Yes unem ...**
You have . . .	*formal*	**Duk' oinek' ...**
	informal	**K'o mot ...**
a pain		**ts'av**
a sore throat		**kokort'ë mërrsats e**
a temperature		**jermut'yun**
an allergy		**alergia**
an infection		**infekts'ia**
an itch		**k'os**
a rash		**ts'an**
backache		**mejk'ats'av**
constipation		**p'orkap**
diarrhea		**diarea**
fever		**dogh**
hepatitis		**lyart'i borbok'um**
indigestion		**anmarsoghut'yun**
influenza		**grip**
a heart condition		**sërti vich'ak**
pins and needles		**tsakots'**
stomachache		**stamok'si ts'av**
a fracture		**kotërvatsk'**
a toothache		**atamnats'av**
I have a cold.		**Yes mërrsel em.**
You have a cold.	*formal*	**Duk' mërrsel ek'.**
	informal	**Du mërrsel es.**

I have a cough.	**Yes hazum em.**
You have a cough. *formal*	**Duk' haz unek'.**
informal	**Du hazum es.**
I have a headache.	**Gëlukhës ts'avum e.**
You have a headache. *formal*	**Duk' unek' gëlkhats'av.**
informal	**Gëlukhëd ts'avum e.**

I take this medication.	**Yes ays deghn em ënt'unum.**
I need medication for . . .	**Indz petk' e degh ... hamar.**
What type of medication is this?	**Sa inch deghorayk' e?**
What pill is this?	**Sa inch hab e?**
How many times a day must I take it?	**Orekan k'ani ank'am petk' e ënt'unem sa?**
When should I stop?	**Yerp' petk' e avartem?**
I'm on antibiotics.	**Yes ënt'unum em antibiotikner.**
I'm allergic to antibiotics.	**Yes antibiotiknerin alergia unem.**
I'm allergic to penicillin.	**Yes penits'ilinin alergia unem.**
I have been vaccinated.	**Indz vakts'inayov patvastel en.**
I have my own syringe.	**Yes im nerarkots'ë unem.**
Is it possible for me to travel?	**Yes karogh em ch'anaparort'el?**

—Health words

AIDS	**DZIAH**
alcoholism	**alkoholizm**
to amputate	**andamahatel**
anemia	**sakavaryunut'yun**
anesthetic	**ts'avazertsum**
anesthetist	**ts'avazërkogh**
antibiotic	**antibiotik**
antiseptic	**hakanekhich**
appetite	**akhorzhak**
artery	**arteria**
artificial arm	**arhestakan dzerr**
artificial eye	**arhestakan achk'**
artificial leg	**arhestakan vot**
aspirin	**aspirin**
bandage *medical*	**virakap**
Band-Aid	**speghani**
bladder	**park**
blood	**aryun**
blood group	**aryan khumb**
blood pressure	**aryan ch'ënshum**
high blood pressure	**aryan barts'ër ch'ënshum**
low blood pressure	**aryan ts'atsër ch'ënshum**
blood transfusion	**aryan p'okhnerarkum**
bone	**voskor**
brain	**ughegh**
bug *insect*	**michat**
burn *medical*	**ayrvatsk'**
cancer	**k'aghts'kegh**
catheter	**kat'eter**
cholera	**kholera**
clinic	**klinika**
cold *medical*	**ts'ërtarrut'yun**

constipated: Are you constipated?	**Dzez mot p'orkaput'yun e?**
cotton wool	**bambak**
cough	**haz**
cream *ointment*	**k'ësouk'**
dehydration	**jërazërkum**
dentist	**atamnabuyzh**
diarrhea	**diarea**
diet	**dieta**
dressing *medical*	**virakap**
drug *medical*	**deghorayk'**
drug *narcotic*	**t'ëmradegh**
dysentery	**dizenteria**
ear	**akanj**
ears	**akanjner**
eardrum	**t'ëmp'kataghant'**
edema	**aytuts'**
epidemic	**hamach'arak**
eye	**achk'**
eyes	**achk'er**
femur	**azdër**
fever	**dogh**
flea	**lu**
flu	**grip**
frostbite	**tsërtaharel**
gall bladder	**leghapark**
gently!	**zguysh!**
germs	**saghm**
gut	**aghik'**
guts	**aghik'ner**
hand: left hand	**dzakh dzerrk'**
right hand	**ach dzerrk'**
hard! *vigorously*	**uzhegh!**
health	**arroghchut'yun**
heart attack	**sërtaharut'yun**
heel	**kërunk**

hip	**azdër**
hips	**azdrer**
hygiene	**higiyena**
infant	**yerekha**
infected	**varakvats**
It is infected.	**Sa varakvats e.**
infection	**infekts'ia**
intestine(s)	**aghik'ner**
joint	**hod**
kidney	**yerekam**
kidneys	**yerekamner**
lice	**vochil**
limbs	**verjavorut'yunner**
maternity hospital	**tsënëndatun**
milk: *mother's*	**mor kat'**
cow's	**kovi kat'**
goat's	**aytsi kat'**
powdered	**kat'i p'oshi**
mouth	**beran**
muscle	**mëkan**
navel	**port**
needle	**asegh**
nerve	**nyart'**
newborn child	**noratsin yerekha**
nose	**k'it'**
nurse	**dayak**
ointment *cream*	**k'ësuk'**
operating theater/room	**virabuzhakan dahlich'**
(surgical) operation	**virahatut'yun**
organ *of body*	**organ**
oxygen	**t'ët'vatsin**
painkiller	**ts'avazërkogh**
palm *of hand*	**ap'**
pancreas	**yent'astamok'sayin geghdz**
physiotherapy	**fiziot'erapia**

placenta	**ënkerk'**
plaster *medical*	**speghani**
plaster cast *medical*	**gipsakap**
pupil *of eye*	**bib**
rabies	**divaharut'yun**
rash *on skin*	**ts'an**
rib(s)	**koghoskër**
rib cage	**kërtsk'avandak**
saliva	**t'uk'**
shoulder blade	**t'iak**
shrapnel	**shrapnel**
side *of body*	**koghm**
skin	**mashk**
skull	**gang**
sleeping pill	**kënaber degh**
snake bite	**ots'i khayt'um**
sole *of foot*	**t'at'**
spinal column; spine	**voghnashar**
stethoscope	**lësap'oghak**
stump *of limb*	**këch'at votk'/dzerk'**
surgeon	**virabuyzh**
(act of) surgery	**virahatut'yun**
syringe	**nerarkots'**
syrup *medical*	**mik'stoura**
thermometer	**jermachap'**
thigh	**azdër**
thorax	**kërtsk'avandak**
throat	**kokort'**
tibia	**mets sërunk'oskër**
to vomit	**p'ëkhskel**
tooth	**atam**
teeth	**atamner**
torture	**tanjank'**
trachea	**shënchap'ogh**
tranquilizer	**hangëstats'uts'ich deghamijots'**
tuberculosis	**tuberkulyoz**

umbilical cord	**portalar**
urine	**mez**
vein	**yerak**
vertebra	**voghnoskër**
vitamins	**vitaminner**
waist	**iran**
windpipe	**shënchap'ogh**

—Eyecare

I have broken my glasses.	**Yes jart'ets'i aknots'ës.**
Can you repair them?	**Karogh ek' veranorok'el ayn?**
I need new lenses.	**Indz petk' en nor apakiner.**
When will they be ready?	**Yerp' patrast klinen?**
How much do I owe you?	**Inchk'an petk' e věch'arem dzez?**
contact lenses	**kontaktayin linzaner**
contact lens solution	**kontaktayin linzaneri heghuk**

ELECTRICITY — Armenia is 220-volt electric current. However, it may not be constantly at full voltage strength and lengthy power failures may be common, particularly away from the larger towns, where the local transformers of villages that have a supply can overload. Although many buildings may now have their own back-up generators in case of power failure, be sure to keep a flashlight or supply of candles.

24. RELIEF AID

Can you help me?	**Duk' karogh ek' indz ok'nel?**
Can you speak English?	**Duk' khosum ek' angleren?**
Who is in charge?	**Ov e pataskhanatu?**
Fetch the main person in charge.	**Kanchek' karevor pataskhanat'yun.**
What's the name of this town?	**Inch e ays k'aghak'i anunë?**
How many people live there?	**Inchk'an mart' e aystegh aprum?**
What's the name of that river?	**Inche ays geti anunë?**
How deep is it?	**Vorka'n khorn e ayn?**
Is the bridge down?	**Ka nerk'evë kamurj?**
Is the bridge still standing?	**Kamurjë minch ayzhëm ka?**
Where can we ford the river?	**Vortegh karogh enk getë ants'nenk'?**
What is the name of that mountain?	**Inchpes e kochvum ayd lerrë?**
How high is it?	**Vorka'n barts'r e ayn?**
Where is the border?	**Vortegh e sahmanë?**
Is it safe?	**Ayn anvëtang e?**
Show me.	**Ts'uts' tëvek' indz.**
Is there anyone trapped?	**Voreve mekë ayntegh mënats'el e?**
Is the building safe?	**Ays shenk'ë anvëtang e?**
It's going to collapse!	**Ayn k'andvelu e!**

Get out (of the building) now!	**Shtap lëk'ek' shenk'ë!**
Can you hear any sound?	**Duk' voreve dzai lësum ek'?**
Silence!	**Lërrut'yun!**

— Checkpoints

checkpoint	**hert'apah ants'agrayin ket**
roadblock	**oghekal**
Stop!	**Kangnek'!**
Do not move!	**Chsharjvel!**
Go!	**Gënats'ek'!**
Who are you?	**Ov ek' duk'?**
Don't shoot!	**Mi krakek'!**
Help!	**Ok'nets'ek'!**
Help me!	**Ok'nek' indz!**
no entry	**mutk'n ark'elvats e**
emergency exit	**pahestayin yelk'**
straight on	**ughigh**
turn left	**t'ek'vek' dzakh**
turn right	**t'ek'vek' ach**
this way	**aystegh**
that way	**ayntegh**
Keep quiet!	**Lërrek'!**
You are right.	**Duk' iravats'i ek'.**
You are wrong.	**Duk' skhalvum ek'.**
I am ready.	**Yes patrast em.**
I am in a hurry.	**Yes shtapum em.**
What's that?	**Inch e sa?**
Come in!	**Mëtek'!**
That's all!	**Aysk'anë!**

— Food distribution

feeding station	**baregortsakan ch'asharan**

How many people are in your family?	**Dzer ëntanik'um k'ani mart' ka?**
How many children?	**Inchk'an yerekha?**
You must come back . . .	**Duk' petk'e veradarrnak' . . .**
this afternoon	**ays ts'erek**
tonight	**ays yereko**
tomorrow	**vaghë**
the day after tomorrow	**vaghë che myus orë**
next week	**hajort' shap'at'**
There is water for you.	**Dzer hamar jur ka.**
There is grain for you.	**Dzer hamar hats'ahatik ka.**
There is food for you.	**Dzer hamar utelik' ka.**
There is fuel for you.	**Dzer hamar varrelik' ka.**
Please form a line (here/there)!	**Khënt'rum enk hert kangnel aystegh/ ayntegh!**

—Road repair

Is the road passable?	**Ch'anaparë ënt'anali e?**
Is the road blocked?	**Ch'anaparë p'ak e?**
We are repairing the road.	**Menk' norok'um enk ch'anaparë.**
We are repairing the bridge.	**Menk' norok'um enk kamurjë.**
We need . . .	**Mez petk' e . . .**
wood	**p'ayt**
a rock	**k'ar**
rocks	**k'arer**
gravel	**manrakhich'**
sand	**avaz**
fuel	**varrelik'**

Lift!	**Barts'rats'rek'!**
Drop it!	**Gëts'ek'!**
Now!	**Hima!**
All together!	**Miasin!**

— Mines

mine *noun*	**akan**
mines	**akanner**
minefield	**akanadasht**
to lay mines	**akaner dënel**
to hit a mine	**akani vëra kangnel**
to clear a mine	**akanë vnasazertsel**
mine detector	**akanors**
mine disposal	**akaneri dasavorut'yun**
Are there any mines near here?	**Shërjakayk'um kan akanner?**
What type are they?	**Inch tesaki en nërank'?**
anti-vehicle	**hakatankayin**
anti-personnel	**hakahetevakayin**
plastic	**plastik**
magnetic	**magnisayin**
What size are they?	**Inch chap'si en nërank'?**
What color are they?	**Inch guyni en nërank'?**
Are they marked?	**Nërank' nëshvats en?**
How?	**Inchpes?**
How many mines are there?	**Inchk'an akan ka ayntegh?**
When were they laid?	**Yerp' en nërank' dërvel?**
Can you take me to the minefields?	**Duk' karogh ek' indz akanneri dasht tanel?**

Are there any booby traps near there?	**Aystegh shërjakayk'um kan art'ok' akan-t'akardner?**
Are they made from grenades, high explosives, or something else?	**Nërank' patrastvats en nërrnaknerits', payt'ets'utsich nyut'erits', t'e ayl nyut'erits'?**
Are they in a building?	**Nërank' shenk'um en?**
on paths?	**ants'knerin?**
on roads?	**ch'anaparnerin?**
on bridges?	**kamurjnerin?**
or elsewhere?	**ayl tegh?**
Can you show me?	**Karogh ek' indz ts'uyts' tal?**
Don't go near that!	**Mi motikats'ek'!**
Don't touch that!	**Mi këpek'!**

— Other words

airforce	**ot'ayin uzh**
ambulance	**shtap ok'nut'yun**
armored car	**zrahapatvats mek'ena**
army	**banak**
artillery	**hretani**
barbed wire	**p'shalar**
bomb	**rrumb**
bomber	**rrëmbakotsich**
bullet	**gëndak**
cannon	**t'ëndanot'**
cluster bomb	**kasetayin rrumb**
disaster	**aghet**
drought	**yerasht**
earthquake	**yerkrasharzh**
famine	**sov**

fighter		**korstanich**
gun	*pistol*	**atërch'anak**
	rifle	**hrats'an**
	cannon	**t'ëndanot'**
machine-gun		**avtomat**
missile		**hërt'irr**
	missiles	**hërt'irrner**
mortar *weapon*		**akananet**
natural disaster		**bënakan aghet**
navy		**navatorm**
nuclear power		**atomayin energia**
nuclear power station		**atomayin elektrakayan**
officer		**spa**
parachute		**ot'aparik**
peace		**khaghaghut'yun**
people		**zhoghovurd**
pistol		**atërch'anak**
refugee camp		**p'akhstakanneri ch'ambar**
refugee		**p'akhstakan**
refugees		**p'akhstakanner**
relief aid		**humanitar ok'nut'yun**
sack		**park**
shell		**ark**
shelter		**apastan**
submachine gun		**gëndats'ir**
tank		**tank**
troops		**zork'er**
unexploded ammunition		**chpayt'ats handerts'ank'**
unexploded bomb		**chëpayt'ats rrumb**
unexploded ordnance		**chëpayt'ats hretani**
war		**paterazm**
weapon		**zenk'**

25. TOOLS

binoculars	**herraditak**
brick	**aghyus**
brush	**vĕrts'in**
cable	**malukh**
cooker	**plita**
crane	**ambarts'ich**
crowbar	**ling**
drill	**shaghap'ich**
gas bottle/canister	**balon**
hammer	**murch'**
handle	**bĕrrnak**
hose	**kashep'ogh**
insecticide	**insektits'id**
ladder	**astich'an**
machine	**mek'ena**
microscope	**manraditak**
nail	**mekh**
padlock	**koghpek'**
paint	**nerk**
pickaxe	**sorani**
plank	**dzoghik**
plastic	**plastik**
rope	**paran**
rubber	**rretin**
rust	**shang**
saw	**sĕghots'**
scissors	**mĕkrat**
screw	**pĕtutak**
screwdriver	**pĕtutakich**
sieve	**magh**
spade	**bah**
spanner *wrench*	**pĕtutakabanali**
string	**t'el**
telescope	**astghaditak**
varnish	**lak'**
wire	**lar**

26. THE CAR

Where can I rent a car?	**Vortgh karogh em mek'ena varts'el?**
Where can I rent a car with a driver?	**Vortgh karogh em varort'ov mek'ena varts'el?**
How much is it per day?	**Inchk'an e oravarts'ë?**
How much is it per week?	**Inchk'an e shp'at'va varts'ë?**
Can I park here?	**Karogh em aystegh mek'enan kangnets'nel?**
Are we on the right road for . . . ?	**Sa e ch'anaparë depi ...?**
Where is the nearest gas station?	**Vortegh e amenamotik lëts'akayanë?**
Fill the tank please.	**Lits'k'avorek', khënt'rum em.**
normal/diesel	**sovorakan/dizel**
Check the oil/tires/ battery, please.	**Khënt'rum em stugel yughë/anvadogherë/ uzhakutakichë.**

– Emergencies

I've broken down.	**Mek'enas p'ëchats'el e.**
I have a puncture/flat tire.	**Im anvadoghë tsakvel e.**

I have run out of gas.	**Benzinë verchats'el e.**
Our car is stuck.	**Mer mek'enan khërvel e.**
There's something wrong with this car.	**Ays mek'enan ansark' e.**
We need a mechanic.	**Mez petk' e mek'enaget.**
Where is the nearest garage?	**Vortegh e motaka garazhë?**
Can you tow us?	**Duk' karogh ek' mez buk'sirel?**
Can you jumpstart the car (by pushing)?	**Karogh ek' mek'enan hërelov gortsi k'ëts'el?**
There's been an accident.	**Aystegh patahar e teghi unets'el.**
My car has been stolen.	**Im mek'enan goghats'el en.**
Call the police.	**Vostikanut'yun kachek'.**
The tire is flat.	**Anvadoghë ichats e.**

—Car words

driver's license	**varort'akan iravunk'**
insurance policy	**apahovagrakan polis**
car papers	**mek'enayi p'astat'ukht'**
car registration/numberplate	**mek'enai petakan hamarë**
accelerator	**aragarar**
air	**ot'**
anti-freeze	**antifriz**
battery	**martkots'**

THE CAR

bonnet/hood	**tsatskots'**
boot/trunk	**bagazhategh**
brake	**ark'elak**
bumper/fender	**bamper**
car park	**kayanategh**
clutch	**këts'ort'ich**
driver	**varort'**
engine	**sharzhich**
exhaust	**artazhayt'k'um**
fan belt	**haghordap'ok**
gear	**p'okhants'man tup'**
indicator light	**lusayin indikator**
inner-tube	**ot'apahpanich**
jack	**ambarts'ich**
mechanic	**mek'enaget**
neutral drive	**parap ënt'ats'k'**
oil	**yugh**
oilcan	**yughamas**
passenger	**ughevor**
petrol	**benzin**
radiator	**rradiator**
reverse	**yetadarts'**
seat	**nëstategh**
spare tyre/tire	**pahestayin anvadogh**
speed	**aragut'yun**
steering wheel	**ghek**
tank	**benzinabak'**
tyre/tire	**anvadogh**
tow rope	**buk'sirayin ch'opan**
windscreen wipers	**dimats'i apakineri mak'rich**
windscreen/windshield	**aftomek'enayi dimats'i apaki**

27. SPORTS

The Armenians are avid followers of a wide variety of sports, especially when it comes to soccer — the country has been a member of FIFA since 1992. During the Soviet days Armenia produced its fair share of Olympic medalists, especially in the field of gymnastics, wrestling, boxing and weightlifting. "All-Time Great" weightlifter Yuri Sarkisian, born in Armenia but now living in Australia, has chalked up some remarkable successes in his career, winning more than 600 medals in international and national competitions and setting over 23 world records. Other world-class sportsmen of Armenian descent on the international circuit include chess grandmaster Gary Kasparov (chess and backgammon are extremely popular pastimes for Armenians), Steve Bedrossian, baseball pitcher with the Atlanta Braves and Philadelphia Phillies, soccer player Alain Boghossian, who played in the French team which won the 1998 World Cup, and world tennis champion Andre Agassi.

athletics	**at'letika**
ball	**gëndak**
backgammon	**nardi**
basketball	**bask'etbol**
chess	**shakhmat**
cricket	**kriket**
goal	**gol**
horse racing	**dziarshav**
horseback-riding	**dziagënats'ut'yun**
match/game	**mërts'akhagh**
soccer match	**futbol**
	mërts'akhagh
pitch	**netum**
referee	**mërts'avar**
rugby	**regbi**
skiing	**dahuknerov vazk'**
soccer	**futbol**
stadium	**stadion**

SPORTS

swimming	**logh**
team	**t'im**
wrestling	**ëmpshamartik**

Who won?	**Ov haght'ets'?**
What's the score?	**Inchk'an e hashivë?**
Who scored?	**Ov khëp'ets' gëndakë?**

Weights & measures . . .

Armenia uses the metric system. Here is a list of international units — for reference translations are included for the most common imperial units:

kilometer	**kilometër**
meter	**metër**
mile	**mëghon**
foot	**fut**
yard	**yard**
acre	**akër**
gallon	**galon**
liter	**litër**
kilogram	**kilogram**
ton; tonne	**tonna**
gram	**gram**

28. THE BODY

ankle	**koch'**
arm	**dzerrk'**
back	**mechk'**
beard	**moruk'**
blood	**aryun**
body	**marmin**
bone	**voskor**
bottom	**hetuyk'**
breast	**kurtsk'**
chest	**kërtsk'avandak**
calf *leg*	**hort'**
cheek(s)	**ayt(er)**
chin	**dunch**
ear	**akanj**
elbow	**armunk**
eye	**achk'**
eyebrow	**unk'**
eyelashes	**t'art'ichner**
face	**demk'**
finger	**mat**
fingers	**mater**
fist	**bërruntsk'**
foot	**t'at'**
feet	**t'at'er**
genitals	**serrakan organner**
hair	**mazer**
a hair	**maz**
hand	**dastak**
head	**gëlukh**
heart	**sirt**
index finger	**ts'uts'amat**
jaw	**tsënot'**
kidney	**yerekam**

THE BODY

knee	**tsunk**
leg	**vot**
lip	**shërt'unk**
liver	**lyart'**
lung	**t'ok'**
mustache	**begh**
mouth	**beran**
nail *of finger/toe*	**yeghung**
navel	**port**
neck	**viz**
nose	**k'it'**
rib	**koghoskër**
ribs	**koghoskrer**
shoulder	**us**
skin	**mashk**
stomach	**stamok's**
throat	**kokort'**
thumb	**bët'amat**
toe	**voti mat**
tongue	**lezu**
tooth	**atam**
teeth	**atamner**
womb	**argand**
wrist	**dastak**

29. POLITICS

aid worker	**ok'nakan**
ambassador	**despan**
to arrest	**dzerp'akalel**
assassination	**spanut'yun**
assembly *meeting*	**zhoghov**
parliament	**khorërt'aran**
autonomy	**ink'navarut'yun**
cabinet	**kabinet**
a charity	**baregortsut'yun**
citizen	**k'aghak'ats'i**
civil rights	**k'aghak'ats'iakan**
	iravunk'ner
civil war	**k'aghak'ats'iakan**
	paterazm
coalition	**koalits'ia**
condemn	**datapartel**
constitution	**sahmanadrut'yun**
convoy	**pahakakhumb**
corruption	**korrupts'ia**
coup d'etat	**heghasërjum**
crime	**hants'agortsut'yun**
criminal	**hants'agorts**
crisis	**ch'ëk'nazham**
dictator	**bërrnapet**
debt	**partk'**
democracy	**zhoghovërt'avarut'yun**
dictatorship	**bërrnapetut'yun**
diplomatic ties	**divanagitakan kaper**
displaced person	**teghahanvats andz**
displaced persons/people	**teghahanvats mart'ik**
election	**ëntrut'yunner**
embassy	**despanatun**
ethnic cleansing	**et'nik mak'rumner**
exile	**ak'sorum**

free	**azat**
freedom	**azatut'yun**
government	**karravarut'yun**
guerrilla	**partizan**
hostage	**patand**
humanitarian aid	**humanitar ok'nut'yun**
human rights	**mart'u iravunk'ner**
imam	**imam**
independence	**ankakhut'yun**
independent	**ankakh**
independent state	**ankakh petut'yun**
judge	**datavor**
killer	**mart'aspan**
king	**t'ak'avor**
law	**orenk'**
law court	**dataran**
lawyer	**iravaban**
leader	**ghekavar**
left-wing	**dzakh**
liberation	**azatagrum**
majority	**metsamasnut'yun**
mercenary	**varts'kan**
minister	**nakharar**
ministry	**nakhararut'yun**
minority	**p'ok'ramasnut'yun**
ethnic minority	**et'nik p'ok'ramasnut'yun**
minority vote	**p'ok'ramasnut'yan dzayn**
murder	**mart'aspanut'yun**
opposition	**ёndimadir**
parliament	**khorёrt'aran**
upper house	**verin palat**
lower house	**nerk'in palap**
(political) party	**kusakts'ut'yun**
politics	**k'aghak'akanut'yun**
peace	**khaghaghut'yun**

peace-keeping troops	**khaghaghapah zork'er**
politician	**k'aghak'akan gortsich**
president	**nakhagah**
prime minister	**varchapet**
prison	**bant**
prisoner-of-war	**rrazmageri**
POW camp	**rrazmagerineri ch'ambar**
protest	**boghok'arkum**
reactionary *adjective*	**hetadimakan**
Red Cross	**Karmir Khach**
refugee	**p'akhëstakan**
refugees	**p'akhëstakanner**
revolution	**heghap'okhut'yun**
right-wing	**dzakh**
robbery	**koghoput**
seat (in assembly)	**tegh**
secret police	**gakhtni vostikanut'yun**
socialism	**sots'ializm**
socialist	**sots'ialist**
spy	**lërtes**
struggle	**payk'ar**
to testify	**vëkayel**
theft	**goghut'yun**
trade union	**armiut'yun**
treasury	**gandzapetaran**
United Nations	**Miavorvats Azger**
veto	**veto**
vote	**k'vearkel**
vote-rigging	**ëntrut'yunneri kekhtsum**
voting	**k'vearkum**

30. WAR

airplane	**ink'nat'irr**
air-raid	**ot'ayin harts'akum**
ambush	**daran**
ammunition	**zinvorakan handerts'ank'**
anti-aircraft gun	**hakahërt'irrajin t'ëndanot'**
armored car	**zrahapat mek'ena**
arms	**zenk'**
army	**banak**
artillery	**hretani**
assault; attack	**harts'akum**
aviation	**aviats'ia**
bayonet	**svin**
to beat *overcome*	**haght'el**
belt	**goti**
cartridge belt	**p'amp'ështakal**
bomb	**rrumb**
bombardment	**rrëmbakotsut'yun**
butt *of rifle*	**takarr**
to camouflage	**k'ogharkanerkel**
captain	**kapitan**
cartridge	**p'amp'usht**
ceasefire	**zinadat'ar**
chief of staff	**shtabi hramanatar**
to command	**hramayel**
to conquer	**haght'aharel**
dagger	**dashuyn**
defeat	**partut'yun**
to defeat	**partut'yan matnel**
to destroy	**jakhjakhel**
detonation	**andërpayt'um**
enemy	**t'ëshnami**
to evacuate	**evakuats'nel**

to explode	**payt'el**
to free	**azatagrel**
freedom	**azatut'yun**
general	**general**
grenade	**nërrnak**
gun	**hërats'an**
gun barrel	**p'ogh**
helicopter	**ughat'irr**
hostage	**patand**
to invade	**nerkhuzhel**
jihad	**jihad**
to kill	**spanel**
to liberate	**azatagrel**
liberty	**azatut'yun**
lieutenant	**leytenant**
lieutenant-colonel	**general-gëndapet**
lieutenant-general	**general-leytenant**
to loot	**hap'shtakel**
to lose	**partvel**
machine gun	**gëndats'ir**
major-general	**general-mayor**
martyr	**akananet**
military university	**zinvorakan hamalsaran**
military school	**zinvorakan varzharan**
mine	**akan**
anti-personnel mine	**hakahetevakayin akan**
anti-tank mine	**hakatankayin akan**
munitions	**handerts'ank'**
objective	**nëpatak**
opponent	**hakarrakort'**
patrol	**parek**
peace	**khaghaghut'yun**
to make peace	**khaghaghut'yan hasnel**

personnel *military*	**andznakazm**
pilot	**ot'achu**
pistol	**atërch'anak**
plane	**ink'nat'irr**
prisoner	**bantarkyal**
to take prisoner	**dzerp'akalel**
to pursue	**hetapëndel**
raid	**martarshav**
air-raid	**ot'ayin harts'akum**
regiment	**gund**
reinforcements	**hamalërum**
to resist	**dimadrel**
to retreat	**nahanjel**
rifle	**hërats'an**
rocket	**hërt'irr**
rocket-launcher	**hërt'irrayin arts'akich**
shell *military*	**ark**
shelter	**apastan**
to shoot down	**gëndakaharel**
shrapnel	**shrapnel**
siege	**pasharum**
soldier	**zinvor**
spy	**lërtes**
staff *army*	**shtab**
submachine gun	**gëndats'ir**
to surrender	**andznatur linel**
to surround	**shërjapatel**
to take shelter	**patsparvel**
tank	**tank**
tracer bullet	**hetagëtsogh gëndak**
truce	**zinadat'ar**
victory	**haght'anak**
war	**paterazm**
weapon	**zenk'**
to win	**haght'el**
to wound	**viravorel**

31. TIME

century	**dar**
decade	**tasnamyak**
year	**tari**
month	**amis**
week	**shap'at'**
day	**or**
hour	**zham**
minute	**rope**
second	**vayrkyan**

dawn	**lusabats'**
sunrise	**arevatsak'**
morning	**arravot**
daytime	**ts'erek**
noon	**kesor**
afternoon	**ts'erek**
evening	**yereko**
sunset	**mayramut**
night	**gisher**
midnight	**kesgisher**

three days before	**yerek' or arraj**
the day before yesterday	**yerek che arrachi orë**
yesterday	**yerek**
today	**aysor**
tomorrow	**vaghë**
the day after tomorrow	**vachë che myus orë**
three days from now	**yerek' or arraj**
the year before last	**nakhants'ats tari**
last year	**ants'ats tari**
this year	**ays tari**
next year	**hajort' tari**
the year after next	**yerku tari heto**

TIME

last week	**ants'ats shap'at'**
this week	**ays shap'at'**
next week	**hajort' shap'at'**
last night	**ants'ats gisher**
this morning	**ays arravot**
just now	**hents' hima**
now	**hima**
this afternoon	**ays ts'erek**
this evening	**ays yereko**
tonight	**ays gisher**
yesterday morning	**yerek arravotyan**
yesterday afternoon	**yerek ts'erekë**
yesterday night	**yerek gisherë**
tomorrow morning	**vaghë arravotyan**
tomorrow afternoon	**vaghë ts'erekë**
tomorrow night	**vaghë gisherë**
in the morning	**arravotyan**
in the afternoon	**ts'erekë**
in the evening	**yerekoyan**
past	**ants'yal**
present	**nerka**
future	**aparrni**
What day is it?	**Shap'at'va inch or e aysor?**
What date is it today?	**Aysor amsi k'anisne?**
What time is it?	**Zhamë k'anisn e?**
It is . . . o'clock.	**Zhamë ... e.**

—Seasons

summer	**amarr**
autumn	**ashun**
winter	**dzëmerr**
spring	**garun**

—Days of the week

Monday	**Yerkushap'tʻi**
Tuesday	**Yerekʻshap'tʻi**
Wednesday	**Chorekʻshap'tʻi**
Thursday	**Hingshap'tʻi**
Friday	**Urp'atʻ**
Saturday	**Shap'atʻor**
Sunday	**Kiraki**

—Months

January	**Hunvar**
February	**Pʻetervar**
March	**Mart**
April	**April**
May	**Mayis**
June	**Hunis**
July	**Hulis**
August	**Ogostos**
September	**September**
October	**Hoktember**
November	**Noyember**
December	**Dektember**

—Star signs

Aries	**Khoy**
Taurus	**Tsʻul**
Gemini	**Yerkvoryak**
Cancer	**Khetsʻgetin**
Leo	**Arryuts**
Virgo	**Kuys**
Libra	**Kësherrkʻ**
Scorpio	**Karichʻ**
Sagittarius	**Agheghnavor**
Capricorn	**Aytsekhchyur**
Aquarius	**Jërhos**
Pisces	**Dzuk**

32. NUMBERS

0	**zëro**		
1	**mek**	31	**yerresun mek**
2	**yerku**	32	**yerresun yerku**
3	**yerek'**	33	**yerresun yerek'**
4	**chors**	34	**yerresun chors**
5	**hing**	35	**yerresun hing**
6	**vets'**	36	**yerresun vets'**
7	**yot'**	37	**yerresun yot'**
8	**ut'**	38	**yerresun ut'**
9	**inë**	39	**yerresun inë**
10	**tas**	40	**k'arrasun**
11	**tasnëmek**	41	**k'arrasun mek**
12	**tasnëerku**	42	**k'arrasun yerku**
13	**tasnëerek'**	43	**k'arrasun yerek'**
14	**tasnëchors**	44	**k'arrasun chors**
15	**tasnëhing**	45	**k'arrasun hing**
16	**tasnëvets'**	46	**k'arrasun vets'**
17	**tasnëyot'**	47	**k'arrasun yot'**
18	**tasnëut'**	48	**k'arrasun ut'**
19	**tasnëinë**	49	**k'arrasun inë**
20	**k'san**	50	**hisun**
21	**k'san mek**	51	**hisun mek**
22	**k'san yerku**	52	**hisun yerku**
23	**k'san yerek'**	53	**hisun yerek'**
24	**k'san chors**	54	**hisun chors**
25	**k'san hing**	55	**hisun hing**
26	**k'san vets'**	56	**hisun vets'**
27	**k'san yot'**	57	**hisun yot'**
28	**k'san ut'**	58	**hisun ut'**
29	**k'san inë**	59	**hisun inë**
30	**yerresun**	60	**vat'sun**

61	vat'sun mek	81	ut'anasun mek
62	vat'sun yerku	82	ut'anasun yerku
63	vat'sun yerek'	83	ut'anasun yerek'
64	vat'sun chors	84	ut'anasun chors
65	vat'sun hing	85	ut'anasun hing
66	vat'sun vets'	86	ut'anasun vets'
67	vat'sun yot'	87	ut'anasun yot'
68	vat'sun ut'	88	ut'anasun ut'
69	vat'sun inë	89	ut'anasun inë
70	yot'anasun	90	inësun
71	yot'anasun mek	91	inësun mek
72	yot'anasun yerku	92	inësun yerku
73	yot'anasun yerek'	93	inësun yerek'
74	yot'anasun chors	94	inësun chors
75	yot'anasun hing	95	inësun hing
76	yot'anasun vets'	96	inësun vets'
77	yot'anasun yot'	97	inësun yot'
78	yot'anasun ut'	98	inësun ut'
79	yot'anasun inë	99	inësun inë
80	ut'anasun	100	haryur

105	haryur mek	2,000	yerku hazar
200	yerku haryur	3,000	yerek' hazar
300	yerek' haryur	4,000	chors hazar
400	chors haryur	5,000	hing hazar
500	hing haryur	6,000	vets' hazar
600	vets' haryur	7,000	yot' hazar
700	yot' haryur	8,000	ut' hazar
800	ut' haryur	9,000	inë hazar
900	inë haryur	10,000	tas hazar
1,000	hazar		

50,000	hisun hazar
100,000	haryur hazar
1,000,000	milion

first	**arrachin**
second	**yerkrort'**
third	**yerort'**
fourth	**chorort'**
fifth	**hingerort'**
sixth	**vets'erort'**
seventh	**yot'erort'**
eighth	**ut'erort'**
ninth	**inerort'**
tenth	**taserort'**
fifteenth	**tasnëhingerort'**
twentieth	**k'sanerort'**
once	**mek ank'am**
twice	**yerku ank'am**
three times	**yerek' ank'am**
one-half	**kes**
one-quarter	**k'arrort'**
three-quarters	**yerek' k'arrort'**
one-third	**mek yerrort'**
two-thirds	**yerku yerrort'**

33. OPPOSITES

beginning—end	**skizb—avart**
clean—dirty	**mak'ur—keghtot**
comfortable — uncomfortable	**harmaravet—anharmaravet**
fertile—barren *land*	**pëtghaber—anberri**
happy—unhappy	**yerjanik—dëzhbakht**
life—death	**kyank'—vakhch'an**
friend—enemy	**ënker—t'ëshnami**
modern—traditional	**zhamanakakits'—avandakan**
modern—ancient	**zhamanakakits'—hënavurts'**
open—shut	**bats'el—tsatskel**
wide—narrow	**layn—negh**
high—low	**barts'ër—ts'atsër**
peace—violence/war	**khaghaghut'yun—paterazm**
polite—rude	**k'aghak'avari—kopit**
silence—noise	**lrrut'yun—aghmuk**
cheap—expensive	**t'ankarzhek'—ezhan**
hot/warm—cold/cool	**tak'—sarrë**
health—disease	**arrokhchut'yun—hivandut'yun**
well—sick	**arroghch—hivand**
night—day	**gisher—ts'erek**
top—bottom	**gagat'—himk'**
backwards—forwards	**arraj—yet**
back—front	**yet—arraj**
dead—alive	**mahats'ats—kent'ani**
near—far	**motik—herru**
left—right	**dzakh—ach**
inside—outside	**ners—durs**
up—down	**verev—nerk'ev**

OPPOSITES

yes—no	**ayo—voch**
here—there	**aystegh—ayntegh**
soft—hard	**p'ap'uk—kosht**
easy—difficult	**hesht—dëzhvar**
quick—slow	**arag—dandagh**
big—small	**mets-p'ok'ër**
old—young	**tser—jahel**
tall—short *people*	**barts'rahasak— ts'atsrahasak**
tall—short *things*	**barts'ër—ts'atsër**
strong—weak	**uzhegh—t'uyl**
success—failure	**hajoghut'yun— anhajoghut'yun**
new—old	**nor—hin**
question—answer	**harts'—pataskhan**
safety—danger	**anvëtangut'yun— vëtang**
good—bad	**lav—vat**
true—false	**ch'ëshmarit— keghtsavor**
light—heavy	**t'et'ev—tsanër**
light—darkness	**luys—mët'ut'yun**
well—badly	**lav—vat**
truth—lie	**ch'ëshmartut'yun— sut**

MAP OF ARMENIA

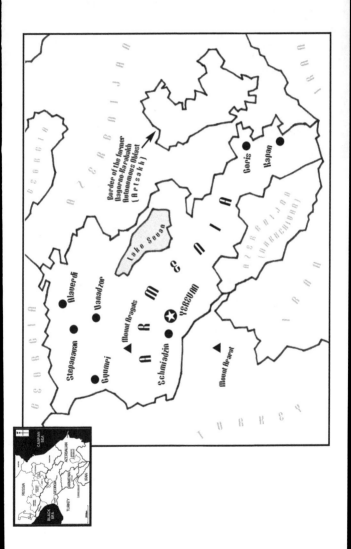

www.ingramcontent.com/pod-product-compliance
Lightning Source LLC
Jackson TN
JSHW011359130125
77033JS00023B/751